William T. Stead

The passion play as it is played today, at Ober Ammergau in 1890

William T. Stead

The passion play as it is played today, at Ober Ammergau in 1890

ISBN/EAN: 9783742888709

Hergestellt in Europa, USA, Kanada, Australien, Japan

Cover: Foto ©Thomas Meinert / pixelio.de

Manufactured and distributed by brebook publishing software (www.brebook.com)

William T. Stead

The passion play as it is played today, at Ober Ammergau in 1890

[Kunst und Verlags Anstalt, Oberammergau.]

ECCE HOMO!

THE PASSION PLAY

AS IT IS PLAYED TO-DAY.

AT OBER AMMERGAU IN 1890

BY

WILLIAM T. STEAD

GERMAN AND ENGLISH
TEXT OF
PASSION PLAY
IN PARALLEL COLUMNS

COPIOUSLY ILLUSTRATED
FROM ORIGINAL
PHOTOGRAPHS BY
SPECIAL PERMISSION.

LONDON: OFFICE OF THE "REVIEW OF REVIEWS,"
MOWBRAY HOUSE, NORFOLK STREET, STRAND, W.C.

NEW YORK: CHARLES E. MERRILL & CO., 52 & 54, LAFAYETTE PLACE
MUNICH & OBERAMMERGAU: HEINRICH KORFF

PREFACE.

WHEN I went to Ober Ammergau to obtain a little rest and to witness a performance which was being somewhat warmly discussed throughout Christendom, nothing was further from my thoughts than to write a book about it. An article for my Review—yes. A book, certainly not.

But here is my book after all, and the best preface is a brief explanation of how it came to be written.

On arriving at Ober Ammergau on June 7th, I asked, as probably every one else does, for the text of the play in German and in English. In a short time I was furnished with a small library in both languages. Official guides, authorized texts, the only authentic version, complete descriptive accounts, illustrated editions, and so forth. Armed with specimens of the best, I made my way to the Passion Play, on Sunday, June 8th.

Imagine then my astonishment on discovering that not one of all the versions sold has the faintest claim to give an account of the Passion Play as it is played to-day; that all of them describe the play as it was presented ten years ago; that in all the mass of Ober Ammergau literature there is not a single German-English edition with the German text printed in parallel columns to the English translation, and that none of the published books about the Passion Play contain any illustrations either of the play as it is played or of the performers as they appear. Nothing is more pathetic than to witness the vain attempts of the audience to follow the play by the aid of books which describe tableaux which have been dropped, give the dialogues of scenes which have been suppressed, and illustrate their text by portraits of players who are no longer on the stage or who are playing different parts.

I went to see the Passion Play a second time on Monday, and decided there and then that as there was no one else who seemed to be preparing to supply the need I would do it myself. Not being a stenographer, and not being able to command on the spot a German shorthand writer who would take down the ipsissima verba of the performers, I cannot profess to present in the following pages in all cases a full verbatim report of the whole play. But by taking all the existing versions to the Theatre and collating them as the play progressed, I am able to produce a version which, although here and there imperfect by reason of my being unable to take down passages omitted in the hitherto published editions, nevertheless does give a fairly complete and faithful account of what is actually to be seen to-day on the stage at Ober Ammergau.

The only original printed basis for the text of the Passion Play is the prose version taken down in shorthand ten years ago by Mr. W. Wyl and published by him in "Maitage in Ober Ammergau," a work which has been through three editions, and which still remains the only German text that is of the slightest use to those who wish to follow the Play book in hand. The two English versions which are useful are both translations from the "Maitage": one by the author of "Charles Lowder," published by Messrs. W. H. Allen & Co., the other by Mary Frances Drew, published by Messrs. Burns & Oates. The book which is usually sold at Ober Ammergau as the text of the Play is a poetical version written by the Geistlicher Rath Daisenberger, the parish priest of the village. He endeavoured in vain to secure the adoption of his poetic version. The villagers refused to abandon their traditional prose. Here and there, however, the omissions in Mr. Wyl's "Maitage," due chiefly to the difficulty of following in shorthand the exceedingly rapid speeches of some of the performers, can be supplied not textually but with sufficient accuracy as to meaning from Father Daisenberger's drama. In one scene which I could not restore by the combination of the "Maitage" and Daisenberger, I was kindly furnished with the manuscript of his "Rolle" by the principal performer. Add to this the additions which I was able to make as I followed every sentence spoken by the performers, pencil in hand, on the second and third occasions on which I witnessed the performance, and you have the materials on which the present edition is based. I think I may say that its only faults are those of omission. Nothing is printed that is not actually spoken on the stage, and where omissions occur I have indicated the hiatus in the usual manner. It will be seen that the hiatus seldom or never occurs in the part of the Christ, and very seldom in those of any of the leading performers, except occasionally in the case of Caiaphas. Those who witness that extraordinary personation will not, however, marvel at the impossibility of catching every word of his rapid and vehement discourse. Altogether, I do not think the omitted passages if printed consecutively would more than fill half a page of the present volume.

As to the English version which I have printed in parallel columns to the German text, it will be observed that I have departed from the usual method of giving a merely textual translation. While translating as closely as possible the actual text I have thrown the speeches of the performers into a narrative, so that while following the movement of the play the accompanying description will enable the spectator at any moment to find his place. Where so much depends upon the action that takes place on the stage, the mere words convey little or no idea of what actually takes place, and the only alternatives were either to perpetually interrupt the text of the drama by numerous stage directions, or to throw the whole of the dialogue into the form of a narrative. I have adopted the latter course, not only because it is most simple but because it will enable thousands who will never visit Ober Ammergau to read the whole story without the difficulty that invariably attends the reading of a drama. I have in all cases collated my translations with those made by the author of "Charles Lowder" and by Mary Frances Drew, and have submitted the result to the revision of one whose knowledge of German is much more profound than mine can pretend to be. The metrical translations of the prologues and the songs have been kindly undertaken for me by Miss Werner.

The photographs which form the illustrations could not possibly have been published until the play was actually on the stage. The photographs of some of the tableaux, for instance, are even now not yet ready. Guides to Ober Ammergau, which were got ready before May, were therefore compelled to fall back upon the photographs of 1880. Since 1880 photography has made so much progress as almost to be a new art. The contrast between the splendid series of photographs, produced by Messrs. Faller, Buchmüller & Co. from the photographs taken by Mr. Stockmann, the Court photographer of Vienna, and those taken ten years ago, needs to be seen to be believed. The right of publishing these photographs has been let to Messrs. Faller, Buchmüller & Co., for the sum of 37,000 marks, and they naturally forbid any reproduction of their pictures excepting by special authorisation. That authorisation I succeeded after some difficulty in obtaining, and I have the exclusive concession for the non-photographic reproduction of the photographs in the British Empire.

The "Passion Play" is witnessed about twice a week by nearly five thousand persons. This week the spacious theatre has been crowded thrice, and there is every sign of the demand for seats increasing. The English summer exodus has hardly begun, but on Sunday there were said to be five hundred English people in Ober Ammergau. As the performance closes with September, it has been indispensable to bring this volume out with a haste which must be my excuse for its many imperfections. If, however, the reception which it meets with from the public accords to the need which it endeavours to supply, I hope to bring out a revised and extended edition in the autumn, in the shape of a Christmas giftbook, under the title of "The Story that Transformed the World."

W. T. STEAD.

LUCERNE, *June* 18*th*, 1890.

CONTENTS.

Frontispiece. Ecce Homo!—Joseph Maier as Christus.

Preface. Why this Book was Written . . . . .

Chap. I. The Story that Transformed the World . . .
   Portrait—Mary, the Mother of Jesus.
     " Christus.

Chap. II. Ober Ammergau and its Vow . . . .
   Illustration—View of Ober Ammergau.

   Plan of the Theatre, with Numbered Seats . . .

Chap. III. The Theatre of the Passion Play . . .
   Portrait—The Chorogus.

   Specimens of the Music . . . . .

   Names of the Performers . . . . .

Chap. IV. The Passion Play—Text in German and English .
   Tableau—The Expulsion from Paradise.
     " The Adoration of the Cross.

   Act 1. The Entry of Christ into Jerusalem . .
    Illustration—Christ driving the Traders out of the Temple.
    Portraits—Ezechiel, Nathanael, and Sadok.

   Act 2. The Sanhedrim . . . . .
    Portraits—Caiaphas and Annas.

   Act 3. The Leave-Taking at Bethany . . .
    Portraits—Martha, Mary, and Mary Magdalene.
      " James, Peter, and John.

   Act 4. The Last Journey to Jerusalem . .
    Portrait—Judas.
    Illustration—Ordering the Passover.

   Act 5. The Last Supper . . . . .
    Illustration—The Last Supper.
    Portraits—James the Less, Thomas, Simon, and Matthew.
      " Andrew, Philip, Bartholomew, Thaddeus.

   Act 6. Judas, the Traitor . . . .
    Illustration—Judas receives the Price of Blood.
    Portraits—Nicodemus, and Joseph of Arimathæa.

CONTENTS

		PAGE
Act 7. IN GETHSEMANE		60
Illustration—JESUS IN THE GARDEN.		
" THE BETRAYAL.		
Act 8. JESUS BEFORE ANNAS		67
Act 9. JESUS BEFORE CAIAPHAS		70
Illustration—JESUS BEFORE CAIAPHAS.		
Act 10. THE DESPAIR OF JUDAS		77
Portrait— JUDAS.		
Act 11. CHRIST BEFORE PILATE		81
Portraits— RABINTH, SAMUEL, AND A RABBI.		
" PILATE AND HEROD.		
Act 12. CHRIST BEFORE HEROD		88
Illustration—BEFORE KING HEROD.		
Act 13. CHRIST SCOURGED AND CROWNED WITH THORNS		92
Illustration—THE CROWNING WITH THORNS.		
Act 14. CHRIST CONDEMNED TO DEATH		96
Portraits—"THIS MAN!" OR BARABBAS?		
Act 15. THE WAY OF THE CROSS		102
Illustration— IN THE VIA DOLOROSA.		
Portraits— VERONICA, THE CENTURION, AND SIMON OF CYRENE.		
Act 16. THE CRUCIFIXION		108
Illustration—ON CALVARY.		
Portraits OF—MARY, THE MOTHER OF JESUS.		
Illustration— THE DESCENT FROM THE CROSS.		
" CHRIST IN THE BOSOM OF MARY.		
Act 17. THE RESURRECTION		118
Illustration—JESUS RISING FROM THE GRAVE.		
Act 18. THE ASCENSION		120
TABLEAU.		
Chap. V. THE GOSPEL ACCORDING TO ST. DAISENBERGER		121
Chap. VI. SOME GENERAL REFLECTIONS		123
Appendix. HOW TO GET TO OBER AMMERGAU		126
TRAVEL HINTS		127
MAP OF DISTRICTS		129
FARES, TIME TABLES, ETC		130

THE PASSION PLAY AS IT IS PLAYED TO-DAY.

I.—THE STORY THAT TRANSFORMED THE WORLD.

OBER AMMERGAU, June 9th, 1890.

This is the story that transformed the world!
    This is the story that transformed the world!
Yes, and will yet transform it!
Yes, thank God, so the answer comes; and will yet transform it, until Thy Kingdom comes!
This is the story that transformed the world. I awoke shortly after midnight, after seeing the Passion Play at Ober Ammergau, with these words floating backwards and forwards in my head like a peal of bells from some distant spire. Backwards and forwards they went and came, and came and went!
This is the story that transformed the world!
This is the story that transformed the world. And then in the midst of the reiterated monotone of this insistant message came this glad response from I know not where.—Yes, and will yet transform it! And then the two met and mingled, strophe and antistrophe, one answering the other, "This is the story that has transformed the world. Yes, and will yet transform the world!"
I tried to sleep, but could not. It was as if church bells were pealing their sweet but imperious music within my brain. So I got up and wrote.

All is silent save the ticking of the watch by my bed-side; silent as the stars which gleam down from the blue sky above the cross-crowned crag, which stands like some gaunt sentinel keeping watch over the village at its foot. Herod, our host, sleeps soundly, and Johannes, wearied by his double service of waiter at the hotel and his rôle in the sacred play, is oblivious of all. The crowded thousands who watched for hours yesterday the unfolding of the Passion of Christ Jesus of Galilee have disappeared, and I am alone.

But not alone. For as real and as vivid as that same crowd of yesterday seem to me the thronging memories of other days, of the centuries that rise between the time when Jesus really lived on earth and to-day. Nearly nineteen hundred years have gone since all that we saw represented yesterday was no mere mimic show but deadly tragic fact; nineteen hundred years during which the shaping power of the world has been that story. The old, old story, never before so vividly realised in all its human significance and its Divine import.

Its human significance, for, thank God, we have at last seen Jesus as a man among men, a human being with no halo round his brow, no radiance not of this world marking him off apart from the rest of us his fellow-men, but simply Jesus, the Galilean, gibbeted on the gallows of his time, side by side with the scum of mankind.

And it was this story that transformed the world! "Thou hast conquered, O pale Galilean!" Over how many tribes and nations and kindreds of men? On this very spot, by the side of the swift-flowing Ammer, what strange rites were being celebrated long centuries after the cry of victory over death burst from the lips of the Crucified, and yet here we stand to-day.

Oh, the wonder of it all, the miracle of miracles surely is this! That this story should have transformed the world. For after all, what was the Passion? Looked at as we looked at it yesterday, not from the standpoint of those who see the sacred story through the vista of centuries that have risen in splendour and set in the glory of the Cross, but from the standpoint which the actors on the stage assumed yesterday, what was the Passion? It was merely a passing episode in the unceasing martyrdom of man. Think you that of the thirty thousand Jews whom the humane Titus by a mere stroke of his stylus condemned to be crucified round the walls of Jerusalem forty years after that scene on Calvary, none suffered like this? For them also was reared the horrid cross, nor were they spared the mockings and the scourgings, the cruel thirst, and the slow-drawn agony of days of death. And among all that unnamed multitude how few were there but had some distracted mother to mourn for him, some agonised Mary to swoon at the news of his death? Jews they were; as was he. Hero souls, no doubt faithful unto death, and now, let us hope, wearing a crown of life; patriots who knew how to die in the service of the land which their fathers had received from God, and of the Temple in which was preserved His Holy Law. But their self-sacrifice availed not even to save their names from oblivion. Their martyrdom was as powerless to avert the doom of the chosen people as the bursting of the foam-flakes on the sand is to arrest the rush of the returning tide.

Why, then, should the death of one Jew have transformed the world, while the death of these uncounted thousands failed even to save the synagogue?

Why? That is the question that the Passion Play forces home — a question which never even comes to the mind of those who are accustomed from childhood to regard this Jew as mysteriously Divine, not so much man as God, cut off from us and our daily littleness by the immeasurable abyss that yawns between the finite and the Infinite. This greatest of all the miracles, the coming of Christendom into being, has become so much a matter of course that we marvel as little at it as we do at the sunrise — which, also, in its way, is wonder-worthy enough. Think, for a moment, of how many myriads of fierce heathen, worshipping all manner of proud ancestral gods, have gone down before the might of that pale form. Civilisations and empires have gone down into the void; darkness covers them and oblivion is fast erasing the very inscriptions which History has traced on their tombs. But the kingdom which this man founded knoweth no end. The voice that echoed from the hills of Galilee is echoing to-day from hills the Romans never trod, and the story of that life is rendered in tongues unknown at Pentecost. The more you look at it from the standpoint of the contemporaries of the Carpenter of Nazareth, the more incredibly marvellous it appears.

And that is the great gain of the Passion Play. It takes us clear back across the ages to the standpoint of those who saw Jesus the Galilean was but a man among men. It compels us to see him without the aureole of Divinity, as he appeared to those who knew him from his boyhood and who said — Are not his brethren still with us? It is true that it is still not real enough. The dresses are too beautiful; everything is conventional. We have here not the real Christ, the Jew, the outcast, and the vagabond. For him we must wait till Vereschagin or some other realist painter may bring us reality. But even behind all the disguises of conventional Christian art, we have at least a sufficiently human figure to elicit sympathy, compassion, and love. We get near enough to Christ to hear the blows that fall upon his face, to appreciate the superior respectability of the

MARY, THE MOTHER OF JESUS.

high priests, and to understand the contempt of Herod for "the king of fools." Not until we start low enough do we understand the heights to which the Crucified has risen. It is only after realising the depth of his humiliation we can even begin to understand the miracle of the transformation which he has wrought.

Nor is that all. It is the greatest thing, but it does not stand alone. For besides enabling us to realise the story which transformed the world, it enables us to understand the agency by which that story effected its beneficent revolution. I learned more of the inner secret of the Catholic Church in Ober-Ammergau than ever I learnt in Rome. Yet there is nothing distinctively Roman about the Passion Play. With the exception of the legend of St. Veronica, with which Gabriel Max's picture has familiarised every Protestant who looks into a photograph-shop, and sees the strange face on the handkerchief, whose eyes reveal themselves beneath your gaze; there is nothing from first to last to which the Protestant Alliance could take exception. And yet it is all there. There, condensed into eight hours and less, is the whole stock-in-trade of the Christian Church. It was in its effort to impress that story upon the heart of man that there came into being all that is distinctively Roman. To teach truth by symbols, to speak through the eye as much as the ear, to leave no gate of approach unsummoned by the bearer of the glad tidings of great joy, and, above all, in so doing to use every human element of pathos, of tragedy, and of awe that can touch the heart or impress the imagination—that was the mission of the Church; and as it got further and further afield, and had to deal with ruder and ruder barbarians, the tendency grew to print in still larger capitals. The Catholic Church, in short, did for religion what the new journalism has done for the press. It has sensationalised in order to get a hearing among the masses.

Protestantism that confines its gaze solely to the sublime central figure of the Gospel story walks with averted face past the beautiful group of the Holy Women. Because others have ignorantly worshipped, therefore we must not even contemplate. But plant Mr. Kensit or Messrs. Morgan and Scott in the theatre of Ober-Ammergau, let them look with dry eyes—if they can — upon the leave-taking at Bethany, and then as the universal sob rises from thousands of gazers, they will realise, perhaps for the first time, how intense is the passion of sympathy which they have sealed up, how powerful the emotion to which they are forbidden to appeal. The most pathetic figure in the Passion Play is not Christ, but His mother. There is in Him also sublimity. She is purely pathetic. And after Mary the Mother comes Mary the Magdalen. Protestantism will have much leeway to make up before it can find any influence so potent for softening the hearts and inspiring the imaginations of men. Even in spite of all the obloquy of centuries of superstition, and of the consequent centuries of angry reaction against this abuse, these two women

CHRISTUS.

stand out against the gloom of the past radiant as the angels of God, and yet the true ideals of the womanhood of the world.

Yes, this was the story that transformed the world! This and no other. This it was which, to make visible, men carved it in stone and built it in the cathedral, and then, lest even the light of Heaven should come to the eye of man without bearing with it the Story of the Cross, they filled their church windows with stained glass, so that the sun should not shine without throwing into brighter relief the leading features of the wonder-working epic of His life and death. Wherever you go in Christendom you come upon endless reproductions of the scenes which yesterday we saw presented with all the vividness of the drama. The cross, the nails, the lance have been built into the architecture of the world, often by the descendants of the men who crucified their Redeemer—not knowing what they did. For centuries Art was but an endless repetition in colour or in stone of the scenes we witnessed yesterday, or of incidents in lives which had been transformed by these scenes. The more utterly we strip the story of the Passion of all supernatural significance, the more irresistibly comes back upon the mind the overwhelming significance of the transformation which it has effected in the world.

Why?—I keep asking why? If there were no divine and therefore natural law behind all that, why should that trivial incident, the crucifixion of one among the unnumbered host of vagabonds executed every year in the reign of Tiberius and the Cæsars that followed him, how comes it that we are here to-day? Why are railways built and special trains organized and six thousand people gathered in curiosity or in awe to see the representation of this simple tale? How comes it, if there were no dynamo at the other end of that long coil of centuries, that the light should still be shining at our end to-day? Shining, alas! not so brightly as could be wished, but to shine at all, is that not in itself miraculous?

Through all the ages it has shone with varying lustre. And still it shines. The dawn of a new day as I write is breaking upon this mountain valley. The cocks are crowing in the village, recalling the Apostle who, in the midst of the threatening soldiery, denied his Lord. And even as Peter went out and wept bitterly, and ever after became the stoutest and bravest disciple of his Master, may it not yet be with those of this generation who also have denied their Redeemer?

Who knows? The transformation would be far less startling than that which converted the Colosseum from the shambles of Imperial Rome into the gigantic monument of triumphant martyrdom, far less violent than that which made the German forbears of these good Ammergauers into Christian folk.

But if the transformation is to be effected, and the light and warmth of a new day of faith, and hope, and love are to irradiate our world, then may it not be confidently asserted that in the old, old story of the Cross lies the secret of the only power which can save mankind?

II.—OBER AMMERGAU AND ITS VOW.

I FEEL grateful to Caspar Schuchler. Poor Caspar Schuchler! He deserved well of posterity, although he played a scurvy trick to his contemporaries, for which the fates promptly exacted capital punishment. Caspar Schuchler was a humble day labourer of Ober Ammergau, who lived in the reigns of our Queen Elizabeth and King James. In old days, as far back, it is said, as the twelfth century, there had been a Passion Play performed in the little village, but towards the close of the sixteenth century, the wars that wasted Germany left but little time even to the dwellers in these remote highlands for dramatic representation. Gustavus Adolphus and his Swedes, good fellows, no doubt, who were fighting on the right side, nevertheless played dreadful havoc with the homes and fortunes of the German folk who were on the other side. Among these unfortunates were the Bavarians of the Tyrol, and as one of the remote after-consequences of that wide-wasting thirty years' war, a great pestilence broke out in the villages surrounding Ober Ammergau. Whole families were swept off. In one village only two married couples were left alive. It was a visitation somewhat similar to our Black Death. While village after village fell a prey to its ravages, the people of Ober Ammergau remained untouched, and enforced a vigorous quarantine against all the outside world. Their preventive measures were for a while successful. But then, as always, the blind instinctive promptings of the human heart broke through the most necessary sanitary regulations in the person of Caspar Schuchler. This good man who was working in the plague-stricken village of Eschenlohe, felt an uncontrollable desire to return to his wife and children who were living in Ober Ammergau. Whether it was that he felt the finger of death upon him, and that he wished to see his loved ones before he died, or whether he merely wished as Housefather to see that they had bread to eat and a roof to cover them, history does not record. All that it says is that Caspar Schuchler evaded the quarantine and returned to his wife and little ones. A terrible retribution followed. In two days he was dead, and the plague which he had brought with him spread with such fatal haste from house to house that in thirty-three days eighty-four of the villagers had perished. At this moment, the Ober Ammergauers in their despair assembled to discuss their desperate plight. Unless the plague were stayed there would soon not be enough living to bury the dead. Sanitary preventive measures had failed. Curative measures were utterly useless. Where the plague struck death followed. It was as men looking into the hollow eye-sockets of Death that the Ober Ammergauers cried aloud to God. They remembered their sins that day. They would repent, and in token of their penitence and as a sign of gratitude for their deliverance—if they were delivered—they would every ten years perform the Passion Play. And then, says the local chronicler, from that hour the plague was stayed. Those who were already smitten of the plague recovered, nor did any others fall victims to the pestilence. Since Moses lifted up the brazen serpent in the wilderness, there had not been so signal a deliverance from mortal illness on such simple terms. Thus it was that the Passion Play became a fixed institution in Ober Ammergau, and has been performed, with a few variations due to wars—such as that which summoned the Christ of 1870 to come down from the cross to serve in the Bavarian artillery—ever since. The performance of the Passion Play, like the angel with the drawn sword which stands on the summit of the Castle of San Angelo, is the pious recognition of a miraculous interposition for the stay of pestilence, a kind of dramatic rainbow set in the hills to commemorate the stay of the pestilential deluge. But for Caspar Schuchler it would have gone the way of all other Passion Plays, if, indeed, it had not already perished even before his time. His offence saved it from the general wreck. He sinned, no doubt, and he suffered. He died, and it is probable that his own family were the first to perish. But out of his sin and of their sorrow has come the Passion Play as we have it to-day, the one solitary survival of what was at one time a great instrument of religious teaching, almost universal throughout Europe. Hence I feel grateful to Caspar Schuchler.

And after Caspar, who was the guilty cause of this unique survival, our gratitude is due chiefly to the good parish priest, Daisenberger, to whom—more than to any other man—is due the conversion of the rude mystery or miracle play of the Middle Ages into this touching and tragic unfolding of the greatest drama in history. For thirty-five years he lived and laboured in the village, presiding as a true father in Israel over the mental, moral, and spiritual development of his parishioners. A born dramatist and a pious Christian, he saw the opportunity which the performance offered, and he made the most of it. Stripping the play of all that was ignoble or farcical—and nothing is more curious than the way in which all miracle plays ran to farce; even at Ober Ammergau, before Daisenberger's time, the Devil excited uproarious hilarity, as he tore open the bowels of the unfortunate suicide, Judas, and produced therefrom strings of sausages—he produced a wonderfully faithful dramatic rendering of the Gospel story. Thus the Geistlicher Rath became the Evangelist of Ober Ammergau. The play which we have been witnessing is the Gospel according to St. Daisenberger. His beatification has not been declared at Rome, and his version is not entitled to rank with the canonical Scriptures; but none the less, generations yet to come may rise up and call him blessed, and his version, unauthorised though it be, enables all who see it to realise more vividly than ever before the human side of the Martyrdom of Jesus.

Ober Ammergau is a beautiful little village standing in a level valley almost on the water-shed of the Bavarian Alps. A mile or two on one side the streams run east towards Munich, but here in the village itself the Ammer runs westward towards the Planer See. Looked at from above, it forms an ideal picture of an ideal village. The clean white walls of the houses, with their green window-shutters, are irregularly grouped round the church, which, with its mosque-like minaret, forms the living centre of the place. It is the rallying point of the villagers, who used to perform their play in the churchyard—architecturally as morally the keystone of the arch. Seen at sunset or at sunrise the red-tiled and grey-

VIEW OF OBER AMMERGAU.

slated roofs which rise among the trees on the other side of the rapid and crystal Ammer seem to nestle together under the shade of the surrounding hills around the protecting spire of the church. High over head gleams the white cross on the lofty Kofel crag which guards the entrance to the valley.

In the irregular streets Tyrolese mountaineers are strolling and laughing in their picturesque costume, but at the solemn Angelus hour, when the music of the bells swings out in the upper air, every hat is raised, and bareheaded all remain until the bells cease to peal. It is a homely, simple, unspoiled village, and that they have been unspoiled by the flood from the outer world which submerges them every week all summer through every ten years is in itself almost as the miracle of the burning bush. The student of social economics might do worse than spend some days observing how life goes with the villagers of Ober Ammergau. They are more like Swiss than Germans. They inhabit the northern fringe of the great mass of mountains which divide the flat lands of Germany from the plains of Italy, and have most of the characteristics of the mountaineers who, whether they be called Swiss or Tyrolese, is one of the most respectworthy species of the human race. Isolation begets independence, and the little community, secure amidst its rocky ramparts against the intermeddling despotism of distant governments, develope the most simple and the most sound system of democratic government. There is a burgomaster, but he is elected, and the government is vested in the hands of the householders. Nearly every man is a landholder—the poorest have about three acres, the richest about sixty. But over and above that they have the inestimable privilege of pasturage on the Alp. Talk about three acres and a cow! That ideal has been more than realized ever so long ago at Ober Ammergau. Never was there such a place for cows. Every night and morning a long procession of cows, each with her tinkling bell hanging from her neck, marches sedately through the principal street to and from the milking shed. They wander on the hills all day, but come home to be milked every evening, and the continuous tinkling of their bells fills the valley with delightful music. The whole population of Ober Ammergau is not more than thirteen hundred, but they own between them some five or six hundred cows. Few more pleasant sights will you meet in all your travels than the coming home of the cows at milking time. The goats also and the horses all have bells, but the cows so far outnumber all the rest that the others pass unnoticed.

The various wayside shrines that pious souls have reared along the public road, wherever accident befell a drunken waggoner or careless woodman, are touching mementoes of the tragic incidents in the uneventful annals of the valley. Ettal used to be a famous place of pilgrimage before its monastery was transformed into a brewery, and even now its miraculous Madonna is an object of reverence to all the country side. The story goes that the image is invisible to the very reprobate, is as heavy as lead to the impenitent sinner, but as light as a feather to all those who are of a contrite heart. It is natural that all the roads leading to such a pilgrim haunt should be studded with these little shrines. We should be none the worse for a few similar memorials in this country.

It is often wet in Ober Ammergau when the sun is shining all around. Of this I had a curious experience the day I drove over to the Bad Anstalt at Kohlgrub. Kohlgrub is but one hour from Ober Ammergau, but it lies much higher. It stands on the other side of the hill, and commands a magnificent prospect over the lakes and mountains of Bavaria. The season was just commencing, and there were therefore but a few of the hundreds of visitors who in a week or two would crowd the roomy and airy establishment which Messrs. Faller and Buchmüller have built on the famous iron spring of the Kohlgrub. The air was most invigorating. The blue waters of the lakes that lay in the valley at the foot of the hills, the quaint old church of St. Martin, the village that clambered up the hillside, the dark green woods that clothed the mountain, all stood out distinct and clear in the brilliant sunlight. But one hour after leaving Kohlgrub we drove right into a horrible pelting rain that had never ceased all the afternoon in the valley of the Ammer. Hence if it rains in Ober Ammergau the visitor never need despair. He may find perfect weather within an hour's drive.

Very quaint and curious is the effect produced by the appearance of the actors in the Passion Play in their every-day costume. Maier, the Christ, an excellent family man, makes his living by carving crucifixes. Lechner, the most famous Judas of our time, lives in this house. Over yonder stands the Burgomaster's, where if you ask for Caiaphas, you will be told by his daughter, the Virgin Mary, that he has just gone across to the inn to drink beer with the village doctor. That is King Herod driving the Zweispanner that just passed us, and that long-haired lad, who is lighting his cigar in the middle of the street, is the Apostle John. I was lodged in the house of Herod, and we were waited upon at table by St. John. "Johannes, Johannes!" you could hear from the kitchen, and thither Johannes would hasten, bringing back the bottles of beer or plates of meat for which hungry guests were clamouring. All is so strange and simple. As I write it is now two days after the Passion Play. The crowd has departed, the village is once more quiet and still. The swallows are twittering in the eaves, and blue and cloudless sky overarches the amphitheatre of hills. All is peace, and the whole dramatic troupe pursue with equanimity the even tenor of their ordinary life. Most of the best players are woodcarvers; the others are peasants or local tradesmen. Their royal robes or their rabbinical costumes laid aside, they go about their ordinary walk in the ordinary way as ordinary mortals. But what a revelation it is of the mine of latent capacity, musical, dramatic, intellectual, in the human race, that a single mountain village can furnish, under a capable guidance, and with adequate inspiration, such a host competent to set forth such a play from its tinkers, tailors, ploughmen, bakers, and the like. It is not native capacity that is lacking to mankind. It is the guiding brain, the patient love, the careful education, and the stimulus and inspiration of a great idea. But, given these, every village of country yokels from Dorset to Caithness might develop artists as noble and as devoted as those of Ober Ammergau.

NUMBERED PLAN OF SEATS.

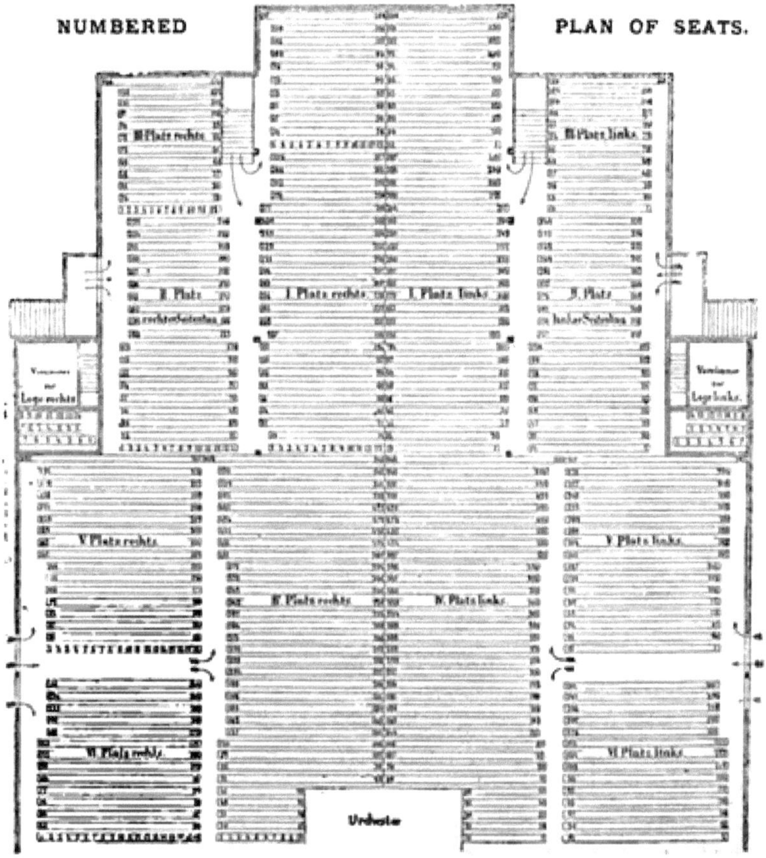

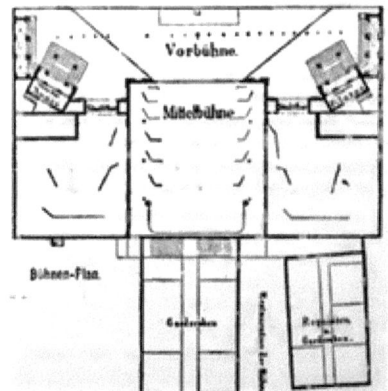

PRICES OF SEATS.

Under Cover.

1st Place	.. ..	10s.
2nd "	.. ..	8s.
3rd "	.. ..	6s.

Without Cover.

4th Place	.. ..	5s.
5th "	.. ..	3s.
6th "	.. ..	1s.

Sixpence extra charged for Booking.

PLAN OF THEATRE

on half-scale of Auditorium.

The Choir of Schuetzgeister stand on the Vorbuehne or Stage, and draw to one side when the Tableaux are exhibited.

III.—THE THEATRE OF THE PASSION PLAY.

The theatre in which the Passion Play is performed is better understood by looking at the accompanying ground-plan than by any verbal description. It stands in a meadow at the far end of the village, and from all parts of the auditorium you see a background of blue sky and fir-crowned hills. Half of the seats are in the open air, half under cover. If it rains the performance goes on, and half the audience is drenched. If the sun blazes the spectators in the open are roasted. But there is no help for it—"rain or shine," the play goes on. Umbrellas are not allowed. The seats are all numbered. If the weather is at all chilly, rugs are almost indispensable. In wet weather you shiver on your seats, and, as you occupy them for four hours at a stretch, you have leisure for regretting your neglect to bring the necessary wrappings. Even with an ample fur rug I felt miserably cold on Sunday morning; yet, on Monday afternoon, in the open I was nearly broiled in the blaze of afternoon sun. Opera-glasses are allowed, and are a necessity to all near-sighted persons. Lunch baskets are not forbidden. But against photographic cameras, kodaks and the like, the regulations are very severe. Not knowing this, I took in a kodak. Caiaphas spied me from the stage, and despatched a messenger to forbid its use; then another to insist upon the confiscation of the plates, and finally, I was at the close of the performance marched off under arrest to the burgomaster's office to render an account to his highness of my misdeeds. I found Caiaphas in quasi-private, or rather, in his local official capacity, very courteous and dignified. He explained that they had sold the monopoly of photographing the play and the performers to three enterprising gentlemen—Messrs. Faller, Buchmüller, and Stockmann, of the Kunst und Verlags-Anstalt, Oberammergau—and it was, therefore, his duty to prevent any other photographs being taken. As I had already received permission to reproduce their photographs from the gentlemen in question, I was released. The experience of being brought up before Caiaphas was, however, a novel and unexpected pleasure—a pleasure enhanced by the opportunity which it afforded me of seeing Caiaphas and the Virgin off the stage in their every-day dress, and of expressing to them the admiration which every one feels who has enjoyed the opportunity of seeing their wonderful performance. What would have happened to me if I had not had permission I do not know. Other visitors who wish to take snap-shots from the auditorium had better trust to small detective cameras, otherwise they may get into serious trouble.

As a rule, most people come early, and stay till the close of the performance. Some, however, behave abominably, arriving late, leaving in the middle of a scene, and generally disturbing all those who are unfortunate enough to be in their neighbourhood.

The play begins at eight, and the first part ends at quarter to twelve. After an hour and a half allowed for luncheon, it is resumed at quarter-past one, and closes about half-past five.

The good priest Daisenberger has left on record that he "undertook the production of the play for the love of my Divine Redeemer, and with only one object in view, the edification of the Christian world." In order to attain this

CHORAGUS.

end he deemed it necessary to follow the scriptural method. Instead of simply setting forth the Gospel story as it stands in the New Testament, he took as his fundamental idea the connection of the Passion, incident by incident, with the types, figures and prophecies of the Old Testament. The whole of the Old Testament is thus made as it were the massive pedestal for the Cross, and the course of the narrative of the Passion is perpetually interrupted or illustrated by scenes from the older Bible, which are supposed to prefigure the next event to be represented on the stage. Thus, in Daisenberger's words, "The representation of the Passion is arranged and performed on the basis of the entire Scriptures."

In order to explain the meaning of the typical tableaux and to prepare the audience for the scene which they are about to witness, resource is had to an ingenious arrangement, whereby the interludes between each scene are filled up with singing in parts and in chorus by a choir of Schutzgeister, or Guardian Angels. The choragus or leader of the choir first recites some verses clearly and impressively, then the choir burst out into song, accompanied by an orchestra concealed from view in front of the stage. The tinkle of a little bell is heard, and the singers draw back so as to reveal the tableau. The curtain rises and the tableau is displayed, during which they sing again. The curtain falls, they resume their old places, and the singing proceeds. Then when they come to the end half file off to the right, half to the left, and the play proper begins. When the curtain falls they again take their places and resume their song. The music is very simple but impressive, and the more frequently it is heard the more you feel its force and pathos. The chorus occupies the stage for fully half the time devoted to the piece.

Their dress is very effective. From the choragus in the centre in bright scarlet, all wear coronets, with the cross in the centre, and are habited in white under-tunic, with golden edging, in yellow leather sandals, and stockings of the same colour as the robe which falls from their shoulders. These robes, held in place by gold decorated cords and tassels round the breast and round the waist, are arranged very artistically and produce a brilliant effect, especially when the wearers are leaving the stage by the wings. Twice, however, these brilliant robes are exchanged for black—immediately before and immediately after the Crucifixion. The bright robes, however, are resumed at the close, when the play closes with a burst of hallelujahs and of jubilant triumph over the Ascension of our Lord.

SPECIMENS OF THE MUSIC.

HOSANNA TO THE SON OF DAVID.

[Act I. Sc. 1.]

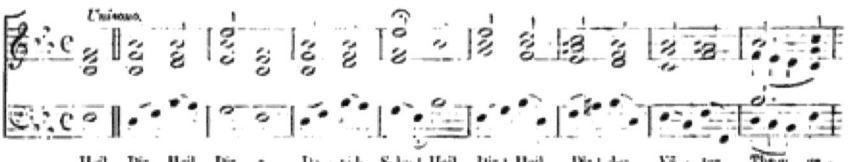

Heil Dir, Heil Dir, o Da- vids Sohn! Heil Dir! Heil Dir! der Vä- ter Thron ge-

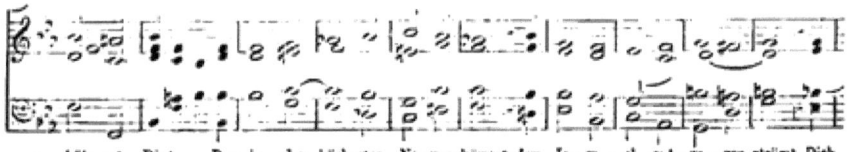

-büh-ret Dir! Der in des höch-sten Na- men kömmt, dem Is- ra- el ent- ge- gen strömt, Dich

THE JOURNEY TO CALVARY.

THE LAMENT OF THE BRIDE.

NAMES OF THE PERFORMERS.

Christus (wiedergewählt zum 3. Male)	Josef Mayr	Schnitzwaarenverleger	alt 47
Johannes (neugewählt)	Peter Rendl	Schnitzer	„ 19
Petrus (wiedergewählt zum 4. Male)	Jacob Hett	Schnitzer	„ 67
Maria (neugewählt)	Rosa Lang	Bürgermeisterstochter	„ 22
Magdalena (neugewählt)	Amalie Deschler	Schnitzerstochter	„ 23
Martha (neugewählt)	Helena Lang	Schnitzerstochter	„ 20
Josef von Arimathaea (wiedrgewählt)	Martin Opperrieder	Schnitzer	„ 32
Nicodemus (wiedergewählt)	Franz Steinbacher	Farbermeister	„ 38
Kaiphas (wiedergewählt)	Bürgermeister Lang	Burgermeister	„ 51
Annas (neugewählt)	Franz Rutz, sen.	Schneidermeister	„ 45
Nathanael (wiedergewählt)	Sebastian Lang, jun.	Messner	„ 49
Rabbi (wiedergewählt)	Sebastian Bauer	Schnitzer	„ —
Judas (neugewählt)	Johann Zwink	Maler	„ 30
Pilatus (wiedergewählt)	Thomas Rendl	Haushofmeister der Frau von Hillern	„ 52
Herodes (neugewählt)	Johann Diemer	Privatier	„ 44
Jakobus (wiedergewählt)	Andreas Braun	Schnitzer	„ —
Richter Schärcher (Dismas, neugewählt)	Peter Lang	Maurer	„ —
Linker Schärcher (neugewählt)	Eduard Bierling	Schäftlermeister	„ —
Barabbas	Joh. Oswald	Taglöhner	„ —
Philippus	Tobias Zwink	———	
Thaddaeus	Josef Kurz	———	
Simon	M. Hohenleitner	———	
Jakobus min.	Josef Klucker	———	
Thomas	Andreas Lang	———	
Matthaeus	Alois Gerold	———	
Bartholomaeus	Martin Albl	———	
Moses	Tobias Zwink	———	
Ezechiel	Rochus Lang	———	
Sadok	Seb. Deschler	———	
Josue	Andr. Wolf	———	
Mererie	Anton Gastl	———	
Samuel	G. Schnellhammer	———	
Rabinth	Eduard Albl	———	
Hauptmann	Anton Bartl	———	
Veronika	Elis. Zundterer	———	
Nathan	Frz. Paul Lang	———	
Dariabdas	Joh. Lang, jun.	———	
Simon von Cyrene	Michael Bauer	Schnitzer	„ —

Prologos oder Chorführer (neugewählt) Jacob Rutz, Huf- und Wagenschmied.

Leiter der Stücke ist Herr Bürgermeister Lang.—Leiter der lebenden Bilder, Herr Zeichenlehrer Lang.

Das Orchester, dessen ausgezeichneter Dirigent Joseph Gruber (Oberlehrer in Oberammergau) ist, wird zweifellos vorzügliche Anerkennung finden.

Hauptsänger und Prolog-Deklamator ist Jakub Rutz, Wagenschmied.

Im Ganzen werden ca. 750 Personen (125 sprechende) mitwirken, darunter 50 Frauen und 230 Kinder.

SCHUTZGEISTER.

Sopran.
Josepha Breitenzauter.
Ludovica Guidhart.
Anna Kornthcuer.
Luzie Lang.
Aloisia Mayr.
Regina Wolf.
Maria Susum.

Alt.
Antonia Albl.
Crescenz Bierling.
Johanna Keller.
Crescenz Klamer.
Magdalena Kopf.

Alt.
Maria Lutz.
Josepha Steidle.

Tenor.
Otto Anderl, Hilfslehrer.
Korbinian Christa.
Alois Lang.
Anton Lechner.
Dominikus Schlieher.

Bass.
Joseph Gabler.
Anton Lutz.
Otto Mangold.
Korbinian Rutz.

IV.—THE PASSION PLAY.

ERSTE ABTHEILUNG.

Vom Einzuge Christi in Jerusalem bis zur Gefangennehmung im Olivengarten.

I. VORSTELLUNG.
PROLOG.

Choragus.—*Recit.*

Wirf zum heiligen Staunen dich nieder,
Von Gottes Fluch gebeugtes Geschlecht!
Friede dir! aus Sion Gnade wieder!
Nicht ewig zürnet Er,
Der Beleidigte, ist sein Zürnen gleich gerecht.
"Ich will," so spricht der Herr,
"Den Tod des Sünders nicht,—vergeben
Will ich ihm—er soll leben!"
Und opfert seinen Sohn, die Welt von Sünde zu befreien.
Preis und Dank dafür wir weihen
Ew'ger, Dir!

TABLEAU.—*Die Vertreibung aus dem Paradies.*

DIE VERTREIBUNG.

[Dieses erste Bild dient als Einführung in das eigentliche Passionspiel und ist so allgemein bekannt, dass es einer Erinnerung nicht bedarf.]

Die Menschheit ist verbannt aus Edens Au'n,
Vom Sünd' umnachtet und von Todesgrau'n.
Zum Lebensbaum ist ihr der Zugang, ach! versperrt.
Es drohet in des Cherubs Hand das Flammenschwert.
Doch von ferne, von Kalvaria's Höhen
Leuchtet durch die Nacht ein Morgenglüh'n.
Von dem Baum des Kreuzes milde wehen
Friedenslüfte durch die Welten hin.

Chorus.

Gott! Erbarmer! Sünder zu begnaden,
Die verachtet frevelnd Dein Gebot,
Giebst Du, sie vom Fluche zu entladen,
Deinen Eingebornen in den Tod.

TABLEAU.—*Die Anbetung des Kreuzes.*

DIE ANBETUNG.

[Das zweite Bild zeigt die Anbetung des Kreuzes durch als Engel gekleidete Kinder.]

Choragus.—*Recit.*

Ew'ger! höre Deiner Kinder Stammeln!
Würdig kein Geschöpf Dich preisen kann.
Die beim grossen Opfer sich versammeln,
Beten Dich voll heil'ger Ehrfurcht an.

Chorus.

Folget dem Versöhner nun zur Seite,
Bis er seinen rauhen Dornenpfad
Durchgelaufen, und im heissen Streite
Hat vollbracht die höchste Siegesthat.

FIRST DIVISION.

From the entry of Jesus into Jerusalem until His arrest in the Garden of Gethsemane.

CHAPTER I.
PROLOGUE.—ACT I.

Cast thyself down in adoring love,
  Race bowed down by the curse of God!
Peace and grace out of Zion above!
  He is not wroth for ever,
Though His wrath be just—though uplifted His rod.
  Thus saith, Who changeth never—
"I will not the death of a sinner, I will forgive—
  Let him live!"
And He gave up his Son, the world from sin to free;
  Praise and thanks we give,
Eternal: to Thee!

[The first tableau is emblematic of the Fall. When the curtain is drawn up, Adam and Eve, a man and woman of the village, hoisted very decently in white sheep-skin, are flying from the Garden of Eden, where stands the tree with the forbidden fruit, while from its branches hangs the Serpent, the Tempter. An angel with a sword painted to look like flame forbids their return.]

Mankind are banished from fair Eden's glades,
Darkened around with sin, and Death's grim shades,
Unto the Tree of Life the way, alas! is barred.
Where the dread cherubim, with flaming sword, keep guard.
Yet afar, from Calvary's height,
Shines a ray of morning through the night,
From the Cross, the Tree of Love, there blow
Winds of peace through all the world below.

God! All-Merciful! Thou, Pardon-Giver—
Though men held Thy law as idle breath—
From the curse the guilty to deliver,
Gavest up Thine only Son to death.

[The second tableau represents the Adoration of the Cross. A cross of wood planted on a rock occupies the centre of the stage. One girl stands with one hand round the Cross, the other holding a palm branch, while another kneels at its foot. Around are grouped fourteen smaller cherubs, charming little creatures. All point to or gaze at the Cross.]

Hear, O Lord, Thy children's voices tremble,
  Worthily no creature Thee can praise.
They, who at the sacrifice assemble,
  Hands of reverent adoration raise.
Follow now the path that He, despising
  Thorns and steepness, trod unflinchingly,
And, in fiercest conflict agonising,
  Won, at last, eternal victory.

TABLEAU—EXPULSION FROM PARADISE.

TABLEAU—THE ADORATION OF THE CROSS.

HANDLUNG.

DER EINZUG IN JERUSALEM.

CHRISTUS *zieht unter dem Jubel des Volkes in Jerusalem ein und entreisst die Käufer und Verkäufer aus den Tempelhallen.*

ERSTE SZENE.

Männer, Frauen, Kinder, dann CHRISTUS, und die APOSTEL, nach ihnen wieder Volk,—aus dem Hintergrunde durch die rechte Seitenscene auf das Proscenium ziehend.

Chor.

Heil Dir, Heil Dir, o Davids Sohn!
Heil Dir, Heil Dir, der Vater Thron
    Gebühret Dir!
Der in des Höchsten Namen kömmt,
Dem Israel entgegenströmt,
    Dich preisen wir!

Hosanna! Der im Himmel wohnet,
Der sende alle Huld auf Dich!
Hosanna: Der dort oben thronet
Erhalte uns Dich ewiglich!

Chor.

Heil Dir, Heil Dir, &c., &c.

Gesegnet sei, das neu auflebet,
Des Vaters David Volk und Reich.
Ihr Völker! segnet, preiset, hebet
Den Sohn empor, dem Vater gleich!

Chor.

Heil Dir, Heil Dir, &c., &c.

Hosanna unserm Königssohne
Ertöne durch die Lüfte weit!
Hosanna! auf des Vaters Throne
Regiere Er voll Herrlichkeit.

Chor.

Heil Dir, Heil Dir, &c., &c.

ZWEITE SZENE.

CHRISTUS, *die* Apostel *und* Volk. Priester, Pharisäer, *und* Händler, *in der Tempelhalle.*

Christus. Was sehe ich hier? So wird das Haus meines Vaters verunehrt! Ist das Gottes Haus? Oder ist es ein Marktplatz? Die Fremdlinge, die aus den Ländern der Heiden kommen, Gott anzubeten, in diesem Gewühle des Wuchers hier sollen sie ihre Andacht verrichten? Und Ihr, Priester, Wächter des Heiligthums! Ihr seht den Gräuel an und duldet ihn? Weh' Euch! Der die Herzen erforscht, weiss es, warum Ihr selbst solchen Unfug fördert!

Händler. Wer ist wohl dieser?

Volk. Es ist der grosse Prophet aus Nazareth in Galiläa.

Chorus.

Hail to Thee! Hail! O David's Son!
Hail to Thee! Hail! Thy Father's throne
    Belongs to thee!
Thou who comest in name of the Lord,
With the throngs of Israel to meet thee outpoured,
    Thy praise sing we!

Hosanna! May He in the Heavens dwelling
Send all His blessings down on Thee;
May He whose glory the angels are telling
Keep Thee for us eternally!

CHORUS—Hail to Thee! &c.

Blest be the realm and folk of David,
Living again after long disgrace.
Praise Him and bless, ye nations saved,
Exalt the Son to the Father's place.

CHORUS—Hail to Thee! &c.

Hosanna to our Prince! The Story
Re-echo through the air again!
Hosanna! let him come in glory
Upon His Father's throne to reign.

CHORUS—Hail to Thee! &c.

THE ENTRY INTO JERUSALEM AND THE CLEANSING OF THE TEMPLE.

AND lo, there was heard a noise of singing and of joyful acclamation. A great multitude came pouring down the narrow street that runs past Pilate's house, chanting as they came. "Hail to thee, O Son of David!" Little children, old men, and maidens ran forward, some raising palm-branches, but all ever looking backwards to one who should come. More and over more streamed down the street into the open space in front of the Temple, but still the Hosanna song went on. At last, in the midst of the jubilant throng, Jesus appeared, clad in a long garment of grey, over which was cast a flowing robe. His face was composed and pensive. His long black hair and beard surrounded features somewhat swarthy from the rays of the hot sun, and he sat as he rode on the side of an ass's colt that seemed almost too small to support his weight. John, the beloved disciple, dressed in green raiment with a red mantle, led the little ass, carrying in his hand a long pilgrim staff. The mob pressed tumultuously around, singing and crying, "Hosanna to the Son of David!" Jesus blessed them as he rode through their midst. After passing the house of Pilate he suddenly dismounted. Then Jesus advanced to the front of the Temple. The Hosannas died away and he contemplated the busy scene. There were the priests busily engaged with the money-changers. Nathanael, chief orator of the Sanhedrim, stood conspicuous among the chaffering throng. There were baskets with pigeons for sale as sacrifices. There were the tables of the dealers. Buying and selling, haggling and bargaining were in full swing in the market-place. For a moment Jesus, who was above the average height and whose mien was dignified and commanding, stood as if amazed and indignant, and then suddenly burst out upon the astonished throng of priests and merchants with the following protest:—

"What see I here? Shall my Father's house be thus dishonoured? Is this the house of God, or is it a market-place? How can the strangers who come from the land of the Gentiles to worship God perform their devotions in this tumult of usury? And you," he continued, advancing a step towards the priests, who stared at him in amazement, "You priests, guardians of the Temple, can you see this abomination and permit it to continue? Woe be unto you! He who searches the heart knows why you encourage such disorder." The crowd, silent now, watched with eager interest the money-changers and priests, who but imperfectly understanding what had been said to them, stared at the intruder. "Who can this man be?" they asked. And then from the lips of all the multitude there went

Christus. [*Zu den Händlern.*] Fort von hier, Diener des Mammons! Ich gebiete es Euch. Nehmet was Euer ist und verlasset die heilige Stätte!

Die Priester. Was störst du diese Leute? — Dieses Alles ist zum Opfer bestimmt.—Wie kannst du verbieten, was der Hohe Rath erlaubt?

Händler. Darf man nicht mehr opfern?

Christus. Ausserhalb des Tempels sind der Plätze genug zu Eurem Geschäfte. Mein Haus, so spricht der Herr, soll ein Bethaus genannt werden für alle Völker: Ihr aber habt es zu einer Räuberhöhle gemacht. [*Stösst die Tische um.*] Hinweg mit diesem Allen!

Händler. Mein Geld, ach mein Geld! — Meine Tauben! [*Die Tauben fliegen davon.*] — Wer ersetzt mir den Schaden?

Christus. [*Mit einer Geissel aus Stricken.*] Hinweg! Ich will, dass diese entweihte Stätte der Anbetung des Vaters wieder gegeben werde!

Priester. Durch welches Wunderzeichen beweisest du, dass du die Macht hast, dieses zu thun?

Christus. Ihr verlangt Wunderzeichen? Ja, eines wird Euch gegeben werden: Zerstöret diesen Tempel hier, und in drei Tagen werde ich ihn wieder aufgebaut haben.

Priester. Welche prahlerische Rede? Sechsundvierzig Jahre hat man an diesem Tempel gebaut und du wolltest ihn in drei Tagen wieder aufbauen?

Volk. Gepriesen sei der da kommt im Namen des Herrn!

Priester. Hörst du diese? Verbiete es ihnen!

Christus. Ich sage Euch: Wenn diese schweigen würden, so würden die Steine reden.

Kinder. Hosannah dem Sohne David's!

Pharisäer. Wollt Ihr schweigen, Ihr Einfältigen!

Christus. Habt Ihr nie gelesen: Aus dem Munde der Kinder und Säuglinge hast du dir dein Lob bereitet? Was den Stolzen verborgen ist, den Kleinen ist es geoffenbaret. Und es wird sich die Schrift erfüllen: Der Stein, den die Bauleute verworfen haben, ist zum Ecksteine geworden: Das Reich Gottes wird von Euch genommen werden, und es wird einem Volke gegeben werden, welches dessen Früchte bringet. Jener Stein aber, — wer auf ihn fällt, wird sich an ihm zerstossen, und auf wen er fällt, den wird er zermalmen. Kommt, meine Jünger! Ich habe gethan, was der Vater mich geheissen hat. Ich habe seines Hauses Ehre vertheidiget. Die Finsterniss bleibt Finsterniss; aber in vielen Herzen wird es bald Tag werden. Lasst uns in das Innere des Heiligthumes gehen, um dort den Vater anzubeten! [*Ab.*]

Volk. Gepriesen sei der Gesalbte!

Priester. Schweigt, Nichtswürdige!

Pharisäer. Ihr sollt Alle mit ihm zu Grunde gehen!

Volk. Gesegnet sei David's Reich, das wieder erscheint!

up the simultaneous response, as if the whole throng had but one voice, "It is the great Prophet from Nazareth, in Galilee!"

Jesus then moving forward into the midst of the astonished merchants in the Temple, exclaimed, in words of imperious authority: "Away with you from here, servants of Mammon! I command it. Take what belongs to you and quit the Holy Place!"

Then the Priests, recovering somewhat their self-possession, stepped forward to remonstrate. "Why troublest thou this people?" they asked. "Everything here is for sacrifice. How canst thou forbid that which the Council has allowed?" And then the Traders, led by one Bathan, chimed in, in eager chorus, "Must there then be no more sacrifices?"

For answer Jesus stood forth, and exclaimed: "There is room enough outside the Temple for your business. 'My House,' says the Lord, 'shall be called a House of Prayer for all nations,' you have made it a den of thieves." And then, crying, "Away with all this!" with one vigorous movement he overturned the tables of the money-changers. The earthenware vessels fell crashing to the ground, the money was scattered over the floor. Some of the dismayed merchants crying, "My money, oh! my money," scrambled for the glittering coins. Others stared in fury at the unceremonious intruder. Half-a-dozen doves, released from their wicker baskets, took to flight, amid the despairing lamentation of their owners, "Oh, my doves, who will compensate me for this loss?"

Their lamentations were rudely cut short. A small rope was hanging near by. Seizing it in the middle and wrapping it once or twice round his hand, Jesus converted it into a whip of cords, with which he drove out the traders. "Away! get you hence. I will that this desecrated place be restored to the worship of the Father!" The traders fled, but the Priests remained, and, after muttering together, they asked, in angry tones: "By what miraculous sign dost thou prove that thou hast the power to act in this wise?" Jesus answered them: "You seek after a sign; Yes, a sign shall be given unto you. Destroy this Temple and in three days I will have built it up again."

The Priests replied, contempt mingling with indignation in their tones, "What a boastful declaration! Six-and-forty years was this Temple in building and thou wilt build it up again in three days?" At this point the Children, who had been standing around watching the altercation with the dealers, cried out in unison with their elders, "Blessed be he that cometh in the name of the Lord!"

The Priests, shocked at their homage, were sore displeased and appealed to Jesus, saying, "Hearest thou what they say? Forbid them!" They paused for his reply. Then Jesus answered and said unto them: "I say unto you, if they were silent the very stones would cry out." Encouraged by this emphatic approval, the Children cried out once more louder than ever, the sound of their childish voices filling the Temple, "Hosanna to the Son of David!" Then the Pharisees, who stood by the overthrown tables of the money-changers, spoke up and said angrily to the little ones, "Silence, you silly children!"

Jesus turned to them and said, "Have you never read, 'Out of the mouths of babes and sucklings thou hast perfected praise. That which is hidden from the proud is revealed unto babes'?" And as the priests and Pharisees muttered in indignation among themselves, he continued, "For the Scripture must be fulfilled. The stone which the builders rejected is become the headstone of the corner. The Kingdom of God shall be taken from you and it shall be given to a people which shall bring forth the fruits thereof. But that stone, whosoever shall fall upon it shall be broken, but on whomsoever it shall fall it shall grind him to powder. Come, my disciples, I have done what the Father has commanded me, I have vindicated the honour of his house. The darkness remains darkness, but in many hearts it will soon be day. Let us go into the inner court of the Temple that we may there pray unto the Father!" Thereupon, Jesus, followed by his disciples, disappeared in the interior of the Temple, while the People cried aloud as with one voice: "Praise be to the Anointed One!" and the Priests said angrily, "Silence, rabble!" The Pharisees adding, "Ye shall all be overthrown with your leader." To which the

THE ENTRY INTO JERUSALEM. 27

JESUS DRIVING THE TRADERS OUT OF THE TEMPLE.

DRITTE SZENE.

Priester und Volk.

Nathanael. Wer es noch mit unseren Vätern Abraham, Isaak und Jacob hält, der stehe zu uns! Allen andern der Fluch Mosis!

Rabbi. Er ist ein Verführer! Ein Feind von Moses. Ein Feind wider's heilige Gesetz!

Volk. Warum habt Ihr ihn nicht ergriffen? Ist er nicht ein Prophet? [*Ein Theil des Volkes geht* JESU *nach.*

Priester. Er ist ein Irrlehrer!

Nathanael. O du verblendetes Volk! Du willst dem Neuerer nachgeben, willst Moses, die Propheten und deine Priester verlassen? Fürchtest du nicht den Fluch, der die Abtrünnigen trifft? Wollt Ihr aufhören, das auserwählte Volk zu sein?

Volk. Das wollen wir nicht.

Nathanael. Wer hat zu wachen über die Reinheit der Lehre? Ist es nicht das heilige Synedrium des Volkes Israel? Wem wollt Ihr hören, uns oder ihn, der sich zum Verkündiger einer neuen Lehre aufgeworfen hat?

Volk. Wir hören Euch, wir folgen Euch!

Nathanael. Wohlan! er geh' zu Grunde—dieser Mensch voll Trug und Irrthum!

Volk. Ja, wir stehen euch zur Seite! Ja, wir sind des Moses Jünger!

Sadok. Der Gott der Väter wird Euch dafür segnen!

VIERTE SZENE.

Die Händler, *den "Oberhändler"* DATHAN *an der Spitze, kommen lärmend.*

Die Händler. Dieser Schimpf werde bestraft. Zur Rache! Er soll seine Verwegenheit büssen! Geld, Oel, Salz, Tauben. Alles muss er vergüten! Wo ist er, er soll unsere Rache fühlen!

Priester. Er hat sich entfernt.

Händler. Wir wollen ihm nach.

Nathanael. Bleibt, Freunde! Der Anhang dieses Menschen is noch zu grosse; es könnte ein gefahrlicher Kampf entstehen, dem das Schwert der Römer ein Ende machen würde. Vertraut auf uns: Er wird seiner Strafe nicht entgehen.

Die Priester. Mit uns, für uns, das ist Euer Heil!

Alle. Nahe ist unser Sieg!

Nathanael. Wir gehen jetzt hin, den Hohen Rath von den heutigen Vorfällen in Kenntniss zu setzen.

Händler. Wir gehen mit Euch, wir wollen Genugthuung.

Nathanael. Kommt nach einer Stunde in den Vorhof des Hohenpriesters. Ich werde im Rath Eure Beschwerde vortragen und befürworten. [*Priester ab.*

Händler und Volk [*abgehend*]. Wir haben Moses! Fort mit jedem Andern! Für Moses Lehre geh'n wir in den Tod! Gelobt, gepriesen seien unsre Väter! Gepriesen unserer Vater Gott!

II. VORSTELLUNG.

Die Anschläge des hohen Rathes.

PROLOG.

Alle seien gegrüsst, welche die Liebe hier
Um den Heiland vereint, trauernd ihm nachzugeh'n
Auf dem Wege des Leidens
Bis zur Stätte der Grabesruh.

Crowd responded by crying louder than ever. "Blessed be the Kingdom of David which again appears!" Then Nathanael, a leading man in the Sanhedrim, tall and well favoured, wearing a horned mitre, and possessing the tongue of an orator, stood forth, and seeing that Jesus had departed and that there was now no one to withstand him, in the hearing of the people, lifted up his voice and cried, "Whoso holds with our fathers, Abraham, Isaac, and Jacob, let him stand by us! The curse of Moses upon all the rest!" Then a Rabbi, in blue velvet apparel, sprang forward and declared with a loud voice, "He is a misleader of the people!" The People answered mockingly, "Then, if so, why did not you arrest him? Is he not a prophet?" Several of the multitude followed Jesus into the Temple, but the rest remained listening to the Priests, who cried more vehemently than ever. "He is a false teacher!" But Nathanael, seizing the opportunity, addressed the remainder of the multitude:

"Oh, thou blinded people, wilt thou run after the innovator, and forsake Moses, the prophets, and thy priests? Fearest thou not the curse which falls upon apostates? Would you cease to be the chosen people?"

The Crowd, shaken by this appeal, responded sullenly, "That would we not."

Nathanael pressed his advantage. "Who," he asked, "has to watch over the purity of the law? Is it not the holy Sanhedrim of the people of Israel? To whom will you listen; to us or to him? To us, or to him who has proclaimed himself the expounder of a new law?" Then the Multitude cried all together, "We hear you! we follow you!" Nathanael: "Down with him then, this man full of deceit and error! People: "Yes, we stand side by side with you! yes, we are Moses' disciples!" and the Priests answered, speaking all together, "The God of your fathers will bless you for that."

At this moment loud and angry voices were heard approaching down the narrow street that led to the house of Annas, the high priest. The priests and Pharisees listened eagerly. As they caught the word "Revenge" they turned to each other with exultant looks. Meanwhile Dathan, a merchant in red and white striped dress and turban, the chief of the Traders who had been driven from the Temple, was seen to be leading on his fellow merchants, who were lifting up their hands and weeping as they recounted their losses. They shouted confusedly as they came, "This insult must be punished! Revenge! Revenge!" He shall repent his insolence. Gold, oil, salt, doves—he must pay for all. Where is he, that he may experience our vengeance?" The Priests replied, "He has conveyed himself away." Then, cried the Traders, "We will pursue him." But Nathanael, seeing what advantage might result from the discontent of the merchants, arrested their pursuit. "Stay, friends," said he; "the faction that follows this man is at present too large. If you attacked them, it might cause a dangerous fight, which the Roman sword would finish. Trust to us. He shall not escape punishment." And the Priests who stood around Nathanael cried, "With us and for us, that is your salvation!" Then Dathan and his friends exclaimed triumphantly, "Our victory is near." Nathanael, assured of the control of the multitude, continued, "We are now going to inform the Council of the Sanhedrim of to-day's events." The Traders impatiently exclaimed, "We will go with you. We must have satisfaction!" But Nathanael dissuaded them, saying, "Come in an hour's time to the forecourt of the high priest. I will plead your cause in the council, and bring forward your complaint." And as Nathanael and the priests and the Pharisees went out, the Traders and the People cheered them, crying aloud, "We have Moses! Down with every other! We are for Moses' law to the death! Praise be to our fathers! praise to our fathers' God!"

CHAPTER II.

PROLOGUE.—ACT II.

Salutation to all here united by love,
Gathered around the Saviour, mourning, to follow Him,
On the pathway of sorrow
To the place of His burial-rest.

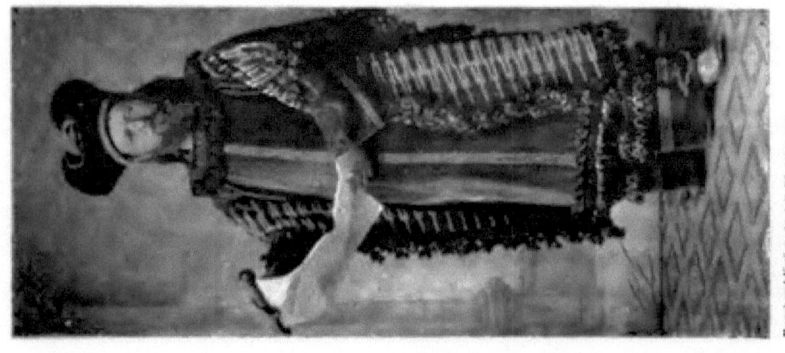

MEMBERS OF THE SANHEDRIM.

Die von nahe und fern heute gekommen sind,
Alle fühlen sich hier Eines in Bruderinn,
    Als die Jünger des Einen
    Der für Alle gelitten hat!

Der sich hingab für uns, treuer Erbarmung voll,
In den bittersten Tod, Ihm sei'n zugewandt
    Unsre Blicke und Herzen
    In einmüthigem Dankgefühl.

Seht! schon füllet sich ihm nahe der Leidenskelch;
Denn der bittere Groll neidischer Schlangenbrut,
    Mit dem Geize verschworen,
    Brütet Tod und Verderben ihm.

Choragus.—*Recit.*

Sie sind nun fort, zur Frevelthat verblendet,
Was sich verbarg im Herzen, hat der Mund verkündet,
Die Maske haben sie sich selber abgerissen,
Getrieben von dem Stachel im Gewissen.

Chor.

"Auf! Lasst uns"—schrei'n sie wild—"auf Rache sinnen,
Das längst geplante Werk beginnen."

A. VORBILD.

Die Söhne des Patriarchen Jakob beschliessen, ihren Jüngeren Bruder Joseph aus dem Wege zu räumen.—1. Moses, 37, 18.

[Joseph ist das Vorbild der Erniedrigung und Erhöhung Christi. Er ist, wie Jesus, der geliebte Sohn seines Vaters, er wird gleich ihm zu seinen Brüdern gesandt, von diesen gehasst, beschimpft, seiner Kleider beraubt und dann um einige Silberlinge an Fremde verkauft.]

Choragus.

Eröffne Gottheit uns das Heiligthum!—
Den bösen Plan im Bilde zeigt das Alterthum.
Wie Jakobs Söhne gegen Joseph sich verschwören,
So werdet ihr von dieser Natternbrut
Den Racheruf nach Jesu Blut
Blindwüthend ausgestossen hören.

ERSTE SZENE.

Die Versammlung des Hohen Rathes.

Kaiphas. Ehrwürdige Brüder, Väter und Lehrer des Volkes! Eine ausserordentliche Begebenheit ist der heutigen Berathung ausserordentlicher Gegenstand. Vernehmt ihn aus dem Munde unseres würdigen Bruders.

Nathanael. Ist es mir erlaubt, o Väter, ein Wort zu sprechen?

Alle. Ja, rede, würdiger Priester!

Nathanael. Wundert Euch nicht, Vater, dass Ihr noch in so später Stunde zur Verhandlung berufen worden seid. Es ist Euch nur zu bekannt, was wir heute zu unserer Schande mit eigenen Augen ansehen mussten. Ihr habt gesehen den Triumphzug des Galiläers durch die ganze heilige Stadt. Ihr habt gehört das Hosanah des bethörten Volkes. Ihr habt vernommen, wie der Hochmüthige sich die hohenpriesterliche Würde angemasst. Was fehlt noch zum Sturze aller staatlichen und kirchlichen Ordnung? Noch einige Schritte weiter und das heilige Gesetz Mosis ist verdrängt durch die Neuerungen dieses Irrlehrers. Die Satzungen unserer Väter sind verachtet, die Fasten und Reinigungen aufgehoben, der Sabbath entweiht, die Priester Gottes ihres Amtes entkleidet, die heiligen Opfer zu Ende.

Those who from near and far have come to-day,
All feel themselves here as one in brothers' love—
    As the disciples of one
    Lord, who has suffered for all;

Who gave Himself up for us, full of unfailing pity,
Even to bitterest death. To Him be turned now
    Our eyes and our hearts,
    In unity of thankfulness.

See! even now the cup of sorrow is filled for Him,—
For the bitter hate of the envious serpent-race
    Conspires with greed of gain
    Together, Him to destroy.

Choragus.

Now they are gone—leagued for the deed unnamed;
What the heart hid the mouth has now proclaimed.
Themselves the mask that hid the evil thing
Have torn away—driven by conscience' sting.

Chorus.

"Up!" they cry wildly, "let us vengeance brood—
The long-planned work make good!"

[The third tableau shows us the children of Jacob in the plain of Dothan conspiring how to kill Joseph, who, in his coat of many colours—in this case plain white with red facings or stripes—is approaching from behind. His brethren are leaning against the well into which they decide to fling their unfortunate victim.]

Choragus.

God open unto us the sacred shrine,
The days of old can show us, as a sign,
The evil plan set forth. As Jacob's sons
Conspired 'gainst Joseph, so this viper's brood
Ye will hear raging after Jesus' blood—
"Vengeance!" their shriek of fury runs.

THE SANHEDRIM.

THEN were the high priests and the rulers and the elders gathered together late in the night, in the Council of the Sanhedrim. In the highest place sat Caiaphas, with his jewelled breast-plate, in robes of white embroidered with gold. A vestment of green and gold covered his shoulders, and on his head he wore a white horned mitre adorned with golden bells, which added to the majesty of his aspect. Annas, the aged high priest, sat on his left. Nathanael, also on the raised dais, was on the right. Below him sat the Rabbis, in blue velvet, while seated around were Pharisees, Scribes, and doctors of the law.

Caiaphas, whose white hair and beard showed that he was well stricken in years, was still in the full vigour of life. As president of the Sanhedrim, he briefly opened the session.

"Honoured Brothers, Fathers, and Teachers of the People, an extraordinary occurrence is the occasion of the present extraordinary assembly. Listen to it from the mouth of our worthy brother."

Then **Nathanael** arose, and standing on the right hand of Caiaphas, said, "Is it allowed, O fathers, to say a word?" All answered, "Yes; speak! speak!" Then said Nathanael, "Marvel not, O fathers, that you should be called together at so late an hour for the transaction of business. It must be only too well known to you what we have with shame been compelled to see to-day with our own eyes. You have seen the triumphal progress of the Galilean through the Holy City. You have heard the Hosannas of the befooled populace. You have perceived how this ambitious man arrogates to himself the office of the high priest. What now lacks for the destruction of all civil and ecclesiastical order? Only a few steps further and the law of Moses is upset by the innovations of this misleader. The sayings of our forefathers are despised, the fasts and purifications abolished, the sabbath desecrated, the priests of God deprived of their office, and the holy sacrifices are at an end.

THE SANHEDRIM. 31

ANNAS.

Alle. Wahr, sehr wahr.

Kaiphas. Ja wohl, noch mehr! Es wird bald dieser Mensch, durch seiner Strebungen Erfolg ermuthigt, aufwerfen sich als König Israels. Dann wird im Lande Zwiespalt sein und Aufruhr. Dann wird mit Heeresmacht der Römer kommen, und wird verderben Land und Leute. Wehe den Kindern Jakobs! Weh der heil'gen Stadt! Jehova's Tempel weh! wann nicht dem Uebel mit Kraft begegnet wird, da es noch Zeit ist! Es ist die höchste Zeit. Noch heute werde ein kräftiger Beschluss gefasst, und was beschlossen ist, vollzogen ungesäumt! Wollt ihr, o Vater, eure Hand dazu mir bieten?

Alle. Ja, wir wollen es! Es werde einhalt gethan dem Treiben des Verführers!

Kaiphas. Sprecht unverholen eure Meinung aus, wie das geschehen soll!

Rabbi. Wir selbst tragen die Mitschuld daran, dass es so weit gekommen ist. Gegen das hereinbrechende Verderben wurden zu gelinde Mittel angewendet. Was haben unsere Disputationen mit ihm geholfen, was hat es gefruchtet, dass wir ihn durch Fragen in Verlegenheit setzten? . . . . Was hat selbst der Bannfluch gewirkt, der ausgesprochen ward über Jeden, der ihn als Messias anerkennen würde? Soll Ruhe werden, so müssen wir uns seiner Person versichern und ihn in's Gefängniss bringen. . . . .

Alle. Ja! dem stimmen wir vollkommen bei!

3. Priester. Ist er einmal im Kerker, wird das leichtgläubige Volk nicht mehr durch seine einnehmende Gestalt und den Zauber seiner Rede geblendet, hat es kein Wunder mehr zu begaffen, dann wird es bald vergessen sein. . . . .

4. Priester. Im Dunkel des Gefängnisses mag er sein Licht leuchten lassen, und sich den Kerkerwanden als Messias ankündigen. . . . .

1. Pharisäer. Lange genug hat er das Volk irre geführt, die strenge Tugend des heiligen Ordens der Pharisäer als Scheinheiligkeit gebrandmarkt. Er busse seine Missachtung in Banden!

2. Pharisäer. Das wird die Schwärmerei seiner Anhänger abkühlen, wenn er, der ihnen die Freiheit verheissen, in Banden liegt!

Annas. Jetzt, ehrwürdige Priester, senkt sich wieder ein Strahl des Trostes und der Freude in mein Herz, da ich eure einstimmige Entschlossenheit sehe. Ach, ein unaussprechlicher Kummer lastete auf meiner Seele, beim Anblick der reissenden Fortschritte des Irrlehren dieses Galiläers! Sollte denn ich unglücklicher Greis nur darum so lange gelebt haben, um selbst noch den Untergang des heiligen Gesetzes zu schauen? Doch nun will ich nicht verzagen. Der Gott unserer Väter lebt noch und ist mit uns. Wenn ihr, o Freunde, Euch jetzt ermannet kräftig einausschreiten, wie Brüder treu und fest zusammensteht, so ist die Rettung nahe. Fasst den Muth, die Retter Israels zu sein!

Alle. Wir sind eines Sinnes!

Priester. Israel muss gerettet werden.

Kaiphas. Ehre Eurem einmüthigen Entschluss! Würdige Brüder! Nun aber steht mir bei mit Eurem weisen Rathe, wie der Verführer am sichersten in unsere Gewalt zu bringen sei.

Rabinth. Ihn jetzt zu fangen, in der Zeit des Festes, dürfte zu gefährlich sein. Auf der Strasse und im Tempel, überall ist er von einer Schaar begeisterter Anhänger umgeben—es könnte leicht ein Aufruhr veranlasst werden.

Ezechiel. Und doch muss es jetzt geschehen, die Sache leidet keinen Aufschub. Vielleicht könnte er zur Zeit des Festes einen Auflauf erregen und dann könnte es kommen, dass wir den Platz einnehmen, den wir ihm bestimmt haben . . . .

As Nathanael concluded, all the fathers of the Council exclaimed with one voice, "True—most true." As he had been speaking they had been interchanging notes of appreciative and sympathetic comment. But it was not until Caiaphas spoke that the Sanhedrim was roused to the highest pitch of excitement. Caiaphas, who spoke with great fire and fervour, thus addressed the rulers of Israel:—

"And more than all this. Encouraged by the success of his efforts, he will proclaim himself King of Israel (murmurs of alarm and indignation), then the land will be distracted with civil war and revolt, and the Romans will come with their armies and bring destruction upon our land and our people. Woe is me for the children of Israel, for the Holy City, and for the Temple of the Lord! It is, indeed, high time that the evil should be arrested. The responsibility lies upon us. To-day must a resolution be passed, and whatever is resolved upon must be carried out without delay. Do we all agree to this?"

And all the Sanhedrim as one man cried out, "We do."

Upsprang a Priest to emphasize his vote: "A stop must be put to the course of this misleader."

Caiaphas then said, "Give your opinion without reserve, as to what should be done."

And thena second Priest arose and said: "We ourselves are to blame that things have come to such a pass. Against this onrushing ruin much too mild measures have been employed. Of what avail have been our disputations with him, or what has it profited that we have, by our questionings, put him in a dilemma? Nay, of what use has been even the excommunication pronounced on all who acknowledged him as the Messiah? To restore peace to Israel we must arrest him and throw him into prison.

The suggestion was hailed with enthusiasm, and springing to their feet they cried, "Yea, that must be done!"

Then a third Priest stood up and said: "Once that he is in prison, the credulous people will no longer be attracted by the fascination of his manner or the charm of his discourse. When they have no more miracles to gape at, all will soon be forgotten."

And a fourth Priest exulted as he added: "In the darkness of his dungeon let him make his light shine and proclaim his Messiahship to the walls of his gaol."

Then it was the turn of the Pharisees. The first said: "He has been allowed long enough to lead the people astray and to denounce as hypocrisy the strict virtue of the Holy Order of the Pharisees. Let him suffer for his contempt in fetters."

A second Pharisee added, complacently: "The enthusiasm of his hangers-on will soon cool down when he who promised them freedom is himself in chains."

By this time it was evident all the Council was of one mind. Then Annas, the venerable high priest, arose and addressed the Sanhedrim with much emotion.

"Now, venerable priests, a ray of confidence and joy penetrates to my breast when I see your unanimous resolution. Alas! an unspeakable grief has weighed down my soul at the sight of the onward progress of the false teachings of this Galilean. It seemed as if I had lived to old age but in order to have the misfortune of seeing the downfall of our Holy Law. But now I will not despair. The God of our fathers still lives, and He is with us. If you have the courage to act boldly, and stand firmly and faithfully together as brothers, there is safety at hand. Take courage and we shall be the deliverers of Israel."

With one accord all answered and said: "We are all of one mind"; while the Priests added, shouting eagerly, "Israel must be saved."

Then Caiaphas began, "All honour to your unanimous resolution, worthy brethren, but now let me have the benefit of your wise counsels how we can most safely bring this deceiver into our power." "It might be dangerous," remarked the first Pharisee, "to seize him now at the time of the Feast, In the streets or in the Temple he is everywhere surrounded by a mob of infatuated followers. It could easily lead to an uproar."

Then cried all the Priests together with a loud voice, as if impatient that one should speak at a time:

"But something must be done at once. The matter brooks no delay. Perhaps, at the Feast, he might raise such a commotion that it might come to pass that we should be consigned to the place which we have destined for him."

Andere Priester. Keine Zögerung! Keinen Aufschub!

Josue. Mit offener Gewalt dürfen wir jetzt allerdings nicht zugreifen. Wir müssen uns seiner in der Stille bemächtigen, mit List. Man müsste auskundschaften, wo er gewöhnlich die Nächte zubringt, da konnte er überfallen und ohne Aufsehen in Gewahrsam gebracht werden. . . .

Nathanael. Den Fuchs in seiner Höhle aufzuspüren, dazu würden sich bald Leute finden lassen, wenn es dem Hohen Rathe gefällt, einen ansehnlichen Preis dafür auszusetzen.

Kaiphas. Wenn Ihr, versammelte Väter, es gut heisst, so will ich im Namen des Hohen Rathes den Befehl ausgehen lassen, dass Jeder, der seinen nächtlichen Aufenthalt weiss, denselben angeben soll; auch soll dem Angeber eine Belohnung zugesichert werden.

Alle. Wir sind ganz einverstanden.

Nathanael. Als Kundschafter könnten uns ohne Zweifel jene Männer dienen, die der Galiläer heute vor allem Volke schwer gekränkt hat. Sie waren von jeher eifrige Anhänger des Gesetzes, und jetzt dürsten sie nach Rache gegen den, der einen so unerhörten Angriff auf ihre Privilegien gemacht hat.

Kaiphas. Wo sind die Händler anzutreffen?

Nathanael. Sie befinden sich bereits im Vorhofe. Ich habe ihnen versprochen, der Verfechter ihrer Rechte vor dem heiligen Synedrium zu sein, und sie warten auf Bescheid.

Kaiphas. Wurdiger Priester, verkündige ihnen, dass der Hohe Rath geneigt sei, ihre Beschwerden zu vernehmen, und führe sie ein. [NATHANAEL ab.

ZWEITE SZENE.

Kaiphas. Noch hat also der Gott unserer Väter seine Hand nicht von uns abgezogen. Noch wacht Moses über uns. Gelingt es einen Kern von Männern aus dem Volke um uns zu sammeln, so ist mir nicht mehr bange. Freunde und Brüder! Lasst uns guten Muthes sein, unsere Väter sehen auf uns herab, aus Abrahams Schoss.

Priester. Gott segne unsern Hohenpriester!

DRITTE SZENE.

Nathanael. Hoher Priester und erwählte Lehrer! Diese Männer, würdig unseres Segens, erscheinen vor dieser Versammlung, um Klage zu führen gegen den bekannten Jesus von Nazareth, der sie heute im Tempel auf unerhörte Weise beleidigt und zu Schaden gebracht hat.

Dathan. Wir bitten den Hohen Rath, uns Genugthuung zu verschaffen. Der Hohe Rath muss unsere gerechte Forderung begünstigen.

Priester und Pharisäer. Euch soll Genugthuung werden; wir stehen Euch dafür.

Die Händler. Hat nicht der Hohe Rath uns erlaubt, Alles zum Opfer Nöthige öffentlich in den Hallen zum Verkaufe auszustellen?

Priester. Ja, das haben wir erlaubt, wehe dem, der Euch in diesem Rechte stört!

Händler. Und der Galiläer hat uns mit einer Griessel vertrieben!—Und die Wechseltische hat er umgestossen und die Taubenbehälter geöffnet!—Wir fordern Genugthuung!

Kaiphas. Dass Euch Genugthuung werde, will das Gesetz. Euer Verlust soll Euch einstweilen aus dem Tempelschatz vergütet werden. Dass aber der Frevler selbst gestraft werde, dazu bedürfen wir Eurer Mitwirkung. Was können wir ihm thun, so lange er nicht in unserer Gewalt ist?

Händler. Er geht ja täglich in den Tempel, da kann er leicht gefangen und weggeführt werden.

Kaiphas. Das geht nicht. Ihr wisst, dass er eine Menge erhitzter Anhänger hat, es könnte da einen gefährlichen Aufruhr geben. Es muss in Stillen geschehen. . . .

Händler. Das ginge am besten zur Nachtzeit.

Kaiphas. Wenn Ihr auskundschaftet, wohin er sich zur Nachtzeit zurückzieht, so wird er bald ohne Geräusch in unsern Händen sein. Dann werdet Ihr nicht nur die Freude haben, ihn gezüchtigt zu sehen, sondern es soll Euch auch eine ansehnliche Belohnung zu Theil werden.

Nathanael. Auch um das heilige Gesetz Mosis werdet Ihr Euch Verdienste erwerben.

"No delay!" cried some other priests, "No delay!"

Then the second **Pharisee** stood up and said, "We cannot now seize him openly with the strong hand. We must carry out our scheme cunningly and in secret. Let us find out where he usually spends the night, then we could fall upon him and, unobserved, take him into custody."

Nathanael sprang to his feet, for the auspicious moment had come,—the furious merchants from the Temple were without in the courtyard. "To track the fox to his lair will not be difficult. We shall find plenty of people to help if it should please the High Council to offer a suitable reward."

Caiaphas at once put the resolution to the Sanhedrim. Rising from his seat he said, "If you, assembled fathers, agree, then, in the name of the High Council, I will issue notice that whoever knows of his nightly resort, and will inform us of the same, will be rewarded for his pains."

With one voice the rulers and chief priests and scribes cried out, rising from their seats, "We are all agreed!"

"Without doubt we could secure the services, as informers, of those men whom the Galilean to-day has injured so deeply in the sight of all the people. From of old they were zealous of the Law, but now they are thirsting for revenge against him who has made so unheard-of an attack upon their privileges."

"But where," asked **Caiaphas** "are these traders to be found?"

"They are waiting," said **Nathanael**, "in readiness in the outer court. I have promised them to be the advocate of their cause before the holy Sanhedrim, and they await our decision."

"Worthy priest," said **Caiaphas**, "inform them that the High Council is disposed to listen to their grievance, and bring them in."

When Nathanael left the hall **Caiaphas** addressed the council with words of cheer: "The God of our fathers has not withdrawn his hand from us. Moses still watches over us. If only we can succeed in gathering around us a nucleus of men out of the people, then I no longer dread the result. Friends and brethren, let us be of good courage, our fathers look down upon us from Abraham's bosom." "God bless our High Priest!" rang through the hall, as **Nathanael**, followed by Dathan and the other traders, returned to his place. He introduced them thus: "High priests and chosen teachers! These men, worthy of our blessing, appear before this assembly, in order to lodge a complaint against the notorious Jesus of Nazareth, who has to-day insulted them in the Temple in an unheard-of fashion and brought them to grief."

Then with one voice the **Traders** led by Dathan, cried out, "We beseech the Council to procure us satisfaction. The Council ought to support our righteous demands." The priests and Pharisees responded eagerly, "You shall have satisfaction, we will answer for that."

Then ensued the following dialogue between the traders and the Sanhedrim:

The Traders. Has not the Council authorised us to display openly in the Court of the Temple all things needful for the sacrifice?

A Priest. Yes, that has been sanctioned. Woe be to those who disturb you in the exercise of this right!

The Traders. And the Galilean has driven us out with a scourge. And the table of the money-changers has he overturned, and released the doves. We demand satisfaction.

Caiaphas. That you should have satisfaction the law decrees. Your losses will be made good in the meantime out of the Temple treasury (joy among the traders). But that the offender himself may be punished, it is necessary for us to have your help. What can we do, so long as he is not in our power?

The Traders. He goes daily to the Temple; there he can easily be arrested and carried off.

Caiaphas. That will not do. You know that as he has a multitude of excited followers, such a course might lead to a dangerous uproar. The thing must be done quietly.

The Traders. That could be done best at night time.

Caiaphas. If you could find out where he retires at night, he would soon be without tumult in our hands. Then would you not only have the delight of seeing him chastised, but also a considerable reward would fall to your lot.

Nathanael. And you would also have rendered good service

Händler. An uns soll es nicht fehlen.
Ephraim. Wir wollen keine Mühe scheuen.
Dathan. Ich kenne einen seiner Anhänger, durch den ich wohl etwas erfahren kann, wenn ich ihm einen entsprechenden Lohn bieten kann.
Kaiphas. Wenn Ihr einen anfündet, dem macht alle Versprechungen in unserem Namen. Nur säumt nicht, dass wir noch vor dem Feste an's Ziel kommen.
Annas. Und beobachtet tiefes Schweigen.
Händler. Wir geloben es.
Kaiphas. Wollt Ihr aber, liebe Männer, dass das Gefühl der Rache vollkommen befriedigt werde, so gebt Euch auch sonst alle Mühe, mit der heiligen Glut, die in Euch lodert, noch viele Andere zu entzünden.
Händler. Wir haben seit jenem Vorfalle jeden Augenblick dazu benützt, und bereits Viele auf unsere Seite gebracht.— Wir werden nicht ruhen, bis alles Volk wider ihn aufsteht!
Annas. Dadurch werdet Ihr Euch den Hohen Rath zum grössten Dank verpflichten.
Kaiphas. Oeffentlich sollt Ihr dann vor allem Volke geehrt werden, wie Ihr von ihm öffentlich beschimpft worden seid. . .
Händler. Unser Leben für das Gesetz Mosis und das heilige Synedrium.
Kaiphas. Der Gott Abrahams geleite Euch!
Händler. Es lebe Moses, es lebe der Hohenpriester und das Synedrium!
Ein Händler. Heute noch mag der Galiläer seine Rolle ausgespielt haben! [Ab.

VIERTE SZENE.

Kaiphas. Wie vom süssen Schlummer gestärkt, lebe ich wieder auf. Mit solchen Männern lässt sich Alles durchführen. Nun wollen wir sehen, wer obsiegt: Er mit seinem Anhang, dem er ohne Unterlass Liebe vorpredigt, eine Liebe, die selbst Sünder und Zöllner, ja sogar die Heiden umfassen soll—oder wir, mit dieser Schaar des Hasses und der Rache, die wir gegen ihn aussenden.
Annas. Den Sieg verleihe uns der Gott unserer Väter! Wie wird in meinen alten Tagen die Freude mich verjüngen!
Kaiphas. Lasst uns aufbrechen und der Siegesfreude getrost entgegensehen. Gepriesen seien die Väter!
Alle. Gepriesen sei der Gott Abrahams, Isaaks und Jakobs!

III. VORSTELLUNG.

Der Abschied zu Bethania.

PROLOG.

Der mit hellem Blicke durchschaut der Zukunft
Schleier, sieht schon nahen das Ungewitter,
Das sich drohend sammelt, ob seinem Haupte
    Sich zu entladen.

Weilend noch im Kreise der Seinen, kündet
Er den lieben Freunden das Wort des Scheidens,
Ach! ein Wort, das schmerzlichst der treuen Mutter
    Seele verwundet.

Seht, wie tiefbetrübt des Tobias Mutter
Nachblicket noch dem scheidenden Herzenssohne
Und in Thränenströmen ergiesst den Kummer
    Zärtlicher Liebe;

So auch weint die Mutter des Gottessohnes
Dem Geliebten nach, der entschlossen hingeht,
Durch der Liebe sühnenden Tod der Menschheit
    Sünde zu tilgen.

Chor.

Ach! sie kommt—die Scheidestunde,
Und sie schlägt die tiefste Wunde,
O Maria! in dein Herz.
Ach! dein Sohn muss dich verlassen,
Um am Kreuze zu erblassen,
Wer ermisst den Mutterschmerz!

---

to the law of Moses. Then all the traders cried out together: "You can depend on us, we will spare no trouble," and all the priests and Pharisees congratulated themselves that the business was going well. Dathan, conspicuous by his apparel, then volunteered a statement. He said, "I know one of his followers, from whom I could easily gain some information if I could offer him a sufficient reward."
Caiaphas at once authorized him, "If thou findest such a one make all necessary promises in our name. Only don't loiter; we must attain our end before the feast."
Annas enjoined the strictest silence, to which with one voice the traders responded, "We swear it," and then Caiaphas proceeded to urge upon them the need of creating a party on their side among the people.
"If, my good fellows, you really desire fully to glut your longing for revenge, then take care and use every means to kindle in others the same holy zeal which glows in you."
They answered that they had not waited for his prompting, but had already brought several others over to their side. "We will not rest until the whole populace is roused against him," Annas and Caiaphas applauded their zeal. "You will thereby merit the greatest gratitude from the council," said Annas and Caiaphas chimed in, "Openly will ye then be honoured before all the people as you have been to-day put to shame before them by him."
"Our life for the law of Moses," then cried the traders, "and the holy Sanhedrim." "The God of Abraham guide you," said Caiaphas, dismissing them, and they left the hall crying aloud, "Long live Moses, long live the high priests and the Sanhedrim. Even to-day may the rôle of the Galilean be played out."
Then **Caiaphas** addressed these parting words to the council. "As though refreshed by sweet slumbers, I live once more. With such men as these we can put everything through. Now we shall see who will triumph—He with his followers to whom he is always preaching love, a love which is to include publicans and sinners and even the Gentiles also, or we with this troop inspired by hate and revenge which we are sending against him."
"The God of our fathers give us the victory!" said **Annas**, "joy in my old age will renew my youth."
Then said **Caiaphas**, "Let us now break up, looking forward with confidence to the joy of victory. Praised be our fathers." And all the assembly with a deep sonorous voice exclaimed, "Praised be the God of Abraham, of Isaac, and of Jacob."

CHAPTER III.

PROLOGUE.—ACT III.

He Who clear-eyed looks through the future's mystery,
Sees the lowering tempest which, threatening, gathers,
Sees the clouds approaching, which o'er His head will
    Burst with their thunders.

Lingering yet while in the midst of His loved ones,
He hath said to those friends the word of parting—
Word—ah, me!—the soul of His faithful mother
    Cruelly wounding.

See how, deeply grieving, Tobias' mother
Gazes after the son of her heart in parting,
And pours forth the sorrow of love so tender
    In tears down-streaming.

Thus, too, weeps the Mother of our Redeemer,
Gazing after her loved One, who goes unflinching
In His love, to blot out men's sins for ever
    By His death's ransom.

Chorus.

See! the parting hour has come,
Hour of anguish and of gloom;
Mary! 'tis the sharpest blow
To thy heart: Thy Son must leave thee!
On the cross His pain shall grieve thee,
Who can sound such depths of woe?

THE LEAVE-TAKING AT BETHANY.—ACT III.

MARY MAGDALENE.

MARY.

MARTHA.

VORBILD.

Der junge Tobias nimmt Abschied von seinen Eltern.

[Das Bild erinnert an den Abschied Christi von seiner Mutter, um nach Jerusalem zu gehen.]

Solo.

Freunde! welch ein herber Schmerz
Folterte das Mutterherz,
Als Tobias an der Hand
Raphaels in fremdes Land
Auf Befehl des Vaters eilte!

Unter tausend Weh und Ach
Ruft sie dem Geliebten nach:
Komme, ach! verweile nicht,
Meines Herzens Trost und Licht!
Bald und glücklich kehre wieder!

Ach, Tobias! Theuerster!
Eil' in meine Arme her!
Liebster Sohn! an dir allein
Wird mein Herz sich wieder freu'n,
Freuen sich der schönsten Freude!

Chor.

Trostlos jammert sie nun so,
Nimmer ihres Lebens froh,
Bis ein sel'ger Augenblick
An das Mutterherz zurück
Den geliebten Sohn wird führen.

2. Die liebende Braut beklagt den Verlust ihres Bräutigams.
Hohes. 5, 17.

[In einem wunderlieblichen Blumengarten sehen wir in einer Rosenlaube die Braut des hohen Liedes, umgeben von ihren treuen Freundinnen in weissen Gewändern und mit Blumen geziert, eine Anspielung auf die Kirche als jungfräuliche Braut. Oder auch ein Bild des Abschieds Christi von den Seinen, — oder Marie beiammert den Abzug ihres geliebten Sohnes, ihrer einzigen Freude.]

Solo.

Wo ist er hin? Wo ist er hin,
Der Schöne aller Schönen?
Mein Auge weinet, ach! um ihn
Der Liebe heisse Thränen.

"Seht ihr ihn nicht, Der mich beglückt,
Vor tausend auserkoren,
Den aller Liebreiz schmückt?
Ihn hab ich, ach! verloren!

O komme doch, o komm' zu mir,
Im Auge Thränen thauen,
Die Seele sehnet sich nach Dir,
Dein Angesicht zu schauen.

Mein Auge forschet überall
Nach Dir auf allen Wegen:
Und mit der Sonne erstem Strahl
Eilt Dir mein Herz entgegen."

Geliebter! ach, was fühle ich?
Wie ist mein Herz beklommen!

Chor.

Geliebte Freundin! tröste Dich,
Dein Freund wird wieder kommen.

O harre, Freundin! bald kommt er,
Schmiegt sich an Deine Seite,
Dann trübet keine Wolke mehr
Des Wiedersehens Freude.

O komm' in meine Arme her!
O weil' an meiner Seite,
Dann trübet keine Wolke mehr
Des Wiedersehens Freude.

[The fourth tableau, taken from the Apocrypha, represents the departure of Tobias, who with his little dog takes leave of his parents before setting forth with the angel Raphael, who is in undress, with a staff instead of wings. The little dog stands as if stuffed, if, indeed, it is not.]

Solo.

Friends, what bitter pain and woe
Had a mother's heart to know
When her son, by Raphael's hand
Led into a foreign land,
Hastened at his father's hest.

With "Alas!" and "Woe is me!"
Gazing after him, cries she,
"Tarry not, but soon return,
Leave me not in vain to mourn.
Light and comfort of my breast!

"Ah! Tobias! dearest one,
Haste thou back, mine only son,
To my arms! In thee alone
Can my heart forget her moan
And rejoice with fairest joy!"

Chorus.

So she mourns, and will not be
Comforted—no joy can see
In her life—till one glad day
To her heart, no more to stray,
Brings again her best-loved boy.

[The fifth tableau shows us the Bride in the Song of Solomon, who is lamenting the lost and absent bridegroom. She is gorgeously arrayed in the midst of a bevy of four companions in the traditional flower garden, and while it is displayed the chorus sings a lament as ardent in its passion as the original in Canticles. Christ, of course, is prefigured by the absent bridegroom: the lamenting bride, who appeals to the daughters of Jerusalem, is the Church, the Lamb's Bride of the Apocalypse.]

Solo.

Oh! where is He, the Beautiful,
All glorious once above?
My weary eyes they weep for Him
The burning tears of love.

See you not Him who blesses me?
He is the chosen One
Among ten thousand, crowned with grace—
I've lost Him—am undone.

Oh! come to me! Oh! come to me!
Mine eyes drop tears apace,—
My soul it yearneth after Thee,
To look upon Thy face.

Mine eyes are searching everywhere
For Thee upon all ways,—
My heart to meet Thee forth doth haste,
With daylight's earliest rays.

Beloved! what is it I feel?
How sinks my heart with pain!

Chorus.

Beloved friend, be comforted!
Thy Friend shall come again.

Oh! wait, dear heart, for soon He comes
To take thee to His side;
And then no cloud shall dim the joy,
When He shall meet His bride.

Oh! come! Oh! come into mine arms!
Oh! stay but by my side!
And then no cloud shall dim our joy
When Thou shalt meet Thy bride!

THE LEAVE-TAKING AT BETHANY.—ACT III.

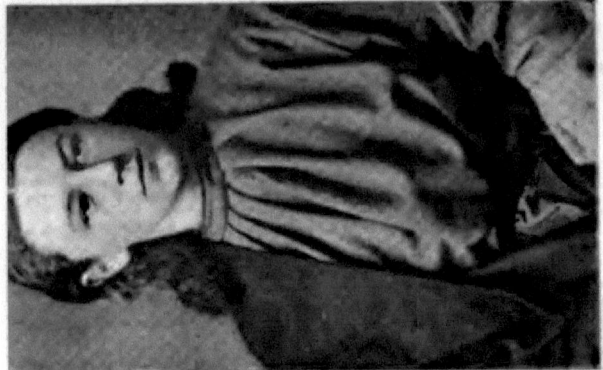

JOHN.

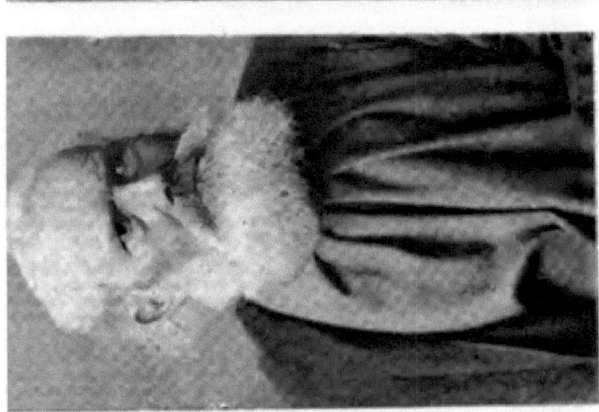

PETER.

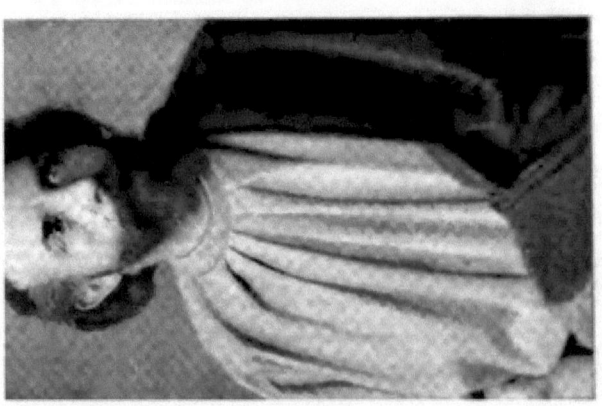

JAMES.

HANDLUNG.

Christus in *Bethanien* wird von Maria *gesalbt, worüber* Judas *murrt.* Christus *nimmt Abschied von seiner Mutter und von den Freunden zu Bethanien.*

ERSTE SZENE.

Christus und die Zwölfe.

Christus. Ihr wisset, liebe Jünger, dass nach zwei Tagen Ostern ist. So lasst uns nun unsere letzte Einkehr nehmen bei unsern Freunden zu Bethanien, und dann hingehen nach Jerusalem, wo in diesen Tagen Alles sich erfüllen wird, was durch die Propheten vom Menschensohne geschrieben ist.

Philippus. So ist denn endlich der Tag gekommen, da du das Reich Israel wieder herstellen wirst?

Christus. Da wird der Menschensohn den Heiden überliefert, verspottet und verspieen werden, und sie werden ihn kreuzigen; er aber wird am dritten Tage wieder auferstehen.

Johannes. Meister, welche dunkle, schauervolle Worte sprichst du! Wie ist es zu verstehen? Erkläre es uns.

Christus. Die Stunde is gekommen, dass des Menschen Sohn verherrlichet werde! Wahrlich, wahrlich, sage ich Euch: Wenn das Weizenkörnlein nicht in die Erde fällt und stirbt, so bleibt es allein, wenn es aber stirbt, so bringt es viele Frucht. Jetzt ergeht das Gericht über die Welt; jetzt wird der Fürst dieser Welt hinausgestossen. Und ich, wenn ich von der Erde erhöht sein werde, so werde ich Alles an mich ziehen.

Thaddäus. Was meint er wohl mit dieser Rede?

Simon. Warum vergleicht er sich mit dem Weizenkörnlein?

Andreas. Herr, du redest zugleich von Schmach und Sieg. Ich weiss das in meinen Gedanken nicht zu vereinigen.

Christus. Was Euch dunkel ist wie die Nacht, wird Euch hell werden, wie der Tag. Ich habe es Euch gesagt, damit Ihr nicht verzaget, was immer auch kommen mag. Glaubet und hoffet! Ist die Trübsal vorbeigezogen, dann werdet Ihr sehen und verstehen.

Thomas. Das geht mir nicht ein, was du vom Leiden und vom Sterben sagst. Was können deine Feinde dir thun? Ein einziges Wort von dir zermalmt sie.

Christus. Thomas! Bete die Rathschlüsse Gottes an, die du nicht ergründest! Noch eine kurze Zeit ist das Licht bei Euch. Wandelt, so lange Ihr das Licht habet, damit Euch die Finsterniss nicht überfalle.

ZWEITE SZENE.

Die Vorigen. Simon, *dann* Lazarus, Martha, Maria Magdalena.

Simon. Mein Lehrer! sei gegrüsst! O welche Freude, dass Du mein Haus beglückst mit Deiner Einkehr! Seid, liebe Freunde, alle mir gegrüsst!

Christus. Simon, zum letzten Male nehme ich mit den Meinigen deine Gastfreundschaft in Anspruch.

Simon. Rede nicht so, Herr. Oft noch soll Bethania dir eine kurze Rast gewähren.

Christus. Siehe da, unser Freund Lazarus.

Lazarus. O Todesüberwinder! Lebenspender! O Herr! Dich seh' ich wieder! Und die Stimme vernehme ich, die aus dem Grab mich rief!

[*Birgt sein Angesicht an der Brust des Herrn.*]

Magdalena. Rabbi!

Martha. Rabbi, sei mir gegrüsst.

THE LEAVETAKING AT BETHANY.

Jesus, accompanied by all his disciples, set out to pay his last visit to Bethany. Peter, with his staff in hand, walked with John beside the Master. Judas was present, with dishevelled locks and haggard mien. James the Greater and James the Less, and Andrew and Thomas, and the rest of the disciples.

Then Jesus spoke unto them, and said, "You know, dear disciples, that after two days is the feast of the passover. So now let us make one last visit to our friends in Bethany, and then go into Jerusalem, where in three days all will be fulfilled which has been written by the prophets concerning the Son of Man."

The disciples understood not his saying, and after some questioning among themselves Philip ventured to address Jesus, saying unto him, "Has the day then really come at last when thou wilt restore the kingdom to Israel?" Jesus looked upon Philip with tender compassion, and said unto him, "Then shall the Son of Man be delivered up to the Gentiles, and shall be mocked and spat upon, and they will crucify him; but on the third day he will rise again." Then said John, in a voice that trembled with emotion, as the other disciples gazed at each other in horror, "Dear master, what dark and terrible words thou speakest. What are we to understand by them? Make it clear unto us."

Then Jesus answered and said unto him, "The hour is now come when the Son of Man shall be glorified. Verily, Verily, I say unto you, if a corn of wheat does not fall into the ground and die it abideth alone, but if it die it bringeth forth much fruit. Now is the judgment of the world. Now shall the prince of the world be cast out. And I, if I be lifted up from the earth, will draw all men unto me."

Then were the breasts of the disciples troubled, for they could not understand what these things meant. Thaddeus said to Simon, "What does he mean by this speech?"

Simon replied with a puzzled air, "Why does he compare himself to a grain of corn."

Then said **Andrew** unto him, "Lord, thou speakest at once of shame and of victory. I know not how to reconcile those ideas in my mind."

Jesus said, "That which is now dark to you as the night, will be as clear as the day. I have told you before that you may not lose courage whatever may happen. Believe and hope. When the tribulation is passed, then you will see and understand."

Thomas answered and said unto him, "What I cannot understand is that thou shouldst speak of suffering and of death. What can thine enemies do unto thee? One single word from thee would annihilate them all."

Jesus said unto him, "Thomas, reverence the secret counsels of God which thou canst not fathom."

Then, turning to the others, he said, "Yet a little while is the light with you. Walk while you have the light, lest darkness overtake you."

By this time they had approached near the village of Bethany, and there met them one Simon, after whom there came Lazarus, who was raised from the dead, with Martha, his sister, and Mary Magdalene, the latter tall, dark, with long black hair, in dark blue dress with a yellow mantle.

Simon pressed forward; he was an old man, and he hastened to meet Jesus. "Welcome, best of teachers. O what joy that thou shouldest honour my house with thy entrance. Dear friends, be also welcome," he exclaimed; but he was startled to hear the reply, "Simon, for the last time, I, with my disciples, lay claim to thy hospitality."

Simon replied in grief, "Say not so, Lord. Often still shall Bethany afford thee a brief repose."

By this time Lazarus drew near; he was of less than middle stature, and silent as if his sojourn in the other world left him little to speak of in this. "See," said Jesus, "there is our friend Lazarus." "My Lord," cried Lazarus, embracing him, "the Vanquisher of Death, Lifegiver and Lord, I see thee once again, and hear the voice that called me from the grave."

Then hastened the **Magdalen** to his side, and, kneeling down. "Rabbi," she exclaimed; **Martha** also said "Welcome, Rabbi."

THE LEAVE-TAKING AT BETHANY.—ACT III., SC. 3.

Christus. Gottes Segen über Euch!
Martha. Werde ich dich, O Herr, bedienen dürfen? ...
Magdalena. Wirst du auch von mir ein Zeichen der Liebe nicht verschmähen?
Christus. Thut, gute Seelen, was Ihr zu thun vorhabt.
Simon. Bester Meister, gehe unter mein Dach ein und erquicke dich und die deinen.

DRITTE SZENE.
Speisezimmer des Simon.

Christus. Der Friede sei diesem Hause.
Jünger. Und Allen, die darin wohnen.
Simon. Herr, es ist Alles bereitet. Setze dich zu Tische und erlaube es auch deinen Jüngern.
Christus. So lasst uns denn, liebe Jünger, mit Dank die Gaben geniessen, die der Vater vom Himmel uns durch Simon, seinen Diener, gewährt. Ach Jerusalem! Möchte dir meine Ankunft so lieb sein, wie sie es diesen meinen Freunden ist! Aber du bist mit Blindheit geschlagen.
Lazarus. Bester Meister! Dort droh'n Gefahren. Voll Erwartung steh'n die Pharisäer, ob Du kommen werdest zum grossen Feste. Gierig lauern sie auf Deinen Untergang.
Simon. Bleibe hier, hier bist du sicher.
Petrus. Herr, hier ist gut sein. Bleibe hier, in diesem Hause Verborgenheit, bedient von treuer Liebe, bis der Sturm vertobt hat, der sich erheben will!
Christus. Bleibe von mir, Versucher! Du hast keinen Sinn für das, was Gottes ist, sondern für das, was des Menschen ist. Darf der Schnitter im Schatten ruhen, während die reife Ernte winkt? Des Menschen Sohn ist nicht gekommen, dass er sich bedienen lasse, sondern dass er diene und sein Leben hingebe als Lösegeld für Viele.
Judas. Aber Meister, was wird aus uns werden, wenn du dein Leben hingiebst?
Apostel. Ach, alle unsere Hoffnungen sind dann vernichtet.
Christus. Beruhiget Euch! Ich habe Macht, mein Leben hinzugeben, und ich habe Macht, es wieder zu nehmen. Diesen Auftrag habe ich von meinem Vater erhalten.
Magdalena. [*Kommt und giesst Salbe auf Christi Haupt.*] Rabbi!
Christus. Maria!
Thomas. Welch' köstlicher Geruch!
Bartholomäus. Das ist köstliches, echtes Nardenöl.
Judas. Wozu solcher Aufwand? man hätte das Geld dafür besser verwenden können.
Thomas. Mich dünkt es fast auch so. [*Magdalena küsst und salbt Christi Füsse.*]
Christus. Was redet Ihr unter einander? Warum tadelt Ihr, was nur aus dankbarer Liebe geschah?
Judas. Eine so kostbare Salbe auszugiessen! Welche Verschwendung!
Christus. Freund Juda! Sieh' mich an! Auch an mir, an deinem Meister, Verschwendung?
Judas. Ich weiss, dass du unnützen Aufwand nicht liebst. Man hätte die Salbe verkaufen und die Armen unterstützen können.
Christus. Juda, die Hand auf's Herz! Ist es nur das Mitleid für die Armen, was dich so sehr bewegt?
Judas. Wenigstens 300 Denare waren damit zu gewinnen. Welcher Verlust für die Armen und für uns!
Christus. Die Armen habt Ihr immer um Euch, aber mich habt Ihr nicht immer. Lasset sie! Sie hat ein gutes Werk

Then Jesus blessed them saying, "God's blessing be upon you!"
Then Martha asked, "May I dare to serve thee, Lord?" while the Magdalena timidly inquired, "Wilt thou not despise a token of love from me?"
And Jesus replied with tenderness, "Do, good souls, that which you purpose to do."
Then said Simon, "Best of masters, come under my roof, and refresh thyself and thy disciples."
So Jesus entered into Simon's house, exclaiming, "Peace be upon this house," to which the disciples added, speaking together, "And to all that dwell therein." Then said Simon, "Lord, all is ready, set thee down at table and bid thy disciples sit down also."
Then Jesus sat down to meat, saying, "Let us now, beloved disciples, enjoy with thanks the gifts which our Father in Heaven bestows upon us through Simon, his servant."
And Jesus said, "Oh, Jerusalem, would that my coming were as dear to thee as it is to these, my friends. But thou art stricken with blindness."
"Yes, Lord," remarked Lazarus; "O best of masters, dangers threaten from afar. The Pharisees stand anxiously expecting whether thou wilt come up to the Passover. They are eagerly counting upon thy destruction." Simon said, "Stay here, Lord, here thou art safe."
Then Peter interposed with an entreaty, "Lord, it is good to be here. Remain here till the gathering storm be passed."
But Jesus rebuked him sternly, saying, "Get thee behind me, tempter. Thou savourest not of the things that are of God, but those that be of men. Can the reaper tarry in the shade while the harvest is ripe? The Son of Man came not to be ministered unto and rule, but to minister and to give his life as a ransom for many."
Then the dark-browed Judas spoke, uttering this time the thought of all. "But, Master, what will become of us if thou givest up thy life?"
A chorus of approval burst from all the disciples, "Ah, all our hopes would then be destroyed."
"Trouble not yourselves," said Jesus. "I have power to lay down my life and I have power to take it again. This commandment have I received of my father."
And lo, while they were yet speaking, Mary Magdalene silently approached Jesus, carrying in her hand a bottle of ointment of spikenard, very precious, which she poured over his head as she murmured but one word, "Rabbi." And Jesus also said but one word, "Mary"; but his tone was full of tenderness and love.
As the perfume of the ointment filled the room, the disciples spoke among themselves. "What an exquisite odour!" said Thomas. "It is spikenard, very costly," said Bartholomew. But Judas could not contain himself. He growled from his distant seat, "To what purpose is this waste? The money might have been much better expended." "Yes," said Thomas, "I almost think so too."
Then Magdalen, heedless of the murmurs of the disciples, knelt down and anointed Jesus's feet and wiped them with her long black tresses. Jesus, after a little while, noticing the muttering down the table, asked, "What are you saying to each other? Why do you condemn that which is done only from grateful love?" The Magdalen knelt back, sheltering herself as it were behind her Lord. Judas blurted out impetuously his dissatisfaction. "To pour out so much costly ointment, what wasteful extravagance!"
"Friend Judas," said Jesus, "look at me and say that what is done for me, thy master, is waste."
Judas said, "I know that thou lovest not useless expense; the ointment might have been sold and the money given to the poor."
"Judas," said Jesus, somewhat sternly, "hand upon thy heart now! Is it only pity for the poor which moves thee so much?"
Judas replied, "At least three hundred pence could have been got for it. What a loss both for the poor and for us."
Then Jesus answered and said, "The poor you have always with you, Me, you have not always."
Then, he said, "Let her alone, she has wrought a good work on me, for in that she has poured out the ointment upon me,

an mir gethan. Denn dass sie diese Salbe über meinen Leib ausgoss, das hat sie im Voraus zu meinem Begräbnisse gethan. Fürwahr, ich sage Euch: Wo man immer in der ganzen Welt dieses Evangelium verkünden wird, da wird man auch in ihrem Andenken sagen, was sie gethan hat! [Zu Simon.] Dank dir, wohlthätiger Mann für die Bewirthung! Der Vater wird dir's lohnen.

Simon. Sage nichts von Dank, Meister. Ich weiss, was ich dir schulde.

Christus. Es ist Zeit, von hinnen zu gehen. Ihr Bewohner dieses gastlichen Hauses, lebet alle wohl! Meine Jünger, folget mir!

Petrus. Herr, wohin du willst, nur nicht nach Jerusalem!

Christus. Ich gehe, wohin mich mein Vater ruft. Petrus, gefällt es dir, hier zu bleiben, so bleibe!

Petrus. Herr, wo du bleibst, da bleibe auch ich, wo du hingehest, da gehe auch ich hin.

Christus. So komme!

VIERTE SZENE.

Christus [zu Magdalena und Martha.] Bleibet, Ihr Lieben! Nochmals: Lebet wohl! Liebes, stilles Bethania! Ich werde nie mehr in deinem friedlichen Thale weilen.

Simon. So willst du wirklich von hier scheiden, Meister?

Magdalena. Ach, ich ahne schreckliche Dinge.

Christus. Stehe auf, Maria! Die Nacht bricht ein, und die winterlichen Stürme brausen heran! Doch—sei getrost! In der Morgenfrühe, im Frühlings-garten wirst du mich wieder sehen.

Martha. Ach, du gehst und kommst nimmermehr?

Christus. Der Vater will es, Ihr Lieben! Wo ich bin, trage ich Euch in meinem Herzen, und wo Ihr seid, wird mein Segen Euch begleiten. Lebet wohl!

[*Indem er gehen will, kommt Maria mit ihren Begleiterinnen.*]

FUENFTE SZENE.

Maria. Jesus, liebster Sohn, mit Sehnsucht eilte ich dir nach mit meinen Freundinnen, dich nochmals zu sehen, ehe du hingehst, ach!

Christus. Mutter, ich bin auf dem Wege nach Jerusalem.

Maria. Nach Jerusalem—dort ist der Tempel Jehova's, wo ich dich einst auf meinen Armen trug, dich dem Herrn zu opfern.

Christus. Mutter! Jetzt ist die Zeit gekommen, da ich nach dem Willen des Vaters selbst mich opfern soll. Ich bin bereit, das Opfer zu vollbringen, das der Vater von mir fordert.

Maria. Ach, ich ahne es, was für ein Opfer dieses sein wird!

Magdalena. O wie sehr wünschten wir, den Meister bei uns zurückzubehalten.

Simon. Sein Entschluss ist gefasst.

Christus. Meine Stunde ist gekommen.

Alle Jünger. Bitte doch den Vater, dass er sie vorübersende!

Alle Frauen. Der Vater wird, wie immer, Dich erhören.

Christus. Meine Seele ist jetzt betrübt und was soll ich sagen: Vater! Rette mich von dieser Stunde? Denn dieser Stunde wegen bin ich ja in die Welt gekommen.

Maria. O Simon, ehrwürdiger Greis, jetzt wird sich erfüllen, was du mir einst vorhergesagt hast: "Ein Schwert wird deine Seele durchdringen!"

Christus. Mutter! Der Wille des Vaters war auch dir stets heilig.

Maria. Er ist mir's. Ich bin eine Magd des Herrn. Aber um Eines, mein Sohn, bitte ich dich.

Christus. Was begehrst du, meine Mutter?

Maria. Dass ich mit dir in den Tod gehen darf.

she has anointed me for my burial. Verily I say unto you, wheresoever this gospel will be preached through the whole world, there also shall that which she hath done be told for a memorial of her."

Then turning to Simon his host he said, "I thank thee, benevolent man, for thy hospitality. The Father will repay it unto thee."

"Say nothing of thanks, Master," said Simon, "I know what I owe to thee."

Then Jesus arose and said, "It is time to go hence. Farewell, all ye dwellers in this hospitable house. My disciples follow me."

Peter said unto him, "Lord, wherever thou wilt, only not to Jerusalem."

Jesus answered, "I go where my Father calls me. If it please thee to remain here, Peter, do so." Then Peter declared, "Lord, where thou abidest there will I also abide, whither thou goest, there go I also."

Jesus said, "Come then." The disciples arose and clasping their staffs were ready to depart. Then Jesus turned to Mary Magdalene and Martha, and said, "Remain here, beloved! Once more, fare ye well. Dear peaceful Bethany, never more shall I tarry in thy quiet vale."

Simon, sore troubled in speech as he heard these words, said unto him, "Then thou wilt really depart hence?" Mary Magdalene threw herself at his feet, and said, "Alas, I am filled with terrible forebodings."

Jesus said unto her, "Stand up, Mary. The night cometh and the winter storms bluster overhead. But be comforted. In the early morning, in the garden of spring, thou wilt see me no again."

"Alas," cried Martha, "thou art going and comest thou back never more?"

Jesus said, "The Father wills it, beloved. Wherever I am, I bear you ever with me in my heart, and wherever you are, my blessing will follow you. Farewell."

And behold as they turned to go, there met them Mary the mother of Jesus with her companions. Mary had a white mantle round her head, from beneath which her long dark hair hung down. She hastened to her son, crying:

"Jesus, dearest son, I hastened after thee with eager longing to see thee once more before thou goest, ah—whither?"

Jesus clasped her hands gently and replied, "Mother, I am on the way to Jerusalem."

"To Jerusalem," said his mother. "There is the Temple of Jehovah, whither I once carried thee in my arms to offer thee to the Lord."

"Mother," said Jesus, in solemn sadness, "the hour is come when revealing to the will of the Father I shall offer myself. I am ready to complete the sacrifice which the Father demands from me."

"Ah," cried Mary, with a bitter and piteous cry, "I foresee what kind of a sacrifice that will be." John and Mary Magdalene had joined the mother of Jesus, and the two Marys standing together united their lament. "How much we had wished," said the Magdalen, "to keep back the Master and make him remain with us." "It is of no use," said Simon, gloomily, "His purpose is fixed."

Then said Jesus to his mother, tenderly beholding her, "My hour is come." All the disciples cried, "O ask the Father that he should let it pass by." Then all the women said, "The Father has always listened to thee." But Jesus said, "Now is my soul troubled and what shall I say? Father, deliver me from this hour! But for this hour came I into the world."

But Mary, hearing him, exclaimed as in a trance, "Oh, venerable Simon, now will be fulfilled that which thou once prophesiedst unto me. 'A sword shall pierce through thine own soul.'" And as she spoke the Magdalen gently supported her from falling.

Jesus said in terms of gentle reproach, "Mother, the will of the Father was also ever sacred to thee." His word rallied her courage, and she replied, "It is so to me still. I am thy handmaid of the Lord. But one thing I beg of thee, my son."

"What desirest thou, my mother?"

"That I may die with thee!"

Johannes. Welche Liebe!
Christus. Du wirst, liebe Mutter, mit mir leiden, wirst meinen Todeskampf mitkämpfen, dann aber auch meinen Sieg mitfeiern. Darum tröste dich!
Maria. O Gott, gieb mir Stärke! . . . .
Die heil. Frauen. Beste Mutter, wir weinen mit dir.
Maria. So gehe ich, mein Sohn, mit dir nach Jerusalem.
Die Frauen. Beste Mutter, wir gehen mit dir.
Christus. Ihr möget später dahin gehen; für jetzt bleibet bei unsern Freunden zu Bethanien! Ich empfehle Euch, Ihr treuen Seelen, meine liebe Mutter nebst denen, die sie hieher begleitet haben.
Magdalena. Nach dir ist uns nichts theurer als deine Mutter.
Lazarus. Wenn du, o Meister, doch verbleiben könntest!
Christus. Tröstet Euch unter einander! Nach zwei Tagen aber möget ihr gemeinsam den Weg nach Jerusalem antreten, um auf den grossen Festtag dort zu sein.
Maria. Wie du willst, mein Sohn.
Frauen. Ach, wie traurig werden uns fern von dir die Stunden verfliessen!
Christus. Mutter! Mutter! für die zärtliche Liebe und mütterliche Sorgfalt, die du mir in den dreiunddreissig Jahren meines Lebens erwiesen hast, empfange den heissen Dank deines Sohnes! Der Vater ruft mich. Lebe wohl, beste Mutter!
Maria. Mein Sohn, wo werde ich dich wieder sehen?
Christus. Dort, liebe Mutter, wo sich das Wort der Schrift erfüllt! Er wurd wie ein Lamm, das zur Schlachtbank geführt wird und seinen Mund nicht öffnet.
Maria. Jesus! deine Mutter—ach! Ach Gott!—mein Sohn—
Frauen. [*Zur Mutter Maria eilend, um sie zu unterstützen*]. O liebe, treue Mutter!
Jünger [*Im Abgehen*]. Wir halten es nicht aus. Was wird das werden!
Alle. Welche Trübsal steht uns Allen bevor!
Christus. Unterlieget nicht beim ersten Kampfe! Haltet Euch fest an mich! [*Geht ab.*]
Lazarus. Frauen [*Cumstro nachabend*]. O unser lieber Lehrer!
Simon. Beglücker meines Hauses! [*Zu Maria.*] Komm, Mutter, und würd'ge mich auch du, es zu betreten!
Magdalena. Ein Trost ist in der Trübsal uns geblieben.
Martha. Die Mutter unsers Herrn bei uns zu haben.
Lazarus. (*Zu den Frauen*). Auch ihr Geliebte, kommt mit uns! Wir wollen Wehmuth und Thränen miteinander theilen.
[*Sie gehen in das Haus.*]

IV. VORSTELLUNG.

Der letzte Gang nach Jerusalem.

PROLOG.

Volk Gottes! sich'! dein Retter ist nahe dir;
Gekommen ist der langst dir Verheissene.
   O hör' ihn! folge seiner Führung!
   Segen und Leben wird Er dir bringen.

Doch blind und taub erzeigt sich Jerusalem;
Es stösst die dargebotene Hand zurück.
   D'rum kehrt sich auch von ihm der Höchste,
   Lässt es versinken in sein Verderben.

Der Vasthi Stolz verschmähet das Königsmahl;
D'rob schwer erzürnt, verweist der König sie
   Aus seinen Augen, wählt sich eine
   Edlere Seele zur Eh'genossin.

"Oh what love!" exclaimed John, who stood tearfully beside the two Marys, wistfully looking for some ray of hope to illuminate the darkness beyond.

Jesus embraced her lovingly. "Dear Mother, thou wilt suffer with me, thou wilt fight with me in my death-struggle, but thou wilt also rejoice with me in my victory, therefore be comforted."

"Oh, God," she cried in heartrending accents, "give me strength!"

"We all weep with thee, thou best of mothers," said the Holy Women, adding their tears to those of the Mother of Jesus.

"I go then with thee, my Son, to Jerusalem," said Mary.

And the Holy Women declared they also would go with her. But Jesus, holding her hand, tenderly forbade her: "Later you may go thither, but not now. For the present stay with our friends at Bethany. I commend to you, O faithful souls, my beloved Mother, with those who have followed her here."

Eagerly the Magdalene accepted the charge.

"After thee," she exclaimed, "there is no one dearer to us than thy Mother."

But even at the eleventh hour Lazarus interposed one last word of entreaty: "If only thou, O Master, couldst remain!"

Not noticing this, Jesus said, "Comfort ye one another. After two days you may come up together to Jerusalem, to be there on the great day of the feast."

Mary said, "As thou willest, my Son."

But the Holy Women said, "How sadly will the hours pass when thou art far from us."

Then Jesus spoke to his Mother and said, "Mother, Mother, for the tender love and motherly care which thou hast shown to me for the three and thirty years of my life receive the warmest thanks of thy Son." And stooping down he kissed her. Then raising his head he said, "The Father calls me. Fare thee well, best of mothers."

Mary asked him, "My son, where shall I see thee again?"

And Jesus replied, "There, beloved mother, where the Scripture shall be fulfilled: 'He was led as a lamb to the slaughter, and he opened not his mouth.'"

Mary, sobbing, cried aloud, "Jesus, thy mother, oh. Oh, God, say so!"

Half fainting she was held up by the Holy Women, who exclaimed, "Oh, beloved, faithful mother!"

The Disciples departing muttered, "We cannot endure it. What will be the end of all this?"

Then burst from their lips the despairing cry, "Alas, what affliction lies before us all!"

But Jesus said, "Sink not in the first combat. Hold ye fast by me."

Lazarus and the women looking back after Christ as he passed out of sight, exclaimed, "Ah! our dear teacher," while Simon said, "He brought happiness to my house."

Simon then turned tenderly to Mary, and said, "Come, Mother, and condescend to enter in." "One consolation remains to us in tribulation," said Mary Magdalene, and Martha added, "To have the Mother of our Lord with us." Turning to the other women, Lazarus said, "And you, beloved ones, come with us, we will share our woe and tears together."

All then together went into the house, Mary Magdalene supporting the Mother of Jesus.

CHAPTER IV.

PROLOGUE.

People of God! behold! thy Saviour is nigh to thee!
He is come, who was promised thee long ago.
   Oh! hear Him, follow His guidance!
   Blessing and life will He bring to thee.

But blind and deaf Jerusalem has shown herself;
She has thrust back the Hand held out to her in love.
   Therefore also the Highest has turned away His face,
   And lets her sink to destruction.

Queen Vashti, in her pride, despised the royal feast;—
The king, in his grievous wrath, hath banished her
   Out of his presence, and chosen
   A nobler soul to be his mate.

So wird die Synagoge verstossen auch;
Von ihr hinweggenommen, wird Gottes Reich
An and're Völker hingegeben,
Die der Gerechtigkeit Früchte bringen.
Choragus.—Recit.
Jerusalem! Jerusalem! erwache!
Erkenne, was zum Frieden dir noch werden kann!
Doch zögerst du, so fangt die Zeit der Rache
Unselige! mit fürchterlichen Schlagen an.
Chor.
Jerusalem! Jerusalem!
Bekehre dich zu deinem Gott!
Verachte nicht mit Frevelspott
Den Mahnungsruf der Gnade!
Dass nicht, Unsel'ge, über dich
Des Höchsten Grimm entlade!
Doch ach!—ach! die Prophetenmörderin—
Sie taumelt fort in ihrem bösen Sinn.
Darum, so spricht der Herr,
Dies Volk will ich nicht mehr.

VORBILD.

König Asuer verstösst die Vasthi und erhebt die Esther. [Esth. 1, u 2.]

[Die stolze Königin Vasthi versinnbildlicht Jerusalem und das Judenthum, während Esther das Christenthum bedeutet. Wie Vasthi vom König verstossen wurde, so wendet sich Christus von den Juden zu den Heiden und lässt ihnen durch seine Jünger die Segnungen des Glaubens welchen die Juden verschmähen, zu Theil werden.]

Choragus.—Recit.
Seht Vasthi—seht! Die Stolze wird verstossen!
Ein Bild, was mit der Synagog der Herr beschlossen.
"Entferne dich von meinem Throne—
Du stolzes Weib, unwerth der Krone,"
So spricht Assuerus tief ergrimmt;
"Du Esther, tritt an meine Seite,
Durch's Leben gib mir das Geleite,
Der Thron hier ist für dich bestimmt!"

"Die Zeit der Gnade ist verflossen;
Dies stolze Volk will ich verstossen.
So wahr ich lebe," spricht der Herr,
"Ein besseres Volk will ich mir wählen,
Mit ihm auf ewig mich vermählen,
Wie mit der Esther Assuer."

Chor.
Jerusalem, Jerusalem!
O, Sünd'nvoll, hör' Gottes Wort:
Wollt ihr noch Gnade finden,
So schafft aus eurem Herzen fort
Den Sauerteig der Sünden!

HANDLUNG.

CHRISTUS geht mit seinen Jüngern wieder nach Jerusalem,—weint bei dem Anblick der sündigen Stadt, schickt zwei von den Jüngern voraus, das Osterlamm zu bereiten,—JUDAS fasst den Gedanken, seinen Meister zu verrathen.

ERSTE SZENE.

CHRISTUS und die Zwölfe auf dem Wege nach Jerusalem.
Johannes. Meister, sieh', welch herrliche Aussicht auf Jerusalem!
Matthäus. Und der majestätische Tempel, welches Prachtgebäude!
Christus. Jerusalem, Jerusalem! O dass du es doch erkenntest und zwar an diesem Deinem Tage, was Dir zum Frieden dient! Aber es ist vor Deinen Augen verborgen.
[*Weint.*
Petrus. Meister, warum betrübst du dich so sehr?
Christus. Mein Petrus! Das Schicksal dieser unglücklichen Stadt geht mir zu Herzen.
Johannes. Herr, sage es uns, was wird dies für ein Schicksal sein?
Christus. Tage werden kommen, da die Feinde rings um sie Walle aufwerfen, sie einschliessen und von allen Seiten

Thus also the Synagogue has been cast away,
And the Kingdom of God, taken away from her,
Is given to other nations
Who shall bring forth fruits of righteousness.

Jerusalem! Jerusalem! awake!
Know what belongs unto thy peace, ere the day come
When, if thou lingerest, God will vengeance take,
Unhappy one! in fearful strokes of doom.

Jerusalem! Jerusalem!
Oh! turn unto thy God again!
Despise thou not, with mockery vain,
His mercy's warning call.
Lest on thee, cursed of the Lord,
In fulness measureless outpoured,
The wrath Almighty fall.

But she, alas! she who the prophets slew,
Reels on in her mad course, to outrage new:
Therefore, thus saith the Lord,
This people is abhorr'd.

[The sixth tableau, which is supposed to typify the doom of Jerusalem for the rejection of the Saviour, presents us with a picture of the Court of Ahasuerus at the moment when Vashti the Queen is falling before the wrath of her Royal consort, who is welcoming Esther to the vacant throne. Judging from the tableau, Ahasuerus could not be congratulated upon the change. Poor Vashti's beauty is all exposed to the assembled banqueters, but exposed in shame and disgrace instead of being exhibited as the glory of her lord's harem. Her fate is declared by the chorus to foreshadow that of the Synagogue.]

See Vashti—see the haughty one, outcast—
Symbol of what befell the Synagogue at last.
"Depart thou from before my throne,
O haughty woman, of the crown
Unworthy!" spake the king in wrath.
"Thou, Esther, come unto my side,
This throne's for thee, my chosen bride;
Through life our feet shall tread one path."

Even so, the day of grace is past—
"This haughty people is outcast
From me," so doth the Lord declare.
A better nation He will choose
Eternally to be His spouse,
As Ahasuerus Esther fair.

Jerusalem! Jerusalem!
Ye sinners! hearken to God's word,
If ye would mercy win,
And put away from out your hearts
The leavened bread of sin.

CHRIST AND HIS DISCIPLES ON THE WAY TO JERUSALEM.

Now as they came nigh unto Jerusalem they looked down upon the whole city which lay before them. Then said John unto Jesus, "Master, behold what a splendid view of Jerusalem!" Matthew said, "The majestic Temple, how splendidly it is built!" Jesus was troubled in spirit, and after gazing for a moment over the city, clasped his hands in grief and cried. "O, Jerusalem, Jerusalem, O that thou hadst known even in this thy day the things that belong unto thy peace! but now they are hidden from thine eyes!" Jesus wept.
His disciples, beholding him weep, were amazed. At last Peter ventured to say, "Master, why grievest thou so sorely." Jesus answered, "My Peter, the fate of this unhappy city goes to my heart." Then said John, "Lord, tell us, what shall this fate be?" Jesus answered and said unto them, "The days

THE LAST JOURNEY TO JERUSALEM.—ACT IV., SC. 1.

ängstigen werden. Sie werden sie und ihre Kinder, die in ihren Mauern sind, zu Boden schmettern und keinen Stein auf dem andern lassen.

Andreas. Warum wird die Stadt ein so trauriges Schicksal haben?

Christus. Weil sie die Zeit ihrer Heimsuchung nicht erkannt hat. Ach! die Prophetenmörderin wird selbst den Messias tödten.

Alle. Welch' schreckliche That!

Jakobus der Aeltere. Verhüte Gott, dass die Stadt Gottes nicht solchen Fluch auf sich lade!

Johannes. Meister, um der heiligen Stadt willen, um des Tempels willen bitte ich Dich, gehe nicht hin, damit den Bösen die Gelegenheit fehle, das Schrecklichste zu vollbringen.

Petrus. Oder gehe hin und offenbare Dich ihnen in Deiner ganzen Herrlichkeit, dass die Guten jubeln und die Bösen zittern.

Alle. Ja, das thue.

Philippus. Schmettere Deine Feinde nieder!

Alle. Und richte Gottes Reich unter den Menschen auf!

Christus. Kinder, was Ihr wünschet, wird geschehn zu seiner Zeit. Aber meine Wege sind mir von meinem Vater vorgezeichnet und—so spricht der Herr: Meine Gedanken sind nicht Eure Gedanken, und Eure Wege sind nicht meine Wege.

Petrus. Meister!

Christus. Es ist heute der erste Tag der angesäuerten Brode, an welchem das Gesetz befiehlt, das Ostermahl zu halten. Ihr Beide, Du Petrus und Johannes, gehet voraus und bereitet uns das Osterlamm, dass wir in der Abendstunde es essen können.

Petrus and Johannes. Wie willst du, Herr, dass wir es zurichten?

Christus. Wenn Ihr in die Stadt hineinkommt, so wird euch Jemand begegnen, der einen Krug mit Wasser trägt. Diesem gehet nach in das Haus, wo er hineingeht und saget zum Hausvater: Der Meister lasst dich fragen: Wo ist das Zimmer, da ich mit meinen Jüngern das Osterlamm essen kann? Er wird euch dann einen zugerichteten Speisesaal zeigen; da bereitet es zu.

Petrus. Deinen Segen, bester Meister!

[PETRUS and JOHANNES knien.

Christus. Gottes Segen sei mit Euch!

[Die beiden Apostel ab.

(Kunst und Verlags Anstalt, Oberammergau.)   (Carl Stockmann, Photo.

JUDAS.

will come when her enemies will make a trench about her walls, and close her in on every side and lay her even with the ground. She and her children within her walls will be dashed to the earth, and not one stone will be left upon another." Andrew, giving expression to the general consternation, asked, "Wherefore shall the city have so sad a doom." Jesus said, "Because she hath not known the day of her visitation. Alas! she who hath slain the prophets will kill the Messiah himself." Then spoke all the disciples together, "What a terrible deed!" James the Elder said, "God forbid that the city of Jehovah should bring such a curse upon herself." And John, with pleading voice, added, "Dearest Master, for the sake of the Holy City and the Temple I beg of thee go not thither, so that the opportunity may be wanting to these evil men to do the worst." "Or," said Peter, "Go thither and display thyself in all thy majesty, so that the good may rejoice and the evil tremble." "Yes," cried all the twelve eagerly, "do that." Philip said, "Strike down thine enemies!" and all added earnestly. "And set up the kingdom among men." Jesus answered, "Children, that which you desire shall come to pass in due time, but my ways are appointed to me by my Father and, —thus saith the Lord, My thoughts are not as your thoughts, and your ways are not as my ways."

Then as if to cut short a useless discussion, he said, "It is now the first day of unleavened bread, in which the law commands that we should eat the Passover; you, both Peter and John, go forward and prepare the Passover that we may eat it in the evening." Peter and John, who stood the one on his left and the other on his right, asked, "Where wilt thou that we go to prepare the Passover?" And Jesus said, "When you come into the city there shall meet you a man bearing a pitcher of water, follow ye him, and wheresoever he shall go in, say ye to the good man of the house, 'The Master says, Where is the guest-chamber where I may eat the Passover with my disciples?' and he will show you a large upper chamber furnished and prepared; there make ready the Passover." "Thy blessing, O best of masters!" said Peter. He and John knelt down on either side of their Lord, Jesus placed his right hand on the head of John and his left on the head of Peter, exclaiming, "God's blessing be with you."

ZWEITE SZENE.

Christus. Ihr Uebrigen begleitet mich zum letzten Male in das Haus meines Vaters! Heute geht Ihr noch mit mir dahin. Morgen — —

Judas. Aber Meister, erlaube mir, wenn du wirklich uns verlassen willst, so triff doch wenigstens Anstalten für unsere künftige Versorgung. Sieh hier [zeigt den Seckel], dieses reicht für keinen Tag mehr hin.

Christus. Juda! sei nicht mehr besorgt als nöthig ist!

Judas. Wie gut lage jetzt der Werth jener Salbe da drinnen! Dreihundert Denare! Wie lange konnten wir ohne Sorgen leben!

Christus. Es hat euch nie an etwas gemangelt, und — glaubet mir — es wird euch zu keiner Zeit etwas mangeln.

Judas. Ja, Meister, wenn du nicht mehr bei uns bist, werden sich die guten Freunde bald zurückziehen, und dann—

Christus. Freund Juda! sieh zu, dass nicht der Versucher Dich überfalle!

Alle. Beunruhige doch, Juda, den Meister nicht so sehr.

Judas. Wer sorgt, wenn ich nicht sorge? Bin ich nicht zum Seckelmeister vom Meister bestellt?

Christus. Das bist du, aber ich fürchte — —

Judas. Auch ich fürchte, dass es hier bald leer sein und bleiben wird.

Christus. Juda! Vergiss nicht meiner Warnung! Nun lasst uns weiter gehen! Mich verlangt es, im Hause meines Vaters zu sein. [*Geht ab mit den Jüngern*, JUDAS *bleibt zurück.*

DRITTE SZENE.

JUDAS *allein*.

Was will ich ihm noch nachgeh'n? Ich habe keine Lust dazu. Das Benehmen des Meisters ist mir unerklärlich. Seine grossen Thaten liessen hoffen, er werde das Reich Israels wiederherstellen. Aber er ergreift die Gelegenheiten nicht, die sich darbieten, und jetzt redet er von Scheiden und Sterben und vertröstet uns in geheimnissvollen Worten auf eine dunkle Zukunft. Ich bin es müde, zu glauben und zu hoffen. Nichts steht bei ihm in Aussicht, als fortwährende Armuth und Niedrigkeit, und anstatt der erwarteten Theilnahme an seinem Reich vielleicht gar Verfolgungen und Kerker. Ich will mich zurückziehen. Zum Glück war ich immer vorsichtig und habe aus dem Seckel hie und da eine Kleinigkeit für den Fall der Noth bei Seite gelegt. Hätte die Thörin den Werth jener Salbe in den Seckel gelegt, so würden jetzt, wenn sich die Gesellschaft — wie es scheint — auflösen muss, die dreihundert Denare in meinen Händen bleiben. Dann wäre ich geborgen auf lange Zeit! So aber muss ich auf Mittel sinnen, wie ich einen Erwerb finden könnte. Wo oder wie? [*bleibt sinnend stehen.*]

VIERTE SZENE.

JUDAS. *Der Händler* DATHAN.

Dathan. Judas — die Lage ist günstig, er ist allein. Er scheint sehr verwirrt. Ich muss Alles aufwenden, ihn zu gewinnen. Freund Judas!

Judas. Wer ruft?

Dathan. Ein Freund. Ist dir etwas Trauriges begegnet? Du denkst so tief nach.

Judas. Wer bist du?

Dathan. Dein Freund, dein Bruder.

Judas. Du? Mein Freund, mein Bruder?

Dathan. Wenigstens wünsche ich es zu werden. Wie steht es mit dem Meister? Auch ich möchte in seine Gesellschaft kommen.

Judas. In seine Gesellschaft? ...

Dathan. Hast du ihn etwa verlassen? Steht es schlimm mit ihm? Sage es mir, damit ich mich darnach richte.

Judas. Wenn du schweigen kannst —

Dathan. Sei versichert.

Judas. Es steht nicht mehr gut mit ihm. Er sagt es selbst, seine letzte Stunde sei gekommen. Ich will ihn verlassen. Ich bin Seckelmeister — sich' her, wie es hier steht.

Dathan. Freund, dann bleibe ich dir wie ich bin.

Peter and John having departed, Jesus said to the others, "Accompany me for the last time to the House of my Father, To-day you will go with me thither; to-morrow —" Then Judas, who had for some time past stood apart, came forward and said, " But, Master, allow me; if thou wilt really leave us, make some arrangement for our future support. Look here," he added, pointing to the small bag almost empty of coin, which he carried in his girdle, "there is just enough here for one day more." But Judas went on muttering, and looking, not at his Lord, but at the bag, " How well the value of that ointment would have lain therein! how long we could have lived on it without care!" Jesus reproved him, saying, "You have never lacked anything hitherto and, believe me, that what is necessary will not fail you in time to come." Judas said, " But, Master, when thou art no longer with us our good friends will soon draw back, and then——" Jesus said unto, him "Friend Judas, beware! lest thou fall into temptation." The other Disciples who had listened to this conversation then interrupted, saying all together, "Judas, trouble not the Master so much." Judas retorted, " Who will take thought if I do not? Have I not been appointed by the Master to carry the bag?" "Thou hast," said Jesus, " but I fear——" " And I also fear," interrupted Judas, "that soon it will be empty and remain so." Then said Jesus unto him, "Judas, forget not my warning. Arise, now let us go hence." Jesus then, followed by his disciples, excepting Judas, passed on to the city.

Judas, being left alone, said to himself —

"And shall I follow? I have but half a mind. No roses here will ever bloom for me! The great deeds of the Master once raised hopes that he would restore Israel's ancient fame. But this great scheme He seems of late to waive, His words are all of parting and of death. With dark, mysterious words, he puts us off with promises of a future that lies too far off in the distance to please me. Long have I fed, too long, upon these dreams, and now I am tired of hoping. To Him and His what prospects are held out? An abject state, and poverty forsooth — ay, and perhaps even a prison! I'll withdraw; but how? Ah! now I miss that goodly, goodly sum of full three hundred pence. Oh, were it mine, that were provision for a rainy day! Now for subsistence; I must look about, and know not where!"

As he stood alone under the trees, perplexed and troubled, Dathan appeared in the background, and spying Judas, said to himself, "The occasion is favourable. He is alone and seems much perplexed. I must try everything in order to secure him." Then stepping forward he laid his hand upon the shoulder of Judas, exclaiming " Friend Judas!" Judas started as if a serpent had stung him, and striking his head with his hand cried, " Who calls?" "A friend," said Dathan: " has anything sad happened to thee? Thou art so absorbed in thought." Judas, staring wildly, asked, " Who art thou ?" " Thy friend, thy brother," said Dathan. Judas, starting backward, exclaimed, " Thou my friend, my brother?" " At least," said Dathan, " I wish to be so. How is it with the Master? Could I also become one of his disciples?" Judas said, " One of his disciples?" " Why?" said Dathan; " hast thou then forsaken him? Are things not well with him? Tell me that I may know how to act." Then Judas said unto him, "Canst thou keep silence?" " Be assured of that," said Dathan. "Then," answered Judas, "it is no longer going well with him. He says himself his last hour has come." And then Judas rapidly ran over the various predictions of disaster which he had heard from the lips of Jesus. "I intend to forsake him. See here," said he, producing the almost empty purse, "see how it stands with us." "Friend," said Dathan, shrugging his shoulders, "I shall remain as I am." At this moment six of Dathan's companions came up

THE LAST JOURNEY TO JERUSALEM.—ACT IV., SC. 4.

OBSERVING THE PASSOVER.

FUENFTE SZENE.

Dathan's Genossen schleichen herbei.

Judas. Wer sind diese? Ich will nicht weiter reden.
Händler. Bleibe, Freund, es wird dich nicht gereuen.
Judas. Warum seid ihr hiehergekommen?
Händler. Wir wollen nach Jerusalem zurück und die Gesellschaft leisten, wenn es dir gefällt.
Judas. Wollt ihr vielleicht dem Meister nachgehn?
Händler. Ist er nach Jerusalem?
Judas. Zum letzten Male, wie er sagt.
Händler. Will er denn das Judenland verlassen?
Judas. Was fragt ihr so eifrig? Wollt ihr seine Anhänger werden?
Händler. Warum nicht, wenn günstige Aussichten da sind?
Dathan. . . . .
Judas. Davon sehe ich nichts. Er sagt uns immer, sorgt nicht für Morgen—wenn ihm aber heute etwas widerfährt, stehen wir Alle bettelarm da. Sorgt ein Meister so für die Seinen?
Händler. Da sieht es freilich schlimm aus.

[JUDAS *erzählt die Geschichte von der Salbe.*]

Händler. Und du kannst ihm noch gut sein?—Du solltest selbst für deine Zukunft sorgen, es wäre an der Zeit.
Judas. Darauf sinne ich eben. Aber wo gleich ein gutes Fortkommen finden?
Dathan. Da brauchst du nicht lange zu suchen, die schönste Gelegenheit bietet sich dar.
Judas. Wo, wie?
Händler. Hast du nichts gehört von dem Ausschreiben des Hohen Rathes? Eine schönere Gelegenheit findest du dein Lebtag nicht mehr.
Judas. Welches Ausschreiben.
Händler. Wer den nächtlichen Aufenthalt des Jesus von Nazareth anzeigt, soll eine grosse Belohnung erhalten.
Judas. Eine grosse Belohnung?
Händler. Wer kann sie leichter verdienen als du?
Dathan. *(für sich):* Wir sind nahe am Ziel.
Händler. Bruder, verscherze dein Glück nicht!
Judas. Eine schöne Gelegenheit—soll ich sie aus den Händen lassen? . . . .
Dathan. Und bedenke: mit der Belohnung ist es nicht abgethan. Der Hohe Rath wird weiter für dich sorgen. Wer weiss, was aus dir noch wird!
Händler. Schlag ein, Freund!
Judas. Wohlan, es sei!
Dathan. Komm, Juda, wir führen dich sofort zum Hohen Rath.
Judas. Für jetzt muss ich dem Meister nach. Ich will zuerst auskundschaften, um sicher zu gehen. Meldet mich vorläufig beim Hohen Rath. In drei Stunden findet Ihr mich in der Tempelgasse.
Dathan. Bruder, ein Wort — —
Judas. Ein Mann! [*Die Hand er ab.*]

SECHSTE SZENE.

Judas allein.

Das Wort ist gegeben. Es wird mich nicht reuen. Soll ich etwa dem entgegenkommenden Glücke aus dem Wege gehen? . . . Ja, mein Glück ist gemacht! Ich thue, was ich versprochen, lasse mich aber im Vorrus bezahlen. Gelingt es dann der Priesterschaft, ihn gefangen zu setzen, geht es zu Ende mit ihm, so habe ich mein Schäflein im Trocknen, und werde noch dazu ein berühmter Mann, als Einer, der geholfen hat, das Gesetz Mosis zu retten. Siegt aber der Meister . . . . dann werde ich mich ihm reumüthig zu Füssen werfen. Er ist ja gut; ich habe nie gewhen, dass er einem Reumüthigen von sich gestossen. Er wird mich wieder aufnehmen und ich habe dann das Verdienst, dass ich die Entscheidung herbeigeführt habe. . . . . Judas, du bist ein kluger Mann . . . . aber bange ist mir doch, vor den Meister zu treten. Ich werde seinen durchdringenden Blick nicht ertragen können, und meine Gefährten werden es mir am Gesicht ansehen, dass ich ein — nein! das will ich nicht sein, ich bin kein Verrather! Was thue ich denn, als dass ich den Juden anzeige, wo der Meister zu treffen ist? das ist doch kein Verrath, dazu gehört mehr. Weg mit diesen Grillen! Muth, Judas, es handelt sich um deine Versorgung!

Judas, alarmed, asked, "Who are these? I will not say another word." "Stay, friend," said one of the new comers, "you will not regret it." Judas said, "Why have you come here?" "We were going back to Jerusalem, and we will bear thee company if it please thee." Judas, suspiciously eyeing them, asked, "Do you also, perhaps, wish to go after the Master?" Then said the Traders, "Has he gone to Jerusalem?" "For the last time," said Judas; "so he says." "What?" said they, "is he then going to leave the land of Judea?" "Why do you ask me that so eagerly?" said Judas. "Do you wish to become his followers?" "Why not?" said the Traders with a laugh, "if the prospects are good." "I do not see that they are," said Judas, "he tells us always to take no thought for the morrow; but if to-day anything happened, we should all be as poor as beggars. Doth a master care thus for his own?" "Truly," said the Traders, "the lookout is bad." Then Judas related once more the story of Mary Magdalene's waste of precious ointment. "Three hundred pence," said he, "wasted. Oh, if I only had them." "And thou canst still be faithful to him after that," said the Traders, contemptuously. "Thou shouldst take thought for thine own future; it is high time." "So I have been thinking," said Judas, "but how can I find a good opening?" "Then," said Dathan, "thou hast not long to seek, for the fairest opportunity is awaiting thee." "Where?" said Judas, eagerly. "Hast thou not heard," said the Traders, "of the proclamation of the Council? Fairer opportunity wilt thou never find again in thy whole life long." Judas's eyes gleamed. "What proclamation?" he asked. The Traders said, "Whosoever gives information as to the nightly resort of Jesus of Nazareth shall receive a large reward." "A large reward!" said Judas. "Now who," said they, "can earn it easier than thou?" Dathan muttered to himself. "We have nearly attained our end." The Traders pressed Judas anew, "Brother, don't neglect this good fortune." Judas said, hesitatingly, "A fair opportunity. Shall I let it slip?" Then struck in Dathan, "The reward is not all. The Council will look after thee in the future. Who knows what might not yet come of it for thee?" "Strike the bargain," cried all the Traders together. Judas hesitated one moment and then clasped Dathan's hand saying, "Well, it is done." "Come, Judas," said Dathan, "we will bring thee straightway to the Council." But Judas said, "No, I must first go after the Master, and so obtain information in order to make things sure. Report me to the Council. In three hours you will find me in the street of the Temple." Dathan said, "Brother, one word———." Judas then shook hands all round with the traders. "Done!" exclaimed Judas, as Dathan and the traders left him.

Judas was now alone. He walked to and fro under the trees and said to himself:—

"My word and hand are pledged; I shall not now repent of it. Should I not be a great fool to cast away this bit of profit which I can earn with so little trouble. My fortune's made. It cannot go amiss. I'll keep my promise, then let His priestly foes proceed to capture Him—and should He fall, my prospects are assured. But if the Master should gain the victory, then—yes then—what shall I do? What shall I do? Oh, I will cast me down repentant at His feet, for He is good, and will forgive me for the sin that's past. Nay, I can safely plead my act was wise—by which the issue ripened. Anyhow, I'll take good care to leave a bridge behind, that, should I be unable to go forward, I can return. This plan is well thought out. Judas, thou art a prudent man! And yet I feel a little afraid to meet the Master, for His keen, searching look will pierce my soul, and will read every thought upon my face. What am I going to do, but let the high priest know where the Master is to be found at a certain time? That is no betrayal. Betrayal is—when anyone attempts—No more—such whims serve but to perplex. Courage, Judas! He who wants to make a profit must set to work with a good courage."

Judas who had started with horror when he first mentioned the word traitor, resolved to play his appointed rôle and departed to find Jesus.

SIEBENTE SZENE.

Stadtgasse.—BARUCH. *Gleich darauf* PETRUS *und* JOHANNES. *Dann* MARKUS.

Baruch. [*Geht mit dem Wasserkruge zum Brunnen.*] Es drängen heute die Geschäfte sehr. An diesem Osterfeste wird es nicht an Arbeit fehlen; denn der grosse Zudrang der Pilger lässt nichts Anderes erwarten. Es muss mein Herr auf viele Gäste rechnen, da er sich so geschäftig stets im Hause herumtreibt. [*Er schöpft Wasser.*]

Johannes. [*Mit* PETRUS *von der andern Seite kommend.*] Sieh'! ein Jüngling dort am Brunnen!

Baruch. [*Noch schöpfend.*] Es muss Besonderes für dieses Osterfest im Werke sein, indem die Herren des Rathes so hin und wieder laufen. [*Geht mit dem Kruge seinem Hause zu.*]

Petrus. Dieser ist's. Er trägt den Wasserkrug, wie uns der Meister das Zeichen gab.

Johannes. So wollen wir ihm folgen. [*Gehen nach.*]

Baruch. [*Unsehend vor der Thüre des Hauses.*] Wollt ihr mit mir, o Freunde? Seid willkommen!

Johannes. Wir wünschten gerne deinen Herrn zu sprechen.

Baruch. Gedenket Ihr vielleicht das Ostermahl bei uns zu halten?

Petrus. Ja, der Meister grab uns den Auftrag, bei deinem Herrn die Bitte d'rum vorzutragen.

Baruch. Kommet nur mit mir! Denn meinem Herrn wird's eine Freude sein, Euch aufzunehmen in sein Haus. Doch sieh'! [MARKUS *kommt.*] Da ist er selbst.—Sieh', Herr! hier bring' ich Gäste.

Markus. Willkommen, Fremdlinge! Womit kann ich Euch dienen?

Petrus. Unser Lehrer lässt dir sagen: Wo ist der Saal, dass ich das Osterlamm mit meinen Jüngern essen kann? Denn nahe ist meine Zeit. Bei dir will mit den Meinen ich Ostern halten.

Markus. O der Freude! Jetzt erkenn' ich euch. Ihr seid die Jünger des Wunderthäters, der das Augenlicht mir wieder gab! Wie hab' ich es verdient, dass er vor allen in Jerusalem mein Haus sich auserwählt, das heil'ge Mahl darin zu feiern! O ich Glücklicher! Gesegnet ist dies Haus, das er beehrt mit seiner Einkehr! Kommet, liebe Freunde! Ich will sogleich den Speisesaal euch weisen.

V. VORSTELLUNG.

Das heilige Abendmahl.

PROLOG.

Eh' der göttliche Freund hin in sein Leiden geht,
Gibt, von Liebe gedrängt, Er sich den Seinigen
 Dar zur Speise der Seelen
 Auf der irdischen Pilgerfahrt.

Sich zu opfern bereit, weiht er ein Opfermahl,
Das Jahrtausende fort bis an der Zeiten Schluss
 Der geretteten Menschheit
 Seine Liebe verkünden soll.

Mit des Manna Genuss sättigte wunderbar
In der Wüste der Herr Israels Kinder einst,
 Und erfreute die Herzen
 Mit den Trauben aus Kanaan.

Doch ein besseres Mahl, wahrhaft vom Himmel her,
Bietet Jesus uns dar. Aus dem Geheimnisse
 Seines Leibes und Blutes
 Quillt uns Gnade und Seligkeit.

Solo.—*Recit.*

Nun nahret sich die Stunde
Und die Erfüllung nahet an.
Was längst aus der Propheten Munde
Der Herr der Menschheit kund gethan.

An diesem Volke, spricht der Herr,
Hab' ich kein Wohlgefallen mehr.
Ich will nun keine Opfergaben
Von seinen Händen ferner haben.
Ich stifte mir ein neues Mahl,
Dies spricht der Herr,—und überall
Soll auf der ganzen Erdenrunde
Ein Opfer sein in diesem Bunde.

THE LAST SUPPER.—ACT V.

And it came to pass that when Peter and John were still on their way to Jerusalem, Baruch, the servant of Mark, came out into the street with a pitcher of water which he went to get filled at the well.

As he went he said to himself, "There is a great deal of business to-day, there will be no lack of work this Passover; from the great crowd of pilgrims, we can expect nothing else. My master must expect many guests, as he is already making so much to-do in the house." When he was drawing the water, John and Peter came upon him. "See," said they, "the young man there at the well." Baruch not noticing them went on drawing the water, saying, "There must be something exceptional at this Passover, seeing the way in which the Rulers of the Council hasten about hither and thither." As he lifted the pitcher and turned to go, Peter said, "This is he who carries the pitcher of water that our Master gave us for a sign." "Then," said John, "let us follow him." Baruch looked round as he came to the door of his master's house, and seeing the disciples said, "Will you come in with me, friends? you are welcome." "We wish," said John, "to speak with your master." "Perhaps," said Baruch, "you desire to take the Passover with us?" "Yes," said Peter, "the Master gave us a message about this to your master." "Then," said Baruch, "come with me. It will be a joy to my master to take you into his house. There are," he said, as Mark came out of the house, "there he is himself." "See, master, I bring guests." "Welcome, strangers," said Mark, "how can I serve you?" "Then," said Peter unto him, "Our Teacher sent us to say unto thee, 'Where is the hall where I can eat the Passover with my Disciples, for my time is at hand. I will keep the Passover in thy house with my disciples.'" "O joy!" exclaimed Mark, "now I recognise you as the disciples of the miracle-worker who restored to me the light of my eyes. How have I deserved that he should choose my house before all others that are in Jerusalem in which to celebrate the passover? O, fortunate man that I am, that it should be my house which he honours with his presence. Come, dear friends, I will at once show you the hall." And they went into the house and found all things as Jesus had said unto them.

CHAPTER V.

PROLOGUE.

Ere the Heavenly Friend hence to His Passion goes,
To His own He Himself, urged by constraint of love
 Gives, as food to their spirits
 On their pilgrimage here on earth.

Ready to offer Himself, here He doth consecrate
A sacrificial feast that shall last to the end of time,
 And proclaim His love ever
 Unto the ransomed of Adam's race.

In the desert of old, the Lord fed wondrously,
With the manna from heaven, Israel's children once,
 And with grapes out of Canaan
 Made He their failing hearts rejoice.

But a better food, and truly the bread of heaven,
Jesus offers to us. Out of the mystery
 Of His Body and Blood,
 Flow for us grace and salvation.

Now doth the hour draw near
 When all shall be fulfilled
Which God, by mouth of many a seer,
 Of old to man revealed.
"This people"—thus, O Lord, said'st Thou—
"In them I have no pleasure now,
From sinful hands I will not take
The gifts and offerings that they make.
I consecrate a Banquet new,"
(Thus saith the Lord;) "the whole earth through,
Our sacrifice this feast shall be
In the new Covenant with me."

VORBILD.

Der Herr gibt dem Volke das Manna.—2 Mos., 16.

[Das Manna ist Vorbild des allerheiligsten Altarsakraments. Wie Gott die Israeliten auf ihrem mühevollen Zuge durch die Wüste, so nahrt Jesus die Christen durch die Wüste dieses Lebens mit seiner heiligen Liebe.]

Das Wunder in der Wüste Sin
Zeigt auf das Mahl des neuen Bundes hin.

VORBILD.

Die Weintrauben aus Canaan.—4 Mos., 13.

[Dasselbe wie im vorigen Bilde—ein schönes Gleichniss auf das Brod und den Wein des neuen Bundes.]

Chor.

Gut ist der Herr! Gut ist der Herr!
Das Volk, das hungert, sättigt Er
Mit einer neuen Speise
Auf wunderbare Weise.
Der Tod doch raffte alle hin,
Die assen in der Wüste Sin
Dies Brod im Ueberflusse.
Des neuen Bundes heilig Brod
Bewahrt die Seele vor dem Tod
B im würdigen Genusse.
Gut ist der Herr! Gut ist der Herr!
Dem Volke einstens hatte Er
Den besten Saft der Reben
Aus Kanaan gegeben.
Doch dies Gewächse der Natur
War zum Bedarf des Leibes nur
Bestimmt nach Gottes Willen.
Des neuen Bundes heil'ger Wein
Wird selbst das Blut des Sohnes sein,
Der Seele Durst zu stillen.
Gut ist der Herr! Gut ist der Herr!
Im neuen Bunde reichet Er
Sein Fleisch und Blut im Saale
Zu Salem bei dem Mahle.

HANDLUNG.

Jesus hält mit seinen Jüngern das letzte Paschamahl und stiftet das Mahl des neuen Bundes zu seinem Andenken.

ERSTE SZENE.

Im Speisesaale. Christus und die Zwölfe.
[Stehend an der Tafel.]

Christus. Sehnlichst habe ich darnach verlangt, dieses Osterlamm noch mit Euch zu essen, ehe ich leide. Denn ich sage Euch: Von nun an werde ich es nicht mehr essen, bis es erfüllt sein wird im Reiche Gottes. Vater! Ich danke dir für diesen Trank der Reben. [Trinkt und reicht den Jüngern den Becher.] Nehmet hin und theilet ihn unter Euch, denn ich sage Euch, ich werde von nun an von dem Gewachse des Weinstockes nicht mehr trinken, bis das Reich Gottes kommt.

Die Apostel. Ach Herr, so ist dieses das letzte Osterfest?

Christus. Einen Trank werde ich im Reiche Gottes, meines Vaters, mit Euch trinken, wie geschrieben steht: Aus dem Strome der Seligkeit wirst du sie tranken.

Petrus. Meister, wenn dieses Reich erscheinen wird, wie werden dann die Plätze ausgetheilt?

[The seventh and eighth tableaux foreshadow the Last Supper. Both are marvellous displays of artistic skill in grouping hundreds of persons in a comparatively small space. The first is the gathering of the manna in the wilderness; the second the return of the spies from the Promised Land with a bunch of grapes so colossal as to cause two strong men to stagger beneath its weight. The whole of the stage is a mosaic of heads and hands. Four hundred persons, including 150 children are grouped in these two great living pictures, and so motionless are they that you might almost imagine that they were a group in coloured marble. The tableaux are conventional enough. Moses has his two gilt rays like horns jutting out of his head, the manna falls from above upon the stage like snow in a theatrical winter piece, and there is no attempt to reduce the dimensions of the bunch of grapes to credible proportions. The reference to the manna and to the land that flowed with milk and honey lead up to the institution of the Last Supper.]

The wonder in Sin's Wilderness befell
Is symbol of this blessed feast as well.

The Lord is good! The Lord is good!
The hungry He provides with food,—
With heav'nly food to-day,
In new and wondrous way.

But death all those away has swept
Who in the wilderness were kept.
And with that bread relieved.
But the New Cov'nant's sacred Bread
Preserves the soul that else were dead,
If worthily received.

The Lord is good! The Lord is kind!
For when with thirst His people pined,
He gave the vine's best juice
That Canaan could produce.

But this fair fruit the earth hath grown
God for the body's need alone,
Provided, for our sake,
While the New Cov'nant's blessed wine
Shall be the sacred Blood Divine—
The soul's deep thirst to slake.

The Lord is good! The Lord is good!
He in the Covenant renew'd
Doth give, in Salem's hall,
His Flesh and Blood for all.

THE LAST SUPPER.

In the upper chamber which Mark had prepared for the Passover, Jesus and his disciples stood round a long table. Jesus stood in the centre with Peter on his right and John upon his left. Judas, sullen and scowling, sat next to Peter, and the other disciples were arranged in their order. The table was covered with a white cloth with embroidered edges. On the cloth stood a flagon of wine and several cups, and a plate on which lay a loaf of bread. Jesus, standing in the midst, said unto them, "With longing have I desired to eat this Passover with you before I suffer, for I say unto you I will not any more eat thereof until it be fulfilled in the kingdom of God." Jesus then took the cup, and lifting it with both hands, looked up to heaven and said, "I thank thee for this fruit of the vine." Then drinking of it he passed the cup to Peter, who also drank and passed it to Judas, who in his turn, after drinking, passed it to the next disciple and so on, until it went all round. "Take this," said Jesus, as he passed the cup to Peter, "and divide it amongst yourselves, for I say unto you, I will not drink henceforth of the fruit of the vine until the Kingdom of God comes." Then, exclaimed all the disciples together, "Alas, Lord, is this then the last Passover?" Jesus said unto them, "There is a cup which I will drink with you in the kingdom of God my Father. As it is written, 'Thou shalt make them drink of the river of thy pleasure.'" "Then," said Peter unto him, "Master, when this kingdom shall

THE LAST SUPPER.—ACT V., SC. 1.

50   THE PASSION PLAY AS PLAYED TO-DAY.

Jakobus der Aeltere. War von uns wird den Vorrang haben?

Thomas. Wird etwa Jedem ein besondres Land zur Herrschaft zugetheilt?

Bartholomäus. Das dürfte wohl das beste sein; so würde sich kein Streit mehr unter uns erheben.

Christus. So lange schon bin ich unter Euch und Ihr seid noch so sehr im Irdischen befangen! — Allerdings bereitet ich Euch, die Ihr meine Versuchungen mit mir ausgehalten habt, das Reich zu, wie es mir mein Vater zubereitet hat, dass Ihr in meinem Reiche an meinem Tische esset und trinket, und auf Thronen sitzet, die zwölf Stämme Israels zu richten. Merket aber wohl, die Könige der Völker herrschen über sie und die Gewalthaber werden Wohlthäter genannt. Bei Euch aber soll es nicht so sein. Sondern der Grösste unter Euch sei wie der Geringste, und der Vornehmste, wie Euer Diener! Denn wer ist grösser, der am Tische sitzet, oder der beim Tische dient? Nicht wahr, der am Tische sitzt? Ich aber bin mitten unter Euch, wie einer, welcher dient. [*Legt das Oberkleid ab, umgürtet sich mit einem weissen Tuche, giesst Wasser in ein Becken.*] Nun setzt Euch, liebe Jünger.

Die Apostel. Was will er wohl thun?

Christus. Petrus! Reiche mir deinen Fuss!

Petrus. Herr, die Füsse willst du mir waschen?

Christus. Was ich thue, verstehst du jetzt nicht, du wirst es aber nachher verstehen.

Petrus. Herr! In Ewigkeit sollst du mir die Füsse nicht waschen!

Christus. Wenn ich dich nicht wasche, so wirst du keinen Antheil an mir haben.

Petrus. Herr, wenn das ist, nicht allein die Füsse, sondern auch die Hände und das Haupt!

Christus. Wer gewaschen ist, bedarf mehr nicht, als dass er die Füsse wasche, so ist er ganz rein. [*Wäscht allen Jüngern die Füsse; nachdem er das Oberkleid wieder angethan hat, steht er im Kreise waschrsehend.*] Ihr seid jetzt rein — aber nicht alle! [*Setzt sich.*] Wisset Ihr, was ich Euch gethan habe? Ihr nennt mich Meister und Herr und Ihr redet recht, denn ich bin es. Wenn nun ich Euch die Füsse gewaschen habe, — ich, der Herr und Meister, so sollt auch Ihr, einer dem andern, die Füsse waschen. Denn ich habe Euch ein Beispiel gegeben, dass auch Ihr so thuet, wie ich Euch gethan habe. Fürwahr! Der Diener ist nicht grösser als Derjenige, der ihn gesandt hat. Da Ihr dieses wisset, selig seid Ihr, wenn Ihr es thut. (*Nachdem er wieder aufgestanden ist.*) Kinder! Nicht mehr lange werde ich bei Euch sein. Damit aber mein Andenken niemals unter Euch erstebe, will ich Euch ein ewiges Denkmal hinterlassen und so immer bei Euch und unter Euch wohnen. Der alte Bund, den mein Vater mit Abraham, Isaak und Jakob geschlossen, hat sein Ende erreicht. Und ich sage Euch: Ein neuer Bund fängt an, den ich heute feierlich in meinem Blute stifte, wie der Vater mir aufgetragen — und dieser wird dauern bis alles vollendet sein wird. [*Er nimmt das Brod, segnet und bricht es.*] Nehmet hin und esset! Diess ist mein Leib, der für Euch hingegeben wird. [*Er giebt jedem der Jünger einen kleinen Theil.*]

Thut das zu meinem Gedächtnisse! [*Nimmt den Kelch mit Wein und segnet ihn.*] Nehmet hin und trinket Alle daraus, denn diess ist der Kelch des neuen Bundes in meinem Blute, welches für Euch und für Viele wird vergossen werden zur Vergebung der Sünden. [*Er reicht allen den Kelch.*] So oft Ihr dieses thut, thut es zu meinem Gedächtnisse! [*Setzt sich.*]

appear, how will the offices be portioned out?" "Who amongst us" said James the Elder, "will have the first place?" Then Thomas said, "Will each one of us have lordship over a separate land." "That would be much the best," said Bartholomew, "then no dispute would arise amongst us." Then Jesus looked upon them and said, "So long a time have I been amongst you and are you still entangled in earthly things? Verily, I appoint unto you, which have continued with me in my temptations, the Kingdom which my Father has appointed unto me, that you may eat and drink with me in my Kingdom, and sit on thrones judging the twelve tribes of Israel. But remember, the kings of the Gentiles exercise lordship over them, and they that exercise authority over them are called benefactors, but ye shall not be so. He that is greatest among you let him be as the least and the chief as your servant. For whether is greater, he that sitteth at meat or he that serveth? Is not he that sitteth at meat, but I am among you as he that serveth."

Thereupon John removed the long purple robe from the shoulders of Jesus, and handed him a white linen towel with which he girded himself round the middle. Then came Baruch in, carrying a ewer of water and a basin. As they looked in amazement one at another Jesus said unto them, "Sit you down, beloved disciples." Then said the disciples one to another, "What is He going to do?" Jesus, turning to Peter, said, "Peter, reach me thy foot!" Peter starting backward in amazement, said, "Lord, dost thou wash my feet?" Then said Jesus, "What I do thou knowest not, indeed, but thou shalt know hereafter." Peter replied stoutly, "Lord, thou shalt never to all eternity wash my feet." But Jesus said, "If I wash thee not, thou shalt have no part in Me." Peter said, "Lord, if it be so, then not only my feet only, but also my hands and my head." But Jesus answered, "He that is washed needeth not save to wash his feet but is clean every whit." Then, stooping down, Baruch poured the water over the feet of Peter, and Jesus dried them with a towel. The other disciples took the sandals off their feet, whispering to themselves in wonder as to what this might mean. Jesus washed the feet of Judas as those of the others. Last of all he washed the feet of John also. Then he washed his hands. Baruch pouring the water over them. After which he took off the towel and John placed his mantle once more upon his shoulders. Looking around upon the twelve, He said, "Ye are now clean but not all." Jesus then seated himself in the midst of them.

Then said Jesus unto them, "Do you know what I have done unto you? Ye call me Master and Lord and ye do well, for so I am. If I then, your Lord and Master, have washed your feet, ye also ought to wash one another's foot. For I have given you an example that ye should do as I have done unto you. Verily, verily, the servant is not greater than he that sent him! If ye know these things, happy are ye, if ye do them." Then Jesus stood up again and said, "Children, but for a little while shall I be with you. That my memory shall never perish from among you, I will leave behind an everlasting memorial, and so I shall dwell with you and amongst you. The old Covenant which my Father made with Abraham, Isaac and Jacob has reached its end, and I say unto you, a new Covenant begins which I solemnly consecrate to-day with my blood as the Father has commanded me, and this Covenant will last until all be fulfilled." Jesus then took the bread, lifted it up before him, and replacing it on the table, looked up to heaven and blest it. Then lifting it up again, He broke it in two, saying, "Take, eat, this is my body which was broken for you." Then passing round the table, He placed a morsel of bread with his own hand into the mouth of each of the disciples. All took it reverently, but Judas bit at it almost as a dog snatcheth meat from its master's hand. After Jesus had returned to his place, He said, "This do in remembrance of me." In like manner He took the cup and blest it, and said, "Take this, and drink ye all of it, for this is the cup of the New Testament in my blood which is shed for you and for many, for the remission of sins." Then passing round the table again He gave each of them to drink, and, returning to his place, He said, "As often as ye do this, do it in remembrance of me." During the time Jesus went round the table administering the bread and wine to his disciples, there was heard in the distance a chorus of angels singing.

THE LAST SUPPER.—ACT V., SC. 1.

[Kunst und Verlags Anstalt, Oberammergau.]
JAMES THE LESS.

[Carl Stockmann, Photo.
THOMAS.

[Kunst und Verlags Anstalt, Oberammergau.]
SIMON.

[Carl Stockmann, Photo.
MATTHEW.

ENGELS-CHOR WAEHREND DEM HEILIGEN ABENDMAHLE.

O, der Demuth! o der Liebe!
Sehet dort den Heiland knie'n,
Zu den Füssen seiner Jünger
Knechtesdienste zu vollzieh'n.
O gedenket dieser Liebe!
Liebet auch, wie Er geliebt!
Uebet auch die Liebesdienste,
Die der Heiland hat geübt.

Johannes. Bester Lehrer, nimmer will ich deiner Liebe vergessen, du weisst es, dass ich dich liebe! [*Sinkt an Christi Brust.*]

Die Apostel. O Liebevollster, ewig wollen wir mit dir vereinigt bleiben.

Petrus. Dieses heilige Mahl des neuen Bundes soll nach deiner Anordnung immer so unter uns fortgesetzt werden.

Alle. Geliebtester Lehrer! O göttlicher, o bester Freund und Lehrer!

Christus. Meine Kinder! Bleibet in mir, und ich bleibe in Euch. Gleich wie der Vater mich geliebt hat, so habe auch ich Euch geliebt. Bleibet in meiner Liebe! Wenn ihr meine Gebote haltet, so bleibet ihr in meiner Liebe. Aber — ach! Muss ich es sagen? — Die Hand meines Verrathers ist mit mir auf dem Tisch.

Mehrere Apostel. Wie, ein Verrather zwischen uns?

Petrus. Ist es möglich?

Christus. Wahrlich, wahrlich sage ich Euch: Einer aus Euch wird mich verrathen,

Andreas. Herr, einer von uns Zwölfen?

Christus. Ja, einer von den Zwölfen! Einer, der mit mir die Hand in die Schüssel tunkt, wird mich verrathen. Es wird die Schrift erfüllt werden: Der das Brod mit mir isst, wird seinen Fuss gegen mich aufheben.

Thomas und Simon. Wer sollte dieser Treulose sein?

Die beiden Jakobus. Nenne ihn öffentlich, den Schandlichen!

Judas. Herr, bin ich es?

Thaddäus. Lieber mein Leben für dich, als solch einen Schritt!

Christus. [*Zu Judas.*] Du hast es gesagt. [*Zu Allen.*] Der Menschensohn geht zwar hin, wie es beschlossen ist; weh aber demjenigen, durch welchen der Menschensohn verrathen wird! Besser wäre es diesem Menschen, wenn er nie geboren wäre!

Petrus. [*Leise zu Johannes.*] Wer ist es, von dem er redet?

Johannes. [*Leise zu Jesus.*] Herr, wer ist es?

Christus. [*Leise zu Johannes.*] Der ist's, dem ich das eingetunkte Brod reichen werde.

Mehrere Apostel. Wer mag es doch sein?

Christus. [*Nachdem er Judas das Brod gereicht hat.*] Was du thust, das thue bald! [*Judas eilt aus dem Saale.*]

Thomas. [*Zu Simon.*] Warum geht Judas fort?

Simon. Vermuthlich schickt ihn der Meister, etwas einzukaufen.

Thaddäus. Oder ein Almosen an die Armen auszutheilen.

ZWEITE SCENE.

Christus. Jetzt wird des Menschen Sohn verherrlicht und Gott durch ihn. Wenn nun Gott durch ihn verherrlicht ist, so wird ihn auch Gott bei sich verherrlichen und bald wird er ihn verherrlichen. — Kindlein! Eine kleine Weile bin ich noch bei Euch. Ihr werdet mich suchen, aber, wie ich den Juden gesagt habe: Wo ich hingehe, dahin könnt Ihr nicht kommen, so sage ich jetzt auch Euch.

Petrus. Herr, wo gehst du hin?

Christus. Wohin ich gehe, dahin kannst du mir nicht folgen.

Petrus. Warum kann ich dir jetzt nicht folgen? Für dich gebe ich mein Leben!

Christus. Du willst dein Leben für mich geben? Simon! Der Satan hat verlangt, Euch sieben zu dürfen, wie man den Waizen sicht. Ich habe aber für dich gebeten, dass dein Glaube nicht sinke. Und wenn du einst bekehrt sein wirst, so stärke deine Brüder! In dieser Nacht werdet ihr Alle Euch an mir ärgern, denn es steht geschrieben: Ich werde den Hirten schlagen und die Schafe der Heerde werden zerstreut werden.

Petrus. Wenn sich auch Alle an dir ärgertren, ich werde es nicht thun. Herr, ich bin bereit, mit dir in den Kerker und in den Tod zu geh'n.

CHORUS OF ANGELS.

Oh! the lowly love and tender!
See the Saviour kneeling still
At the feet of His disciples,
Loving service to fulfil.
Oh! this Love remember ever!
Love as He has loved, and do
Unto others loving service
As your Lord has done to you.

Then John in an ecstasy of affection exclaimed, "Oh, best of masters, never will I forget thy love! Thou knowest that I love thee," and leaning forward he laid his head on the breast of Jesus. The rest of the twelve, who were sitting with clasped hands, with the exception of Judas who sat apart moody and sullen, exclaimed together, "Oh, Master, who art so full of love for us, ever will we remain united with thee." Then said Peter, "This holy meal of the new Covenant shall ever be celebrated amongst us according to thy commandment." Then cried they all, "Oh best teacher, Oh divine one! Oh best friend and teacher!" and Jesus looking upon them, said. "Abide in me, and I in you! As the Father has loved me so have I also loved you, continue ye in my love. But, alas, must I say it? the hand of him who betrays me is with me at the table!" Judas started, but the confusion of the disciples caused his guilty look to be unnoticed. Several of the disciples exclaimed, "What! a traitor amongst us." "Is it possible?" said Peter. Then Jesus said, "Verily, verily, I say unto you, one of you shall betray me." "Lord," said Andrew, "one of us twelve?" "Yes," replied Jesus, "one of the twelve who dipped his hand in the dish with me shall betray me. So the scripture shall be fulfilled. He that eateth bread with me hath lifted up his heel against me." Thomas and Simon speaking together with the same thought and same words asked "Who can this faithless one be?" while the two James's said. "Name him publicly, the traitor!" Then while these words were on their lips, Judas fearing lest his silence should be observed, started forward and asked furtively, "Lord. Is it I?" but, excepting by Jesus, his words passed unnoticed. Thaddeus exclaimed, "I would rather give my life for Thee than that such a deed should be done." Jesus looking towards Judas said, "Thou hast said it." Turning to the rest Jesus continued, "The Son of man goeth indeed, as it is written of Him, but woe unto that man by whom the Son of man is betrayed, better were it for him that he had never been born!" Peter leaning over to John whispered to him to ask Jesus who it was. Then John whispered to Jesus, saying, "Lord, who is it?" Jesus answered, speaking so low as to be heard by John alone, "He it is, to whom I shall give a sop, after I have dipped it." The other Apostles who had not heard this kept on asking "Who can it be?" Jesus taking a piece of bread dipped it in the cup, placed it in the mouth of Judas, saying, "What thou doest do quickly." Then Judas arose and hurried from the room. The disciples seeing his departure wondered among themselves and Thomas said to Simon, "Why does Judas go away?" Simon replied, "Probably the Master has sent him to buy something," while Simon added, "Or to distribute alms to the poor."

Judas being now gone, Jesus spoke to the eleven, saying. "Now is the Son of man glorified and God is glorified in him. If God be glorified in him, God shall also glorify him in himself and shall straightway glorify him. Little children, yet a little while I am with you. Ye shall seek me; but, as I have said to the Jews: whither I go ye cannot come, even so now I say it unto you." Then said Peter unto him, "Lord. whither goest thou?" Jesus answered, "Whither I go thou canst not follow me now." Peter passionately cried, "Why can I not follow thee now? I will lay down my life for thy sake." Then Jesus looked upon him with compassion and said, "Wilt thou lay down thy life for my sake? Simon! Simon! Satan hath desired to have thee that he may sift thee as wheat, but I have prayed for thee that thou fall not, and when thou art converted, strengthen thy brethren! This night all ye shall be offended with me, for it is written, 'I shall smite the shepherd and the sheep of his flock shall be scattered abroad.' Peter answered, "Although all shall be offended, yet will not I. Lord, I am ready to go with thee to prison and to death."

THE LAST SUPPER.—ACT V., SC. 2.

ANDREW.

PHILIP.

BARTHOLOMEW.

THADDEUS.

Christus. Wahrlich, wahrlich sage ich dir, Petrus! Heute, in dieser Nacht, noch ehe der Hahn zweimal gekraht hat, wirst du mich drei Mal verleugnen.
Petrus. Und wenn ich mit dir sterben müsste, so würde ich dich doch niemals verleugnen.
Alle. Meister, auch wir bleiben dir ewig treu! Keiner aus uns wird dich jemals verleugnen.
Christus. Hat Euch etwas gemangelt, da ich Euch ohne Seckel, Tasche und Schuhe aussandte?
Alle. Nein! Nichts.
Christus. Jetzt aber nehme jeder seinen Seckel, desgleichen auch die Tasche! Und wer es nicht hat, der verkaufe seinen Rock und kaufe ein Schwert. Denn es beginnt die Zeit der Prüfung, und ich sage Euch: Es muss an mir noch erfüllt werden, was geschrieben steht: Er ist unter die Uebelthäter gerechnet worden.
Petrus und Philippus. Herr, siehe da, zwei Schwerter.
Christus. Genug!—Lasst uns aufstehn und das Dankgebet sprechen. [Mit den Jüngern.] Lobet den Herrn, alle Völker!—Lobet ihn, alle Nationen! denn bestätiget ist über uns seine Barmherzigkeit; die Wahrheit des Herrn bleibet in Ewigkeit! [Geht in den Vordergrund und bleibt dort eine Weile mit zum Himmel erhobenem Blick stehen, die Apostel stehen auf beiden Seiten, betrübt auf ihn hinschend.] Kinder! Was seid Ihr so traurig und seht mich so bekümmert an? Euer Herz betrube sich nicht. Ihr glaubet an Gott, glaubet auch an mich! Im Hause meines Vaters sind viele Wohnungen, und ich gehe hin, Euch einen Ort zu bereiten, und dann werde ich kommen und Euch zu mir nehmen, damit auch Ihr seid, wo ich bin. Ich lasse Euch nicht als Waisen zurück. Ich hinterlasse Euch den Frieden, meinen Frieden gebe ich Euch; nicht wie die Welt ihn giebt, gebe ich ihn Euch. Haltet mein Gebot! Das ist mein Gebot, dass Ihr einander liebet, wie ich Euch geliebt habe. Daran sollen Alle erkennen, dass Ihr meine Jünger seid, wenn Ihr einander liebet.—Nun werde ich nicht mehr viel mit Euch reden; denn der Fürst dieser Welt naht heran, obgleich er nichts an mir zu suchen hat. Aber damit die Welt erkenne, dass ich den Vater liebe und so handle, wie es mir der Vater befohlen hat, so lasst uns von hinnen gehen! [Gehen ab.

Jesus said unto him, "Verily, verily, I say unto thee, Peter, to-day, even this night, before the cock crow twice, thou shalt deny me thrice." Then said Peter, "Even if I should die with thee, I would never deny thee," and the other ten disciples said altogether with a loud voice, "Master, we also will remain faithful to thee, none of us will ever deny thee."
Then said Jesus unto them, "When I sent you out without purse, or scrip, or shoes lacked ye anything?" All replied with one voice, "No, nothing." Then said Jesus, "But now I say unto you, let everyone take his purse and likewise his scrip, and whosoever hath not a sword, let him sell his coat and buy one, for now begins a time of trial, and I say unto you that thus it is written, and it must yet be accomplished in me, 'And he was reckoned among the transgressors!'" Peter then and Philip each drew a sword from the scabbard which hung at his side under his cloak, exclaiming, "Lord, see here are two swords!" Then said Jesus, "It is enough."
"Let us stand up and give thanks." Then standing, Jesus and all the disciples said together with a loud voice, "Praise the Lord all ye people! praise him all ye nations! for his merciful kindness is everlasting, the Truth of the Lord endureth for ever."
Then Jesus leaving the table advanced to the foreground and stood for some time with his eyes raised to heaven, the disciples standing on either side watching him with troubled faces. Then Jesus said unto them, "Children, why are ye so sad and why look ye on me so sorrowfully? Let not your heart be troubled,—ye believe in God, believe also in me. In my Father's house are many mansions and I go to prepare a place for you, and I will come again and receive you unto myself, that where I am, ye may be also. I leave you not as orphans. Peace I leave with you, my peace I give unto you. Keep my commandment. This is my commandment: that ye love one another as I have loved you! By this all men shall know that ye are my disciples, if ye love one another. Hereafter I will not talk much to you, for the Prince of this World cometh, although he hath nothing in me. But that the world may know that I love the Father, and as the Father gave me commandment so do I, let us go hence."

VI. VORSTELLUNG.

Der Verräther.

PROLOG.

Ach! den offnen Feinden gesellt der falsche
Freund sich bei, und etliche Silberlinge
Tilgen aus dem Herzen des Thoren alle
    Liebe und Treue.

Ruchlos geht er hin, dieser Undankbarste,
Abzuschliessen schändlichen Seelenhandel;
Feil ist ihm um schnöden Verrätherlohn der
    Beste der Lehrer.

Gleicher Sinn verhärtete Jakobs Söhne,
Dass sie unbarmherzig den eignen Bruder
Um fluchwürd'gen Preis in der fremden Wuch'rer
    Hände verkauften.

Wo das Herz dem Götzen des Geldes huldigt,
Da ist aller edlere Sinn getödtet,
Ehre wird verkauflich und Mannesswort und
    Liebe und Freundschaft.

Solo.

Bist Judas du denn ganz verblendet
Von ungezahmter Gier nach Gut?
Für schnödes Geld des Meisters Blut
Verkaufen willst du? Schaudert dir die Seele nicht?
Zum Unheil schon dein Loos sich wendet.
Schon bricht herein das Strafgericht.

    "Von euch wird Einer Mich verrathen,"
    Der Herr, auf Judas blickend, spricht,
    Der sinnt die schlimmste alle Thaten;
    Doch sein Gewissen hört es nicht.
    Der Satan herrscht in seiner Brust,
    Nach Sündengold die böse Lust.

CHAPTER VI.

PROLOGUE.—Act VI.

Woe! to open enmity now is added
The false friend, and paltry pieces of silver
Do away, in the heart of the fool, all trace of
    Love and devotion.

In his infamy goes he, this most ungrateful,
Selling a soul, to conclude a shameful traffic;
He for base reward consents to betray the
    Noblest of teachers.

Such a spirit hardened the hearts of Jacob's
Sons, that they, unpitying, their own brother,
For a shameful price and worthy of curses,
    Sold to the stranger.

Where the heart pays homage to Mammon's idol
There all nobler feeling is dead and vanished,—
Honour's bought and sold—and a man's word also,—
    Love, too, and friendship.

O Judas! art thou blinded quite
  By untamed greed of gold and gear?
. And wouldst thou sell thy Master dear
For base gain? Shudders not thy soul in dire affright?
  Thy lot has passed into the night.
  Already doth thy doom appear.

  "'Tis one of you that shall betray"—
    The Lord says—looking full at him,
  Who's purposed his own soul to slay—
    Yet is his conscience dull and dim,
  For Satan rules his heart within,
  And lust for gold that's won by sin.

"O Juda! Juda! welche Sünde!
Vollende nicht die schwarze That!"—

Chor.

Doch nein—vom Geize taub und blind
Eilt Judas fort zum hohen Rath,
Und wiederholt mit bösem Sinn,
Was einst geschah zu Dothain.

VORBILD.

Die Söhne Jakobs verkaufen ihren Bruder Joseph um zwanzig Silberlinge.
1 Mos., 37, 28.

[Dieses Bild deutet auf den Verrath Judas', welcher seinen
Herrn an die Pharisäer um 30 Silberlinge überlieferte.]

Chor.

Was bietet für den Knaben ihr,
So sprechen Brüder, wenn ihn wir
   Euch käuflich übergeben?
Sie geben bald um den Gewinn
Von zwanzig Silberlingen hin
   Des Bruders Blut und Leben.

Solo.

Was gebt ihr mir? Wie lohnt ihr mich,
Spricht der Iskariot, wenn Ich
   Den Meister euch verrathe?
Um dreissig Silberlinge schliesst
Den Blutbund er,—und Jesus ist
   Verkauft dem hohen Rathe.

Chor.

Was hier sich uns vor Augen stellt,
Ist ein getreues Bild der Welt.
Wie oft habt ihr durch eure Thaten
Auch euern Gott verkauft, verrathen?
Den Brüdern eines Joseph hier
Und einem Judas fluchet ihr,
Und wandelt doch auf ihren Wegen;
Denn Neid und Geiz und Bruderhass
Zerstören ohne Unterlass
Der Menschheit Frieden, Glück und Segen.

HANDLUNG.

JUDAS *kommt in das Synedrium und verspricht um dreissig Silberlinge seinen Meister in die Hände der* PHARISÄER *zu liefern; diese beschliess en den Tod* JESU.

ERSTE SZENE.
Der Hohe Rath.

Kaiphas. Eine erfreuliche Kunde, versammelte Väter, habe ich Euch mitzutheilen. Der vermeintliche Prophet aus Galiläa wird hoffentlich bald in unseren Händen sein. Dathan, der eifrige Israelit, hat einen von den vertrautesten Gefährten des Galiläers gewonnen, welcher sich als Wegweiser zum nächtlichen Ueberfalle gebrauchen lassen will. Beide sind bereits hier und harren nur unseres Rufes (*wendet einem Priester,* DATHAN *und* JUDAS *hereinzuführen*).
Mehrere. Man hole sie herein.
Josaphat. Ich will sie rufen.
Kaiphas. Ja, rufe sie! [JOSAPHAT *geht ab.*] Nun will ich aber noch Euren Rath vernehmen über den Preis, der für die That gegeben werden soll.
Nathanael. Das Gesetz Mosis giebt dazu Anweisung. Auf 30 Silberlinge ist ein Sklave gewerthet.
Priester. Ja, ja, solchen Sklavenpreis ist der falsche Messias werth!

ZWEITE SZENE.
DATHAN *und* JUDAS *vor dem Hohen Rathe.*

Dathan. Hochweiser Rath! Hier . . . . ist der Mann, der entschlossen ist, gegen eine angemessene Belohnung Euren und unsern Feind in Eure Gewalt zu liefern. . . .
Kaiphas. (*Zu* JUDAS). Kennst du den Mann, den der Hohe Rath aufsucht?
Judas. Ich bin schon lange in seiner Gesellschaft und kenne ihn und weiss, wo er sich aufzuhalten pflegt.
Kaiphas. Wie ist dein Name?
Judas. Ich heisse Judas und bin Einer von den Zwölfen.

"Oh! Judas! but one moment stay!
  Oh! finish not this foulest deed!"
But no!—for, deaf and blind with greed
  To the Council, Judas hastes away,
And there repeats, in evil trade,
  The bargain once at Dothan made.

[The ninth tableau brings us back to Joseph, whose sale to the Midianites for twenty pieces of silver naturally leads up to Judas's bargain with the Sanhedrim for the betrayal of his Master for thirty.]

"What will ye give for him? now tell,"
Said Joseph's brethren, "if we sell
   The lad to you to-day?"
They gave their brother's life and blood
For twenty silver pieces good,
   And went upon their way.

"What will ye give me? how reward,
If I to you betray the Lord?"
   Iscariot demands.
For thirty shekels, he hath made
The covenant—and Christ's betrayed
   Into the Council's hands.

In this, that's set before our eyes,
A picture true of this world lies;
How often, through your deeds, have you
Betrayed and sold your God anew!
On Judas ye can curses pour,
And Joseph's brethren, evermore.
Yet in their ways ye will not cease
  To walk, for envy, greed and hate
  Destroy unsparing, soon or late,
All blessing, happiness, and peace.

JUDAS BEFORE THE SANHEDRIM.

The Sanhedrim was again in session. Caiaphas presided, Annas as before sat on his left hand and Nathanael on his right. No sooner had all the members of the assembly taken their seats than Caiaphas rose and with radiant countenance began. "Assembled fathers, I have a joyful piece of news to impart to you. The supposed prophet from Galilee will soon, we hope, be in our hands. Dathan, the zealous Israelite, has won over one of the most trusted companions of the Galilean, who will let himself be employed as a guide to his nightly resort. Both are here, only waiting a summons to appear before us." "Bring them in," cried with eager voices the priests and Pharisees. Josue volunteered, "I will call them." "Yes, call them!" said Caiaphas. When Josue left the room, Caiaphas asked their counsel as to the price which should be given for the betrayal of Jesus. Nathanael stood forward and said, "The law of Moses gives direction for such a case: a slave is valued at thirty pieces of silver." The priests laughed thereat and said, "Yes, yes, it is just the price of a slave that the false Messiah is worth."

Then came in Dathan and Judas, Josue conducting them into the presence of the Sanhedrim. Dathan stood forward and said, "Most learned council, here is a man who is determined, for a suitable reward, to deliver your and our enemy into our power." Then said Caiaphas to Judas, "Knowest thou the man whom the council seeks?" Judas answered, "I have now been a long time in his company, and know where he is accustomed to abide." Then said Caiaphas, "What is thy name?" He replied, "I am Judas, and am one of the twelve." "Yes,

Die Priester. Ja, ja, wir sahen dich oft um ihm!
Kaiphas. Bist du nun fest entschlossen, nach unserem Willen zu handeln?
Judas. Darauf gebe ich mein Wort.
Kaiphas. Wird es dich nicht reuen? ....
Judas. Die Freundschaft zwischen ihm und mir ist seit einiger Zeit erkaltet und jetzt habe ich ganz mit ihm gebrochen.
Kaiphas. Was hat dich dazu veranlasst?
Judas. Es ist nichts mehr mit ihm .... and .... Ich bin gesonnen, mich an meine gesetzmässige Obrigkeit zu halten, das ist immer das Beste. Was wollt ihr mir geben, wenn ich ihn Euch überliefere?
Kaiphas. Dreissig Silberlinge und sie sollen dir sogleich ausbezahlt werden.
Dathan. Horr, Juda, 30 Silberlinge! welch' ein Gewinn!
Nathanael. Und merke, Juda, das ist noch nicht Alles. Wenn du dein Werk gut ausführst, so wird weiters für dich gesorgt werden.
Priester. Du kannst noch ein reicher und angesehener Mann werden.
Judas. Ich bin zufrieden. [*Für sich.*] Jetzt ist mein Glück gemacht!
Kaiphas. Rabbi, hole die 30 Silberlinge aus dem Schatzkasten und zahle sie in Gegenwart des Hohen Rathes vor. Ist es so Euer Wille?
Priester. Ja, er ist's.
Nicodemus. Wie, einen so gottlosen Handel mögt Ihr schliessen? [Zu Judas.] Und du, Nichtswürdiger, du errötherst nicht, deinen Herrn und Meister zu verkaufen, du Gottvergessener, Treuloser, den die Erde verschlingen soll? Um 30 Silberlinge ist dir dein liebvollster Freund und Wohlthäter feil? O warte nur! dies Blutgeld wird um Rache gen Himmel schrei'n, und heiss wird's dir dereinst auf die in Geiz versunk'ne Seele brennen. [Judas steht zitternd und wie vernichtet da.
Josue. Kümmere dich nicht, Judas, um die Rede dieses Eiferers. Lass ihn einen Jünger des falschen Propheten sein, du thust deine Pflicht als Jünger Mosis, indem du deiner rechtmässigen Obrigkeit dienst.
Rabbi. [*Kommt mit dem Gelde.*] Komm, Juda, nimm die 30 Silberlinge und mache einen Mann! [zählt sie ihm auf ein steinernes Tischchen hin, dass sie lustig klingen; Judas streicht sie gierig ein].
Judas. Auf mein Wort könnt Ihr Euch verlassen.
Saras. Aber noch vor dem Feste musst du das Werk ausführen.
Judas. Eben jetzt bietet sich die schönste Gelegenheit. Noch in dieser Nacht wird er in Euren Händen sein. Gebt mir bewaffnete Mannschaft mit, damit er gehörig umstellt werde.
Annas. Lassen wir sofort die Tempelwache mitgehn.
Ezechiel. Ja, ja, ordnen wir sie ab!
Kaiphas. Es dürfte auch rathsam sein, einige Mitglieder des heil. Synedriums abzuordnen.
Priester. Wir sind bereit. [Kaiphas wählt 4 Abgeordnete aus.]
Kaiphas. Aber, Juda, wie erkennt die Rotte im nächtlichen Dunkel den Meister?
Judas. Sie sollen mit Fackeln und Laternen auszieh'n, auch werde ich ihnen ein Zeichen geben.
Priester. Vortrefflich, Juda!
Judas. Jetzt eile ich voraus, Alles auszuspähen. Dann komme ich wieder, die Bewaffneten abzuholen.
Dathan. Ich gehe mit dir, Juda, und nicht von deiner Seite, bis dein Werk vollbracht ist.
Judas. Am Thore von Bethphage erwarte ich Eure Leute. [Judas ab mit Dathan und den vier Abgeordneten.

DRITTE SZENE.

Der Hohe Rath.

Kaiphas. Alles geht vortrefflich, ehrwürdige Väter. Nun aber heisst es, die Hauptfrage in's Auge fassen. Was soll mit diesem Menschen gescheh'n, wenn Gott ihn in unsere Hände gegeben haben wird?
Sadok. Man werf' ihn in den Kerker, den tiefsten, finster-

res," cried several of the priests, "We saw thee often with him." Caiaphas asked him, "Art thou steadfastly resolved to do our will?" Judas answered firmly, "I give you my word!" "But, continued Caiaphas, "Wilt thou not repent of it?" Judas answered, "The friendship between him and me has been cooling for some time, and now I have quite broken with him." "What has led to this?" asked Caiaphas. Judas replied, "There is nothing more to be got from him." He continued, "I am resolved to submit myself to lawful authority, that is always the best. What will you give me if I deliver him up to you?" Then Caiaphas, speaking as if he were promising great things, said, "Thirty pieces of silver, which shall be at once paid over to thee!" "Hear that, Judas!" cried Dathan, "thirty pieces of silver, what a gain!" Before Judas could reply, Nathanael sprang to his feet, saying, "And mark well, Judas, this is not all! If thou executest this work right well, thou shalt be cared for still further." "And then mayest become a rich and famous man," added a priest. Judas said aloud, "I am contented," and added to himself, "Now is my fortune made!" Then said Caiaphas to the Rabbi, who sat arrayed in blue velvet and gold below the judgment seat, "Bring the thirty pieces of silver out of the treasury, and pay it over in the presence of the Council." "Is this your will?" he added, putting the question to the Sanhedrim. A great shout went up of "Yes, yes, it is!" But some there were present who did not join in that cry. One of these, Nicodemus, stood up, and asked the Sanhedrim, "How can you conclude so godless a bargain?" Then turning to Judas, he said, "And thou, abject wretch, dost thou not blush to sell thy lord and master, thou God-forgetting traitor whom the earth shall swallow up? For thirty pieces of silver wouldst thou sell that most loving friend and benefactor? O pause while yet there is time: That blood-money will cry to high heaven for vengeance, will burn like hot iron thy avaricious soul!" Judas, surprised by this sudden outburst, stood trembling and amazed; Dathan, Caiaphas, and the rest of the Sanhedrim displayed unmistakable indignation at this unexpected intervention on the part of Nicodemus. Josue said, "Don't trouble yourself, Judas, about the speech of this zealot, let him go and be a follower of the false prophet. Thou dost thy duty as a disciple of Moses in serving the rightful authorities." Then came in the Rabbi with the silver in a dish. "Come, Judas," said he, "take the thirty pieces of silver and play the man," counting the coins out on a stone table so that they chinked merrily as they fell. Judas snatched them up eagerly, testing them now and then to see if they were genuine, and then transferred them piece by piece with feverish haste to his bag, which he tied up when filled, and replaced in his girdle. Then, resuming his place on the left of the judgment seat, he exclaimed, "You can rely upon my word." "But," said the Priests, "the work must be accomplished before the Feast." Judas answered and said, "Even now the fairest opportunity offers itself. This very night he shall be in your hands. Give me an armed band so that he can be duly surrounded." Then said Annas, who up till now had not broken silence, "Let us send with him the Temple Watch." "Yes! Yes!" cried all the Priests, "let us order them to go." Caiaphas said, "It would also be advisable to send some members of the Holy Sanhedrim with them." Half the assembly sprang to their feet crying, "We are ready." From these volunteers Caiaphas chose out four; then, turning to Judas, he said, "But, Judas, how will the band be able to distinguish the Master in the darkness?" Judas answered, "They must come with torches and lanterns, and I will give them a sign." "Excellent, Judas," cried the Priests in approving chorus. "Now," said Judas, "I will hasten away to spy out everything. Then I will come back to fetch the armed men." "I will go with you, Judas," said Dathan, "and will not leave your side until his work is finished." "At the gate of Bethphage I will meet your people," said Judas, as he departed, taking with him Dathan and the four priests told off to accompany him.

When they had left the Sanhedrim, Caiaphas addressed the assembly, "All goes admirably, venerable fathers, but now we are called to look the great question frankly in the face. What shall we do with this man when God has delivered him into our hands?" Then said Zadok, "Let us throw him into the deep-

JUDAS BEFORE THE SANHEDRIM.—ACT VI, SC. 2. 57

JUDAS RECEIVES THE PRICE OF BLOOD.

sten, und halte ihn, beschwert mit Ketten, wohlverwahrt! Er sei lebend'gen Leibes ein Begrabener!

Kaiphas. Wer von Euch bürgt dafür, dass nicht seine Freunde im Gewirre eines von ihnen erregten Aufstandes ihn befreien, oder dass sie die Wächter bestechen? Könnte er nicht durch seine verruchten Zauberkünste seine Fesseln sprengen? [*Die Priester schweigen.*] Ich sehe wohl, dass Ihr keinen Ausweg wisst. So hört denn den Hohenpriester! Es ist besser, dass Ein Mensch sterbe, als dass das ganze Volk zu Grunde gehe. Er muss *sterben*! Bevor er nicht todt ist, ist kein Friede in Israel! Keine Sicherheit für das Gesetz Mosis, keine ruhige Stunde für uns!

Rabbi. Gott hat durch seinen Hohenpriester gesprochen! Nur durch seinen Tod kann und muss das Volk Israel gerettet werden.

Nathanael. Längst lag mir das Wort auf der Zunge. Jetzt ist es ausgesprochen. Er sterbe, der Feind unserer Väter!

Priester. [*Durcheinander.*] Ja, er sterbe! In seinem Tod ist unser Heil.

Annas. Bei meinen grauen Haaren sei es geschworen: ich will nicht ruhen, bis in dem Blute dieses Verführers unsere Schmach getilgt ist!

Nicodemus. O Vater! ist's erlaubt, ein Wort zu reden?

Alle. Ja, rede, rede.

Nicodemus. Also ist über diesen Mann das Urtheil schon gesprochen, ehe er selbst vernommen, ehe eine Untersuchung, ein Zeugenverhör stattgefunden? Ist dies ein Verfahren, würdig der Väter des Volkes Gottes?

Nathanael. Was? du willst den Rath berüchtigen der Ungerechtigkeit?

Sadok. Kennst du das heilige Gesetz? vergleiche—

Nicodemus. Ich kenne das Gesetz; drum weiss ich auch: Eh' Zeugen sind vernommen, darf der Richter nicht Urtheil sprechen.

Josue. Was bedarf es hier der Zeugen noch? Wir waren oft genug Selbst Zeugen seiner Reden, seiner Thaten, durch die er freveind das Gesetz verletzte.

Nicodemus. Ihr seid Alles zugleich, Kläger, Zeugen und Richter. Ich habe seine erhabenen Lehren gehört, seine grossen Thaten gesehn. Sie verdienen Glauben und Bewunderung, nicht Verachtung und Strafe.

Kaiphas. Was, der Bösewicht verdient Bewunderung? Du willst Moses anhängen und doch vertheidigen, was das Gesetz verdammt? Ha! Väter! auf! der Frevel schreit um Rache!

Priester. Fort mit dir aus unserm Kreise!

Joseph von Arimathia. Ich muss dem Nicodemus beistimmen. Man hat ihnen keine That nachgewiesen, die ihn des Todes schuldig machte. Er hat nichts als Gutes gethan.

Kaiphas. Auch du redest so? Ist es nicht überall bekannt, wie er den Sabbath geschändet, wie er das Volk durch aufrührerische Reden verführt hat? Hat er nicht als Betrüger, seine angeblichen Wunder durch Belzebub gewirkt? Hat er sich nicht selbst für einen Gott ausgegeben?

Alle Priester. Hörst du?

Joseph v. A. Neid und Bosheit haben seine Reden verdreht, seinen edelsten Handlungen böse Motive angedichtet. Dass er aus Gott sei, haben seine göttlichen Thaten bewiesen.

Nathanael. Ha, man kennet dich! Schon seit lange bist du ein geheimer Anhänger dieses Galiläers, nun hast du dich völlig entlarvt.

Annas. So haben wir sogar in unserer Mitte Verräther am heiligen Gesetze und bis hieher hat der Verführer seine Netze ausgeworfen?

Kaiphas. Was thut Ihr hier, Abtrünnige? Geht Eurem Propheten nach, ihn nochmals zu sehen, ehe seine Stunde schlägt, denn er muss sterben! Das ist unabänderlich beschlossen.

Priester. Ja, sterben muss er, das ist unser Beschluss!

Nicodemus. Ich verfluche diesen Beschluss. Keinen Antheil will ich haben an diesem schandbaren Blutgerichte.

Joseph v. A. Auch ich will den Ort meiden, wo man die Unschuld mordet. Ich schwöre es bei Gott: Rein ist mein Herz! (NICODEMUS *and* JOSEPH *ab.*

est and darkest of dungeons, and keep him well watched and laden down with chains. Let him be buried while still alive." This, however, did not please Caiaphas, so using the full might of his eloquence and authority he continued, "Which of you would guarantee that his friends would not raise a tumult and free him, or that the guard might not be corrupted, or could he not break his fetters with his abhorred magic arts?" The priests were silent. Caiaphas replied in tones of deepest conviction, "I see well that ye have no other solution. Then listen to the high priest. It is better that one man should die and the whole nation perish not. He must die!" And as the fatal words fell from the lips of Caiaphas the whole Sanhedrim was moved. Caiaphas continued, "Until he is dead there is no peace in Israel, no security for the law of Moses, and no quiet hours for us." Hardly had Caiaphas ended, than the Rabbi sprang to his feet exclaiming in excited tones, "God has spoken through our high priest! Only by his death can and must the people of Israel be delivered." Nathanael exclaimed, "Long has the word lain upon my tongue! now it is uttered. Let him die, the foe of our fathers!" Then sprung all the priests from their seats, and with uplifted hands and eager voices, exclaimed, "Yes, he must die; in his death is our salvation!" When they sat down Annas, the aged high priest, arose, and speaking with intense bitterness, declared, "By my grey hairs let it be sworn, I will never rest until our shame is washed out in the blood of this misleader!"

Then stood up Nicodemus, and said, "O fathers, is it allowed to say one word?" And all cried, "Yes, speak, speak!" Then said Nicodemus, "Is the sentence already pronounced upon this man before he has been tried, before there has been an examination or hearing of the witnesses? Is this a proceeding worthy of the fathers of the people of God?" Nathanael said, "What! wilt thou accuse the Council of injustice?" Zadok exclaimed, "Dost thou know the Holy Law? Compare—" Nicodemus replied, "I know the Law; therefore also I know that the judge may not pass sentence before witnesses are heard." "What need we any further witnesses?" cried Josue. "We ourselves have often enough been witnesses to his speech and his actions, by which he blasphemously outraged the Law." Nicodemus answered, unmoved by the clamour of the assembly, "Them you are in yourselves at once the accusers, the witnesses, and the judges. I have listened to his sublime teachings, I have seen his mighty deeds. They call for belief and admiration, not for condemnation and punishment." "What!" exclaimed Caiaphas indignantly, "this scoundrel deserves admiration! Thou wilt cleave to Moses and yet defendest thou that which the law condemns? Ha! Fathers of Israel, the impious words call for vengeance!" The priests shouted, "Out with thee from our assembly!" when another voice was heard. Joseph of Arimathea stood forth on the opposite side of the hall, and said, "I must also agree with Nicodemus. No one has imputed any deed to Jesus which makes him worthy of death; he has done nothing but good." Then said Caiaphas, "Dost thou also speak in this wise? Is it not known everywhere how he has desecrated the Sabbath, how he has misled the people by his seditious speeches. Hath he not also as a deceiver worked his pretended miracles by the aid of Beelzebub? Has he not given himself out as a God?" "You hear that," cried the priests to Joseph. He remained standing, and continued saying, "Envy and malice have misrepresented his words and imputed evil motives to the noblest acts. That he is a man come from God, his godlike acts testify." "Ha!" cried Nathanael, with a laugh of scorn, "now we know thee. Already for a long time hast thou been a secret follower of this Galilean! Now thou hast shown thyself in thy true colours!" Aged Annas, without leaving his seat, remarked, "So then we have in our very midst traitors to our holy law, and even here has the deceiver cast his net!" "What do you here, apostates?" cried Caiaphas; "be off to your prophet, to see him once more, before the hour strikes when he must die, for that is irrevocably determined." "Yes!" cried all the priests, "yes! die he must, that is our resolve." Then said Nicodemus, "I curse this resolution; I will neither have any part nor lot in this shameful condemnation." "And I also," said Joseph of Arimathea, "will quit the place where the innocent are condemned to death. By God I swear that my hands are clean!" Gathering their robes together, Nicodemus and Joseph of Arimathea walked slowly out of the Sanhedrim.

JUDAS BEFORE THE SANHEDRIM.—ACT VI., SC. 3.

JOSEPH OF ARIMATHEA.

NICODEMUS.

VIERTE SZENE.

Der Hohe Rath.

Josua. Endlich sind wir dieses Verräther los. Wir können uns nun frei aussprechen.

Kaiphas. Es wird allerdings, Brüder, nöthig sein, dass wir über diesen Menschen förmlich zu Gericht sitzen, ihn verhören und Zeugen gegen ihn vorführen, sonst wird das Volk glauben, dass wir ihn nur aus Neid und Hass verfolgten.

Jakob. Zwei Zeugen wenigstens will das Gesetz.

Samuel. An Zeugen wird es nicht fehlen, die will ich besorgen.

Dariabbas. Das Urtheil steht fest. Wir wollen aber, damit die Schwachen sich nicht ärgern, die gerichtlichen Formen wahren.

Ezechiel. Sollten diese Formen nicht ausreichen, so wird unsere Willenskraft den Mangel ersetzen.

Rabbi. Etwas mehr oder weniger schuldig, darauf kommt es nicht an. Das öffentliche Wohl verlangt einmal seinen Tod . . . .

Kaiphas. Was übrigens die Vollziehung des Urtheils anlangt, so wird es wohl das sicherste sein, wenn wir es beim Landpfleger durchsetzen könnten, dass *er* ihn zum Tode brächte —dann wären wir ohne alle Verantwortung.

Nathanael. Wir können es versuchen. Geht es nicht durch, so steht es uns noch immer frei, unser Urtheil durch unsere Getreuen im Gedränge eines Volksauflaufes ausführen zu lassen, ohne dass wir uns offen daran betheiligen.

Rabbi. Und im äussersten Falle wird sich wohl eine Hand finden, die in der Stille des Kerkers das heilige Synedrium von seinem Feinde befreit.

Kaiphas. Die Umstände werden lehren, was geschehen soll. Für jetzt lasst uns aufbrechen. Aber haltet Euch zu jeder Stunde der Nacht bereit—ich könnte Euch rufen lassen. . . . Es ist keine Zeit zu verlieren. Unser Beschluss ist : er sterbe!

Alle (*tumultuarisch*) : Er sterbe, der Feind unseres heiligen Gesetzes!

VII. VORSTELLUNG.

Jesus am Oelberge.

PROLOG.

Wie Adam kämpft mit drückender Lebensmüh,
An Kraft erschöpft, im Schweisse des Angesichts,
Um, ach : die eig'ne Schuld zu büssen,
So drückt den Heiland die fremde Sünde.

Versenkt in einem Meere von Traurigkeit,
Von schwerer Last zur Erde das Haupt gebeugt,
Von blut'gem Angstschweisse überronnen,
Kämpft er den heissesten Kampf aan Oelberg.

Schon nahet auch, als Führer der Häscherschaar,
Der treu-vergess'ne Jünger Ischarioth,
Zum Schergendienste des Verrathes
Schändlich entweihend der Liebe Siegel.

So Böses that auch Joab an Amasa ;
Er drückt zugleich mit heuchelnder Miene ihm
Den Kuss der Freundschaft auf die Lippen
Und in das Herz, ach ! des Dolches Spitze.

Solo.

Judas, ach ! verschlang den Bissen
Bei dem Abendmahle
Mit unheiligem Gewissen
Und der Satan fuhr sogleich in ihn.—

Was du thun willst, sprach der Herr,
Juda, dieses thu' geschwind,—und er
Eilte aus dem Speisesaale
In die Synagoge hin
Und verkaufte seinen Meister.

Bald ist vollbracht,—bald ist vollbracht
Die schrecklichste der Thaten.
Ach ! heute noch, in dieser Nacht,
Wird Judas ihn verrathen.

Then said Josue, "At last we are rid of these traitors. Now we can speak out freely." Caiaphas, however, profiting by the protests of Nicodemus and Joseph of Arimathea, said to the assembly, "It will certainly be necessary that we should sit formally in judgment upon this man, to try him and to bring forth witnesses against him, otherwise the people will believe that we have only persecuted him from hatred and envy." Then said one Jacob, "Two witnesses at least the law requires;" and Samuel answered, "These shall not be lacking, I will provide them myself." Then said Dariabbas, "Our decision stands firm, but in order not to offend the weak it would be well to observe the usual forms of justice." And added Ezechiel complacently, "Should these forms not suffice the strength of our will must supply what is lacking." And a Rabbi said, "A little more or less guilty matters little, since, once for all, the public weal demands his death." Then Caiaphas said, "In securing the execution of our sentence it would be safest if we could so contrive that the sentence of death should be pronounced by the governor, then we should be clear of all responsibility." "We can try," said Nathanael ; "if it miscarries, it is still always open to us to have our sentence carried out by our trusty friends in the commotion of a great tumult, without ourselves being openly responsible for anything." "And then," said the Rabbi, "if the worst come we should have him in our hands, and in the silence of a dungeon it will not be difficult to find a sure hand to deliver the Sanhedrim from its enemy." Then Caiaphas arose and said, "Circumstances will teach us what should be done. Now let us break up. But hold yourselves ready at any hour of the night to be called together. There is no time to be lost. Our resolution is, he must die." And all the members of the High Council cried tumultuously, "Let him die, let him die! The enemy of our Holy Law!"

CHAPTER VII.

PROLOGUE.—Act VII.

As Adam fights against life's burden and weight—
His strength exhausted—in the sweat of his brow,
In expiation of his own guilt,
So is Christ weighed down by the sin of others.

Sunk in a sea of overwhelming sadness,
With heavy load his head bowed down to the earth,
Drenched with the bloody sweat of anguish—
He fights his fiercest fight on the Olive-Mount.

Already approaches, leading the men-at-arms,
The faith-forgetting disciple Iscariot,
Shamefully desecrating the seal of love
To the service of treachery.

A like evil deed did Joab by Amasa.
He pressed, at once, with feigned looks of love,
The kiss of friendship on his lips,
And into his heart, ah me ! the dagger's point.

Judas ate the hallowed bread
   At the holy table,—
With a conscience seared and dead,
And Satan entered into him straightway.

"What thou doest," spake the Lord,
   "Judas, do it quick !"—and he
Hasted forth, as he was able
   To the Synagogue away,
   And betrayed his Master.

The foulest deed will soon be done
   That earth or hell displays,—
Alas ! ere this night's course be run,
   Judas his Lord betrays!

THE GARDEN OF GETHSEMANE.—ACT. VII.

Chor.

O kommet Alle, kommet dann,
Und sehet mit die Leiden an!—
Im Schatten erst und dann im Lichte
Erscheinet sie
Die traurige Geschichte
Von Gethsemani!

VORBILDER.

1. *Adam muss im bittern Schweisse seines Angesichtes sein Brod essen.*
   1. Mos. 3, 17.

[Wie Adam zur Strafe für seine Sünde über seiner Arbeit bittern Schweiss vergoss, so vergiesst Christus am Oelberge Angstschweiss und büsst die Sünden der Menschen.]

Solo.

O wie matt, o wie heiss,
Wird es Vater Adam nicht!
Ach! es fällt ein Strom von Schweiss
Ueber Stirn und Angesicht!
Dieses ist die Frucht der Sünde ;
Gottes Fluch drückt die Natur.

Chor.

Darum gibt bei unserm Schweisse
Und bei mühevollem Fleisse
Sie die Früchte sparsam nur.

Solo.

So wird's unserm Jesus heiss
Wenn Er auf dem Oelberg ringt,
Dass ein Strom von blut'gem Schweiss
Ihm durch alle Glieder dringt.

Chor.

Dieses ist der Kampf der Sünde ;
Für uns kämpfet ihn der Herr,
Kämpfet ihn in seinem Blute,
Zittert, bebet : doch mit Muthe
Trinkt den Kelch der Leiden Er.

2. *Joab, unter dem Scheine, dem Amasa den Freundschaftskuss zu geben, stösst ihm den Dolch durch den Leib.* 2. Kön. 20, 9.

[Das Bild erinnert an den Verrätherkuss mit welchem Judas den Heiland verrieth.]

Choragus.—*Recit.*

Den Auftritt bei dem Felsen Gabaon—
Den wiederholet Judas, Simons Sohn.—

Ihr Felsen Gabaon !
Warum steht ihr ohne Zierde,
Sonst des Landes stolze Würde
Wie mit einem Trauerflor umhüllet da ?
Saget, ich beschwör euch, saget: Was geschah ?
Was geschah ?

Chor.—*In der Ferne.*

Fliehet, Wanderer, fliehet schnell von hier !
Verflucht ist dieser blutgedüngte Ort !
Da fiel, von einer Meuchlerhand durchbohrt,
Ein Amasa.
Vertrauend auf der heil'gen Freundschaft Gruss,
Getäuscht durch Joabs falschen Bruderkuss.
O ruft in unsern Ruf : Der Fluch sei dir !
Der Fluch sei dir !

Choragus.

Die Felsen klagen über dich :
Die blutgedüngte Erde rächet sich.
Verstummet, Felsen Gabaon ! verschrnt mit Grausen,
Was wir dort auf dem Oelberg schauen !

Ihr Felsen Gabaon !
Judas gibt den Menschensohn
Mit dem heuchlerischen Grusse
Und mit einem falschen Kusse
Um den schnöden Geldgewinn
In der Mörder Hände hin !

Oh come, ye faithful souls, come all,
Look on the woes that him befall !
In shadow first, and then in glory
We all shall see
The sorrowful, sweet story
Of Gethsemane.

[The scene in the Garden of Gethsemane is heralded by a double tableau. The first, which is the tenth in order of tableaux, shows Adam under the curse ; the second, Joab's treacherous assassination of Amasa. Adam, clad in a white sheepskin, is represented as sweating and wearied by digging in ungrateful soil. Three of his small children are helping him to pull the thorns and briars from the earth, while Eve, apparently a young girl, with black hair, also skin-clad, is the centre of a group of three very young children, while two in the background are playing with a stuffed lamb. The parallel is worked out by the choir between Adam's sweating and the bloody sweat in Gethsemane.]

Oh what weariness and heat
Is to Father Adam known—
See, there falls a stream of sweat
Over face and forehead down !

Now behold the fruits of sin
'Neath the curse groans Nature sore.
Therefore though he toil in field,
All his pain and labour yield
Scanty fruits for evermore.

Christ the burden and the heat
On the Olive-Mount doth bear,
So that streams of bloody sweat
Drop from brow and body there.

Now behold the fight of sin
That the Lord doth wage for us !
Waged it in his own heart's blood,
Agonised—yet firm he stood—
Drank the cup of suffering thus.

[The eleventh tableau represents Joab making ready to smite Amasa under the fifth rib, while proffering him a friendly kiss. We here come upon several soldiers who do duty in the next scene as the guard who arrest Jesus. The tableau is remarkable, because as the chorus sings there comes an echo from the rocks within, where a concealed choir sing in response to the eager enquiry of the chorus, "What happened ? What happened ?" describing the murder of Amasa, which, of course, needs no link to connect itself with the coming betrayal of Jesus.]

The scene by the rocks of Gibeon
Is repeated by Judas, Simon's son.

Ye rocks of Gibeon !
Why do ye mourning stand,
That once were counted joy of all the land,
As though in gloomy veil enshrouded !—Tell,
Oh tell me, I adjure you, what befell ?
What befell ?

Fly hence, O wanderer, swiftly fly from hence !
This bloodstained spot is cursed in all the land :
Here fell, stabbed through and through by murderer's hand,
An Amasa,
And, trusting in the love of him he greeted,
By Joab with a brother's kiss was cheated.
Oh ! cry now as we cry : "The curse on thee !
The curse on thee !"

The rocks lament for thee,—
The blood-stained earth takes vengeance heavily.
Be dumb, ye rocks of Gibeon, hear with dread,
What now upon the Mount has sped.

Ye rocks of Gibeon !
Judas doth deliver One
Greater yet, with feigned words,
And a kiss that slays like swords,
For the base gain of a day,
Up to those who wait to slay.

Chor.

Ihr Felsen Gaboon!
Verflucht sei, wer den Freund betrügt.
Mit Heuchlermiene Liebe lügt,
Mit Judaskuss die Unschuld kränkt,
Die er nur zu verderben denkt!
Fluch ihm! soll's an die Felsen schallen!
Fluch ihm! vom Felsen widerhallen!

HANDLUNG.

CHRISTUS *leidet bittere Todesangst, wird dann von* JUDAS *mit einem Kusse an die Rotte verrathen, die Ihn gefangen wegführt.*

ERSTE SZENE.

Gegend in der Nähe des Oelberges.—JUDAS, NATHAN, JOSAPHAT, PTOLOMAEUS, SALOMON. *Die* Händler. SELPHA, MALCHUS. *Die Rotte.*

Judas. Nun habet Acht! Wir nahern uns dem Orte, wohin der Meister sich zurückgezogen. . . . .
Salomon. Es werden wohl die Jünger nicht zu früh uns wittern.
Judas. Diese ruhen unbesorgt und ahnen nichts von einem Ueberfalle. An eine Gegenwehr ist nicht zu denken.
Rotte. Und wagen sie's, so werden unsre Arme sie bandigen.
Judas. Ihr werdet ohne Schwertstreich Ihn fangen.
Josaphat. Aber wie erkennen wir im Dunkeln ihn, dass wir nicht eines Andern, statt des Gewünschten, uns bemächtigen?
Judas. Ich will euch dieses als ein Zeichen geben: Wenn wir im Garten sind, so gebet Acht! Ich eile auf ihn zu, und den ich küsse, der ist es; diesen bindet!
Kore. Gut! dies Zeichen lasst uns nicht irre geh'n.
Ptolomaeus. [*Zur Rotte.*] Höret ihr's? Am Kusse werdet ihr den Meister kennen.
Rotte. Ja, ja! wir werden seiner nicht verfehlen.
Judas. Jetzt lasst uns eilen! Es ist Zeit; wir sind nicht weit mehr von dem Mayerhofe.
Josaphat. Juda! Du wirst die Früchte deines Werkes ärnten, wenn uns die heut'ge Nacht dies Glück bescheert.
Händler. Wir auch wollen dir eine grosse Belohnung geben.
Rotte. Nun warte, Volksaufwiegler du! bald wird dein Lohn dir werden. [*Alle ab.*

ZWEITE SZENE.

Der Oelgarten.

CHRISTUS *und die Jünger kommen aus dem Hintergrunde allmälig hervor.*

Christus. Fürwahr! Fürwahr! Ich sage Euch: Ihr werdet weinen und wehklagen, die Welt aber wird frohlocken. Ihr werdet traurig sein, aber Eure Traurigkeit wird in Freude verwandelt werden. Denn ich werde Euch wieder sehen, und Euer Herz wird sich freuen und Eure Freude wird Niemand mehr von Euch nehmen. Ich bin vom Vater ausgegangen und in die Welt gekommen. Ich verlasse die Welt wieder und gehe zum Vater.
Petrus. Sieh, jetzt redest du deutlich und bedienst dich keiner Gleichnisse mehr.
Jakobus der Aeltere. Jetzt sehen wir, dass du Alles weisst.
Thomas. Darum glauben wir, dass du von Gott ausgegangen bist.
Christus. Glaubet Ihr jetzt? Aber sehet! Es kommt die Stunde, und sie ist schon da, da Ihr Euch, Jeder in das Seinige, zerstreuen und mich allein lassen werdet. Doch ich bin nicht allein, denn der Vater ist bei mir. Ja, Vater! Die Stunde ist gekommen! Verherrliche deinen Sohn, damit dein Sohn dich verherrliche! Ich habe das Werk vollbracht, das du mir aufgetragen hast, ich habe deinen Namen den Menschen geoffenbart, die du mir von der Welt gegeben hast! Heiliger Vater! Erhalte sie in deinem Namen. Heilige sie in der Wahrheit! Aber nicht allein für sie bitte ich, sondern auch für Diejenigen, die durch ihr Wort an mich glauben werden, damit Alle eines seien, wie du, Vater, in mir bist, und ich in dir bin. Vater! Ich will, dass, wo ich bin, auch die bei mir seien, die du mir gegeben hast, damit sie meine Herrlichkeit

Ye rocks of Gibeon!
Curst be who his friend betrays,—
Falsely feigning loving ways,—
Innocence, with Judas-kiss,
To destruction leads like this!
"Curst be he!" to the rocks shall sound—
From rock to rock the curse rebound.

THE GARDEN OF GETHSEMANE.

Now when the evening was fully come, there were gathered together in the neighbourhood of the Mount of Olives those who were appointed by the Sanhedrim to seize Jesus. Judas was there with Dathan and the other traders, as well as the four priests appointed by the Sanhedrim to see that all things went well. With them came the Temple Watch under the command of one Selpha, in steel helmet and steel-embossed leather cuirass. The Watch consisted of twenty men in armour, all of whom carried long clubs set with spikes, two bore braziers of burning coals, while the rest carried spears. Conspicuous among the Watch were Malchus, the high priest's servant, and Balbus. They approached stealthily, and Judas addressed them, saying, "Now be careful. We are now approaching the place where the Master has withdrawn himself." Then said Solomon, one of the priests, "I suppose the disciples will not perceive us too soon." "No," said Judas, "they rest unconcerned, and dream nothing of any attack. As to any resistance, there is nothing of that to fear." Then cried the Temple Watch, aloud, "Should they try it, our arms will soon put an end to that." "You will seize him," said Judas, "without a single sword stroke." "But," said Jesue, "how shall we know him in the darkness, so as not to arrest another in place of the one we desire?" "I shall give you a sign," said Judas—"when we are in the garden, then look out: I will hasten up to him, and the man whom I shall kiss, that is he, bind him!" Then said Koras, "Good, this sign will prevent us from making any mistake." Ptolomaeus, the priest, then turned to the Watch and said, "Do you hear? you will know the Master by a kiss!" "Yes! yes!" cried the Soldiers, "we shall not miss him." "Now," said Judas, "let us make haste, it is time. We are not far from the garden." Then said Josue to Judas, "Judas, if to-night brings us good fortune, thou wilt profit by the fruit of thy work." Then cried all the Soldiers together, "Now look out, thou stirrer-up of the people, thou wilt soon have thy reward." Thereupon the whole company moved off into the darkness, and remained hidden in an ambush until the signal should be given.

After a time Jesus and his disciples entered the Garden of Gethsemane. Jesus spoke unto them, saying, "Verily, verily, I say unto you, ye shall weep and lament, but the world shall rejoice; ye shall be sorrowful, but your sorrow shall be turned into joy, for I will see you again, and your heart shall rejoice and your joy no one taketh from you. I came forth from the Father, and am come into the world. I leave the world again and go unto the Father." "Lo," said Peter, "now thou speakest plainly and no more in parables." Then said James the Greater, "Now we see that thou knowest all things." And Thomas added, "Therefore we believe that thou camest forth from God." Jesus answered them, saying, "Do ye now believe? Behold, the hour cometh, yes, is already come, when ye shall be scattered every man to his own, and leave me alone. Yet I am not alone, for the Father is with me. Yes, Father, the hour is come; glorify thy Son, that thy Son may glorify thee. I have finished the work which thou hast given me to do. I have manifested thy name to those whom thou gavest me out of the world. Holy Father, keep them through thy name: sanctify them in the truth. Neither pray I for these alone, but for them also who shall believe on me, through their word, that they all may be one, as thou, Father, art in me, and I in thee. Father, I will that they also whom thou hast given me be with me where I am, that they may behold my glory which thou hast given me, for thou lovedst me before the

THE GARDEN OF GETHSEMANE.—ACT VII, SC 2.

Kunst und Verlags Anstalt, Oberammergau.] [Carl Stockmann, Photo.

JESUS IN THE GARDEN.

schauen, die du mir gegeben hast! Denn du hast mich geliebt, ehe die Welt gegründet war.—[*Nach dem Eintritt in den Oelgarten in sichtbarer Traurigkeit zu den Jüngern*]: Kinder! Setzt Euch hier, während ich dorthin gehe und bete! Betet, dass ihr nicht in Versuchung fallet!—Ihr aber, Petrus, Jakobus und Johannes, gehet mit mir! [*Geht mit den drei Aposteln vorwärts.*]

Bartholomäus. So traurig sah ich ihn noch nie.

Jakobus der Jüngere. Mein Herz ist auch von Traurigkeit belastet!

Matthäus. O dass doch diese Nacht vorüber wäre mit ihren trüben Stunden!

Philippus. Liebe Brüder! Wir wollen hier zur Ruh', bis er zurückkommt, uns niederlassen.

Thomas. Ja, das wollen wir. Ich bin ganz müd' und kraftlos. [*Alle setzen sich.*

Christus. [*Im Vordergrunde.*] O liebe Kinder! Meine Seele ist betrübt bis zum Sterben! Bleibet hier und wachet mit mir! [*Noch einer Pause.*] Ich will mich ein wenig entfernen, um durch die Ansprache an meinen Vater mich zu stärken. [*Geht zur Grotte, langsam und wankenden Schrittes.*]

Petrus. [*Sieht ihm nach.*] O lieber, guter Meister!

Johannes. Meine Seele leidet mit der Seele unseres Lehrers. [*Sie setzen sich.*

Petrus. Mir ist so bang! Wir waren Zeugen seiner Verklärung auf dem Berge, aber jetzt—was werden wir sehen müssen.

Christus. [*In der Nähe der Grotte.*] So soll diese Stunde über mich kommen, die Stunde der Finsternisse! Doch dazu kam ich ja in die Welt! [*Wirft sich in der Grotte auf die Knie.*] Vater! Mein Vater! Wenn es möglich ist, — und dir ist ja Alles möglich — so gehe dieser Kelch an mir vorüber! [*Fällt auf sein Angesicht und bleibt so eine Weile, dann wieder auf den Knien.*] Doch Vater, nicht wie ich will, sondern wie du willst! [*Steht auf, blickt zum Himmel, geht dann zu den drei Jüngern.*] Simon!

Petrus. [*Wie im Traum.*] Ach mein Meister.

Christus. Simon, du schläfst?

Petrus. Meister, hier bin ich.

Christus. Konntet Ihr nicht eine Stunde mit mir wachen?

Petrus. Meister! vergib!

Die Apostel. Der Schlaf, Rabbi, hat uns überwältigt.

Christus. O wachet und betet, dass Ihr nicht in Versuchung fallet!

Die Apostel. Ja Herr, wir wollen beten und wachen.

Christus. Der Geist ist zwar willig, aber das Fleisch ist schwach. [*Geht wieder zur Grotte.*] Mein Vater! Deine Forderung ist gerecht! Deine Rathschlüsse sind heilig! Du forderst dieses Opfer! [*Fällt auf die Knie.*] Vater! Der Kampf ist heiss. [*Fällt auf sein Angesicht, dann sich erhebend.*] Doch wenn sich dieser Kelch von mir nicht entfernen kann, ohne dass ich ihn trinke, so geschehe, Vater, Dein Wille! [*Steht auf.*] Heiligster! Heilig werde es von mir vollbracht! [*Kommt wieder zu den schlafenden Jüngern zurück.*] So sind also Eure Augen noch zu schwer, als dass Ihr wachen könntet? O meine Vertrautesten! Auch bei Euch finde ich keinen Trost! [*Nachdem er einige Schritte auf dem Wege zur Grotte gegangen ist stillstehend.*] Ach! Wie wird jetzt alles dunkel um mich her. Die Angst des Todes umfängt mich! — Die Schwere des göttlichen Gerichtes liegt auf mir! O Sünden, Sünden der Menschheit! Ihr drückt mich nieder! O der furchtbaren Last! O der Bitterkeit dieses Kelches! [*Zur Grotte gekommen.*] Mein Vater! [*Auf den Knien.*] Wenn es nicht möglich ist, dass die Stunde an mir vorüber gehe, so geschehe dein Wille! Dein heiligster Wille! — Vater! — Dein Sohn! — Höre ihn!

DRITTE SZENE.

Ein Engel erscheint.

Engel. Menschensohn, heilige des Vaters Willen! Ueberschaue die Seligkeiten, die aus deinem Kampfe hervorgeh'n! Der Vater hat dir's aufgetragen, du hast es freiwillig auf dich genommen, das Opfer zu werden für die sündige Menschheit, fuhre es aus! Der Vater wird dich verherrlichen.

foundation of the world." Then turning to the disciples who were following him into the garden he said, in a voice which was broken with sorrow, "Children, sit down here, while I go and pray yonder. Pray that you enter not into temptation; but ye, Peter, James, and John, follow me." Eight of the disciples then sat down in the shade under the trees, while Jesus went forward with the three. Bartholomew said, "Never have I seen him so sad"; and James the Less replied, "My heart is also laden down with sadness"; while Matthew cried, "Ah, that this night were past with its weary hours." Philip said, "Dear brothers, we will sit down here and rest until he comes back." "Yes," said Thomas, "that we will, for I am utterly worn out and weary." Then Jesus, who had come forward with Peter, James, and John, said unto them, "Ah, beloved children, my soul is exceeding sorrowful, even unto death. Tarry ye here and watch with me." Then after a pause he added, "I will go a little further apart in order to strengthen myself by communion with the Father." As Jesus with slow and staggering steps went towards the grotto, Peter cried, looking after him, "Ah, dear, good master," and John exclaimed, "My soul is suffering with the soul of our teacher." As they sat down Peter said, "I am very anxious. We were the witnesses of his transfiguration on the mountain, but now, what is it that we have to see?" Slowly Peter, James, and John, who were sitting apart, fell asleep. Jesus, having reached the grotto, said, "This hour must come upon me—the hour of darkness. But for this it was that I came into the world." Then falling upon his knees he clasped his hands, and looking up to heaven cried, with a great and pitiful voice, "Father! my Father! if it be possible, and with thee all things are possible, let this cup pass from me!" Then Jesus fell upon his face on the ground and remained silent for a while. Then again he rose upon his knees and cried, "Yet, Father, not as I will, but as thou wilt!" Then, standing up, he looked towards heaven and slowly returned to the three disciples.

And lo, when he approached he found them asleep. "Simon!" he said. Simon Peter as in a dream, rubbed his head and said, "Alas! my Master." Jesus said, "Simon, dost thou sleep?" Peter, rousing himself, said, "Master, here I am." Jesus said, "Could you not watch with me one hour?" Peter cried, "O Master, forgive." The apostles said, "Rabbi, sleep has overpowered us." Then said Jesus, "Watch and pray that ye enter not into temptation." The apostles answered, "Yes, Lord, we will watch and pray!" Then said Jesus unto them, "The spirit indeed is willing, but the flesh is weak." So saying he turned from them, and again slowly walked towards the grotto.

Praying, he said, "My Father, thy demand is just, thy decrees are holy, thou claimest this sacrifice." Then falling upon his knees he prayed, saying, "Father, the strife is hot." Falling upon his face he remained silent for a time, then raising himself again he cried, "Yet, Father, if this cup may not pass from me unless I drink it, Father, thy will be done." Then standing up he said, "Holy One, it will be completed by me in righteousness!"

Then once more he came back to the sleeping disciples; this time he did not rouse them. "Are also your eyes so heavy that you could not watch?" he said. "Ah! my most trusted ones, even among you I find no consolation!"

Then returning over the rocky road which led to the grotto he paused for a moment in silence while a great sorrow overwhelmed him. "Oh, how dark it grows around me, the anguish of death encompasses me! The burden of God's judgment lies upon me! Oh, the sins! Oh, the sins of mankind! they weigh me down. Oh, the fearful burden! Oh, the bitterness of this cup!" Then coming to the grotto again he cried, "My Father!" and falling down he prayed, "If it is not possible that this hour pass away from me, thy will be done! Thy holiest will! Father! Thy son! Hear him!"

Then from out of the darkness a bright and shining angel in white apparel, and with radiant wings, descended upon him. And out of the silence were heard these words, "O Son of Man, sanctify the Father's will! Consider the blessings which will proceed from thy struggles. The Father has laid it upon thee, and thou hast of thy free will taken it upon thee to become the sacrifice for sinful man. Carry it through to the end. The Father will glorify thee."

THE GARDEN OF GETHSEMANE.—ACT VII., SC. 3. 65

THE BETRAYAL.

Christus. Ja, heiligster Vater! Deine Fügung bete ich an! Vollbringen will ich sie, vollbringen!—Versöhnen, retten, beseligen. [*Steht auf.*] Gestärkt durch dein Wort, o Vater, gehe ich mit Freude dem entgegen, was du mir, dem Stellvertreter der sündigen Menschheit, bestimmt hast! [*Zu den drei Jüngern.*] Jetzt schlafet und ruhet aus!

Petrus. Was ist es, Meister?

Alle drei Apostel. Sieh', wir sind bereit.

Christus. Die Stunde ist gekommen! Der Menschensohn wird in die Hände der Sünder überliefert! Steht auf und lasst uns gehen.

Jünger. Was ist das für ein Getöse?

Philippus. Kommt, wir wollen uns um den Meister sammeln. [*Die Jünger eilen noch vorwärts.*]

Christus. Seht! der mich verrathen wird, ist nahe.
[*Judas erscheint mit der Rotte.*]

Andreas. Was will diese Schaar?

Alle. Ach, es ist um uns gescheh'n!

Johannes. Und seht, Judas an der Spitze.

VIERTE SZENE.

Judas. Rabbi, sei gegrüsset! [*Küsst Jesum.*]

Christus. Freund! Wozu bist du gekommen! Mit einem Kusse verrathest du den Menschensohn? [*Geht der Schaar entgegen.*] Wen suchet Ihr?

Rotte. Jesum von Nazareth!

Christus. Ich bin es.

Rotte. Weh' uns! Was ist das! [*Stürzen zu Boden.*]

Jünger. Ein einziges Wort von ihm stürzt sie nieder!

Christus. [*Zu den Knechten.*] Fürchtet Euch nicht! Stehet auf!

Jünger. Herr, wirf sie nieder, dass sie sich nicht mehr erheben!

Christus. Wen suchet Ihr?

Rotte. Jesum von Nazareth.

Christus. Ich habe es Euch gesagt, dass ich es bin. Wenn Ihr also mich suchet, so lasset diese gehen.

Selpha. Ergreift ihn! [*Die Knechte nähern sich Jesu.*]

Petrus und **Philippus.** Herr, sollen wir mit dem Schwerte d'reinschlagen? [*Petrus schlägt nach Malchus.*]

Malchus. O weh! Ich bin verwundet, ach mein Ohr ist weg!

Christus. [*Zu den Jüngern.*] Lasset ab! Nicht weiter! [*zu Malchus.*] Sei unbesorgt! Du sollst geheilet sein! [*Rührt des Malchus Ohr an. Dann zu Petrus.*] Und du, stecke dein Schwert in die Scheide, denn alle, die das Schwert ergreifen, werden durch das Schwert umkommen. Soll ich den Kelch, den mir der Vater gereicht hat, nicht trinken? Oder meinst du nicht, dass ich meinen Vater bitten könnte, und dass er mir jetzt mehr als zwölf Legionen Engel zu Hilfe schicken würde? Wie würde denn aber die Schrift erfüllt werden, dass es so geschehen müsse? [*Zu den Pharisäern.*] Ihr seid auf mich wie auf einen Räuber ausgegangen, mit Schwertern und mit Knütteln, mich gefangen zu nehmen, und ich sass doch täglich bei Euch im Tempel und lehrte,—und Ihr strecktet Eure Hände nicht nach mir aus und ergriffet mich nicht. Aber das ist Eure Stunde, diess die Macht der Finsterniss! Seht! Hier bin ich.

Selpha. Umgebt ihn, bindet ihn fest, dass er nicht entkommt!

Nathanael. Dafür seid Ihr dem Hohen Rathe verantwortlich. [*Die Jünger verlieren sich.*]

Then said Jesus, "Yes, most holy Father, I adore thy providence, I will complete the work—to reconcile, to save, to bless!" Then standing up he cried in a more joyful tone, "Strengthened by thy word, O Father! I go joyfully to meet that to which thou hast called me, as the substitute for sinful man."

With lighter step he returned to the place where the three disciples lay slumbering peacefully. He looked upon them and said, "Sleep now and take your rest!" Peter hearing his voice, said, "What is it, Master?" Then all three answered, "Behold we are ready." Then said Jesus, "The hour is come, the Son of man is betrayed into the hands of sinners. Rise, let us be going!"

Even as he spoke these words the tramp of armed men was heard in the immediate neighbourhood of the garden mingled with loud cries of denunciation and vengeance. "What is that uproar," said the Apostles. "Come," said Philip, who hurried forward from behind with the rest of the eight, "Come, let us gather round the Master." At that word the disciples hastened forward. "Behold," said Jesus, "he who betrayeth me is at hand." The disciples looked in the direction which Jesus indicated, and there by the flaring light of the braziers carried by the Temple Watch, they saw Judas advancing at the head of the band. "What does this multitude want?" said Andrew. For an answer all the disciples cried as with one voice, "Alas, we are undone!" "And see," cried John, "Judas is at their head!" Even as he said this Judas with long and stealthy steps sprang forward, looking from side to side as he came, until he stopped immediately behind Jesus; then standing on tiptoe he reached over the shoulder of Jesus and kissed him, saying, "Hail, Master!" Jesus answered, "Wherefore art thou come? Betrayest thou the Son of man with a kiss?"

Then, stepping forward to meet the armed band he faced them fearlessly and said, "Whom seek ye?" A loud and angry shout went up from the soldiers, "Jesus of Nazareth!" Jesus said, "I am he." As he uttered these words the soldiers fell backward to the ground, crying, "Woe unto us! What is this?" The disciples exultingly cried, "One single word from him casts them to the ground." But Jesus said to the soldiers, "Fear not, arise." As they regained their feet the disciples whispered eagerly to Jesus, saying, "Lord, cast them down, so that they shall never rise again." But Jesus, a second time, asked, "Whom seek ye?" Again the crowd replied, "Jesus of Nazareth." Then Jesus said, "I have already told you that I am he; if therefore ye seek me, let these go their way."

Selpha, the leader of the band, cried, "Seize him!" The soldiers approached Jesus; Malchus and Balbus, carrying in their hands a small cord, grasped him by the wrists in order to bind him. Peter and Philip asked Jesus, saying, "Lord, shall we smite with the sword?" Before Jesus replied, Peter's sword flashed from its sheath and descended on the head of Malchus. The helmet turned the descending blade, and instead of splitting his skull it only sliced off his ear. "Alas," cried Malchus, "I am wounded; my ear is off!" Then said Jesus to the disciples, "Suffer ye thus far." And reaching forward to Malchus he said, "Be not troubled, thou shalt be healed." And touching his ear, that moment it was made whole. Malchus felt his ear with astonishment. His comrades satisfied themselves that the ear was as the other and stood motionless; while Jesus turned to Peter and said, "Put up thy sword into its sheath; for all they who take the sword shall perish with the sword. The cup which the Father hath given, shall I not drink it? Thinkest thou that I cannot now pray to my Father, and he would presently give me more than twelve legions of angels? But how then would the scriptures be fulfilled, that thus it must be?"

Then, turning to the Pharisees, he said, "Are ye come out as against a thief with swords and staves to take me? I sat daily with ye in the Temple teaching, and ye took me not. But this is your hour and the power of darkness. Behold, I am here!" "Surround him," cried Selpha; "blind him fast, that he escape not." Then said Nathanael, whose eager zeal to destroy Jesus had led him to join the soldiers, "You are responsible to the Council that he does not escape." At Selpha's command Malchus and Balbus had seized Christ, and were busily engaged in tying his hands together with cords. Slowly, one by one,

Rotte. Aus unsern Händen entkommt er nicht.
Die Händler. Jetzt wollen wir unsere Rache kühlen.
Nathanael. Zuerst gehen wir zum Hohenpriester Annas. Dorthin führet ihn!
Händler. [Zu Judas.] Judas, du bist ein Mann! Da verstehst Wort zu halten.
Judas. Sagte ich Euch nicht, dass er noch heute in Eurer Gewalt sein werde?
Pharisäer. Den ganzen Hohen Rath hast du dir verbindlich gemacht. [Ab.
Die Rotte. [Jesum vor sich hertreibend.] Fort mit dir! In Jerusalem wird man über dich entscheiden!
Selpha. Lasst uns eilen, führt ihn behutsam!
Rotte. Ha, lauf nun, wie du im Judenlande umher gelaufen!
Selpha. Schont seiner nicht! Treibt ihn an.
Rotte. Vorwärts, oder man wird dich mit Kolben treiben!
Händler. Hilft dir Belzebub denn nicht mehr? [Alle ab.

ZWEITE ABTHEILUNG.

Von der Gefangennehmung im Olivengarten bis zur Verurtheilung durch Pilatus.

VIII. VORSTELLUNG.

JESUS VOR ANNAS.

PROLOG.

O der schaurigen Nacht! Sehet den Heiland an!
Von Gericht zu Gericht wird Er umhergeschleppt.
Allenthalben kommt Schmähung
Und Misshandlung entgegen Ihm.

Ein freimüthiges Wort, das Er zu Annas spricht
Lohnt ein Bösewicht Ihm, schlägt Ihn mit roher Faust
Um sich Lob zu verdienen,
In's holdselige Angesicht.

Solcher schmähliche Lohn ward dem Michäas auch,
Da er Wahrheit enthüllt Achab dem Könige;
Von den Lügenpropheten
Gibt ihm einer den Backenstreich.

Wahrheit erntet gar oft Hass und Verfolgung nur;
Doch ihr möget ihr Licht schauen und bauen auch—
Endlich wird es obsiegen
Und durchbrechen die Finsterniss.

Chor.

Begonnen ist der Kampf der Schmerzen,
Begonnen in Gethsemani.
O Sünder! nehmet es zu Herzen!
Vergesset dieser Szene nie!

Für euer Heil ist dies gescheh'n
Was auf dem Oelberg wir gesch'n.
Für euch betrübt bis in den Tod,
Sank Er zur Erde nieder.
Für euch drang Ihn, wie Blut so roth,
Der Schweiss durch alle Glieder.

VORBILD.

Michäas, der Prophet, bekommt einen Backenstreich, weil er dem Könige Achab die Wahrheit sagte.—2. Kön., 22, 24.

[Eine Anspielung auf das erste Verhör Jesu bei dem Hohenpriester Annas, woselbst der Heiland einen Backenstreich erduldete.]

Solo.

Wer frei die Wahrheit spricht,
Den schlagt man in's Gesicht.
König, du wirst unterliegen,
Wenn du Ramoth wirst bekriegen.
Dies ist, was Michäas spricht,
Vom Verderben dich zu retten,

the disciples stole away, leaving Jesus alone in the midst of his captors. In reply to Nathanael the soldiers said, "Out of our hands he will not escape." Then cried with a loud voice the traders, with Dathan at their head, "Now we will slake our vengeance!" "First," said Nathanael, "we must go to the High Priest Annas. Lead him thither!" As the band prepared to obey the word of command a trader came up to Judas and said approvingly, "Thou art a man indeed! Thou knowest how to keep thy word." Judas complacently answered, "Did I not tell you that he would be in your power to-day?" The Pharisees said, "Thou hast placed the whole Council under an obligation to thee." The procession then went off, leading Jesus to the palace of Annas. The Temple Watch formed behind Jesus, who, with his hands bound before him was thrown violently forward by Malchus and Balbus, who held the other ends of the cords which bound him, and marched behind him. They cried, "On with thee! In Jerusalem they will settle your affair!" Selpha, who marched at the head of his band, cried, "Let us hasten; lead him away carefully." And all the band shouted, "Ha! run now as thou hast hitherto run to and fro about the land of Judea." "Spare him not!" said Selpha; "drive him on!" "Forward!" shouted the soldiers, shouting together; "otherwise thou shalt be driven on with staves." And as they marched away, driving Jesus before them, the traders derided him, saying, "Doth Beelzebub then aid thee no longer?"

SECOND DIVISION.

CHAPTER VIII.

PROLOGUE.—ACT VIII.

Oh, the terrible night! Look at the Saviour now!
How he is haled about from judgment-seat to judgment-seat!
They meet him with foul abuse
And outrage everywhere.

For one fearless word which he speaks unto Annas,
One, as his reward, strikes him with ruthless hand,
Praise to win from the tyrants,
With ruthless hand on the face.

Such base recompense was given to Micaiah;
When to Ahab the king he prophesied truly,
One of the lying prophets
Smote him then on the face.

Truth wins often hatred and persecution,
Yet see her light; and, banish it as often as ye will,
At the last it will conquer,
And in glory break through the dark.

Now has begun the anguished fight
Begun in dark Gethsemane.
O sinners, never let this night
For evermore forgotten be!

For your salvation this has been,
Which on the mountain we have seen,—
When, sorrowing unto death, He sank
To earth, it was for you;
'Twas for your sake the damp turf drank
Those drops of crimson dew.

[The twelfth tableau shows how Micaiah, the prophet of the Lord, was smitten by Zedekiah, the priest of Baal, for daring to predict, before Ahab and Jehosaphat, the approaching death of the King of Israel at the battle of Ramoth Gilead.]

He who freely dares to speak
Truth, is smitten on the cheek.
"King, if thou wilt still assail
Ramoth, thou shalt ne'er prevail,"
Spake Micaiah on this wise.
"Baal's seers are thy undoing—

Glaube, König, Baals Propheten—
    Dieser Schmeichler Lügen nicht!
Doch des Gottgesandten Stimme
    Schmeichelt einem Achab nicht.
Und ein Lügner schlägt im Grimme
    Ihn dafür in's Angesicht.

Chor.

Lügner, Heuchler, Schmeichler pflücken
    Rosen, Lorbeer ohne Müh'.
Nur die Wahrheit muss sich bucken;
    Denn die Wahrheit schmeichelt nie.

HANDLUNG.

Jesus wird dem Annas vorgestellt und in's Angesicht geschlagen.

ERSTE SZENE.

ANNAS. ESDRAS. SIDRACH. MISAEL.

Annas. Ich kann in dieser Nacht nicht Ruhe finden, bis dass ich weiss, dass dieser Ruhestörer in unsern Handen ist. O war' er doch bereits in Fesseln!—Sehnsuchtsvoll erwarte ich meine Diener mit der frohen Nachricht.

Esdras. Sie können nicht mehr lange weilen; denn geraume Zeit ist's, seit sie abgegangen.

Annas. Vergebens ist mein kummervoller Blick hinausgerichtet nach der Kidronsstrasse. Nichts lasst sich seh'n, nichts hören.—Gich', mein Esdras, geh' dem Kidronsthore zu, und sieh' ob sie nicht nahen.

Esdras. Eilends will ich dahin. [*Ab.*

Annas. Das wäre doch ein Donnerschlag für das Synedrium, wenn diesmal nicht das Werk—

Sidrach. O lass die Sorgen, Hohepriester!

Misael. Es ist ja am Gelingen nicht zu zweifeln.

Annas. Sie haben etwa ihren Weg geändert, und kehren durch die Pforte Siloah zurück? Ich muss doch spähen lassen, auch auf dieser Seite.

Sidrach. Wenn der Hohepriester es wünscht, will ich zur Pforte Siloah—

Annas. Ja, thue es! Doch sieh' zuerst, ob Niemand durch die Synedriumgasse komme!

Sidrach. Herr! Ich säume nicht. [*Ab.*

Annas. Es geht die Nacht vorüber, und immer noch die alte Ungewissheit! Jede Minute dieses bangen Harrens ist eine Stunde mir.—Ich meine—horch!—Es kommt Jemand hergelaufen! Ja! Ja! Man kommt!—Es wird wohl gute Botschaft sein.

Sidrach. [*Hereineilend.*] Herr! Esdras kommt in Eile. Schnellen Fusses sah ich die Gasse ihn heran gesprungen.

Annas. Gewiss ist's frohe Nachricht, die er bringt, da er sich so beeilt. O kein Gefühl ist, wahrlich, mehr in mir, als für den Tod der Missethäter!

Esdras. [*Eilends kommend.*] Heil dem Hohenpriester! Ich sah die abgesandten Vater selbst mit Judas. Alles ist nach Wunsch; in Banden der Galilaer. Ich hört' es aus ihrem Munde und eilte fort, die freudenvolle Kunde geschwind zu überbringen.

Annas. Himmlische Botschaft! Glücksel'ge Stunde! Ein Stein ist von meinem Herzen gelost und ich fühle mich wie neugeboren. Jetzt erst nenne ich mich mit Freude den Hohenpriester des auserwählten Volkes!

ZWEITE SZENE.

Die vier Abgeordneten des Hohen Rathes erscheinen mit JUDAS auf dem Balkon.

Die vier Pharisäer. Es lebe unser Hohepriester!

Nathanael. Der Wunsch des Hohen Rathes ist erfüllt!

Annas. O, ich muss Euch umarmen vor Freude! Judas, dein Name wird in unsern Jahrbüchern eine ehrenvolle Stellung einnehmen. Noch vor dem Feste soll der Galiläer sterben!

Judas. [*Erschreckt.*] Sterben!

Annas. Sein Tod ist beschlossen.

Judas. Für sein Leben und Blut will ich nicht verantwortlich sein.

Annas. Das ist nicht nöthig, er ist in unserer Gewalt.

Judas. Dazu habe ich ihn Euch nicht überliefert.

Wilt thou save thyself from ruin?—
    Hearken not these flatterers' lies."—
But the voice of God's own prophet
    Flatters not proud Ahab's race,
And a lying courtier rising,
    Strikes him, wrathful, in the face.

Roses, laurels, earth's fair glories,
    Are for those who feign and lie;
Truth must go uncrowned in this world,
    She can use no flattery.

JESUS BEFORE ANNAS

It was dark night, and there was silence in the street before the house of Annas, the High Priest, when his door opened and **Annas**, attended by **Esdras**, **Sidrach**, and **Misael**, came upon the balcony. "I can find no rest this night," said **Annas**, looking impatiently up and down the street, "until I know that this disturber of the peace is in our hands. Oh! if he were only safe and in fetters. Full of longing and anxiety I await the arrival of my servants with the joyful news." Then said **Esdras**, "They cannot be much longer, for it is a good while since they went away." "In vain has my troubled gaze looked up and down the street of Kedron. But nothing can I see and nothing hear. Go! my Esdras, go to the Kedron Gate and see." "I will hasten out," said **Esdras**, hurrying away as quickly as his short squat figure would allow. **Annas** walking about impatiently, tormented by misgivings as to the success of the enterprise, began: "It would be a blow to the Sanhedrim, if this time the work should not succeed." **Sidrach** said, "Do not give way to anxiety, High Priest," and **Misael** added, "There is no doubt of our success." **Annas**, heeding not the consolation of his priests, said, "They may have altered their way and returned through the Siloa Gate. I must send to see also on that side." **Sidrach** said, "If the High Priest wishes it, I will go to the Siloa Gate." "Yes, do," said **Annas**, "but first see whether anyone comes through the street of the Sanhedrim." "I will not loiter, my lord," said **Sidrach**, as he disappeared into the darkness. **Annas** resumed his troubled thoughts. "The night is going by, and still the old uncertainty. Every minute of this weary waiting time is as an hour to me. Hark! I think someone comes running! Yes, he comes. May he be a messenger of good." **Sidrach**, bursting into the presence of the High Priest, exclaimed, "My lord, Esdras comes in haste, I saw him just now running down the street with rapid foot." Then said **Annas**, "Surely it is joyful news that he brings, since he hastens so. Truly, I long for nothing now, but the death of this malefactor." Then came **Esdras**, breathless with haste, crying, "Hail to the High Priest. I saw the fathers who were sent with Judas. All has gone according to your wish. The Galilean is in bonds. I heard it from their mouth and hurried as fast as I could to bring the joyful news in haste to thee." **Annas** cried, "Oh, heavenly message! auspicious hour! A stone is lifted from my heart, I feel as if I were born again. Now, for the first time, can I rejoice to call myself High Priest of the chosen people."

There came in to **Annas**, Judas, and the four **Pharisees** who had been sent by the Council to accompany him, crying, "Long live our High Priest!" **Nathanael** exclaimed, "The wish of the Council is accomplished!" **Annas** said. "Oh, I must embrace you for joy. Judas, thy name will take an honourable place in our records of the year. Even before the Feast shall the Galilean die." **Judas**—whom the Pharisees had brought in with them—startled by that word, sprang back, repeating incredulously, "Die!" "His death is decreed," said **Annas**. "For his life and blood," cried **Judas**, "I will not be responsible." "That is unnecessary," said Annas, coolly, "he is in our power." "But," persisted Judas, passionately, "I have not delivered him over to you for that." "Thou hast delivered him over," said the **Pharisees**, "and the rest is our

Pharisäer. Du hast ihn überliefert, das Weitere ist unsere Sache.
Judas. Weh' mir! Was habe ich gethan! Sterben soll er? Nein! Das wollte ich nicht. Das will ich nicht!
[*Eilt hinweg.*
Die Pharisäer. [*Ihm nachspottend.*] Du magst wollen oder nicht, er muss doch sterben.

DRITTE SZENE.

Vorige ausser JUDAS. *Gleich darauf erscheinen* CHRISTUS, *der Rottenführer* SELPHA *und die Tempeldiener* MALCHUS *und* BALBUS *auf dem Balkon. Die Rotte bleibt unten.*

Priester. Hoherpriester, der Gefangene ist vor der Schwelle.
Annas. Man bringe ihn vor mich. [SELPHA *erscheint mit* CHRISTUS.] Habt Ihr ihn allein gefänglich eingebracht?
Balbus. Seine Anhänger zerstreuten sich wie scheue Schafe!
Selpha. Wir fanden es nicht der Mühe werth, sie einzufangen. Jedoch wäre Malchus beinahe um's Leben gekommen.
Annas. Was ist geschehen?
Selpha. Einer seiner Anhänger hieb mit gezücktem Schwerte nach ihm, er traf sein Ohr und weg war es.
Annas. Wie? es lässt sich aber nichts bemerken?
Balbus. [*Halblaut.*] Der Wundermann hat es ihm wieder angekünstelt.
Annas. Was sagst du dazu, Malchus?
Malchus. [*Ernst.*] Ich kann es nicht erklären—es ist Wunderbares an mir geschehn.
Annas. Hat der Betrüger dich etwa auch bezaubert? [*Zu* JESUS.] Sage, durch welche Macht hast du dies gethan?
[CHRISTUS *schweigt.*
Selpha. Rede, wenn dich deine Obrigkeit fragt!
Annas. So rede! Gieb Rechenschaft über deine Jünger, deine Lehre, die du im ganzen Judenlande verbreitet und mit der du das Volk verführt hast!
Christus. Ich habe offentlich vor der Welt geredet; ich habe immer in den Synagogen und im Tempel gelehrt und ich habe nichts im Verborgenen geredet. Was fragst du mich? Frage Diejenigen, welche gehört haben, was ich zu ihnen redete! Sieh, diese wissen, was ich gesagt habe.
Balbus. [*Schlägt* JESUM.] Antwortest du so dem Hohenpriester?
Christus. Habe ich unrecht geredet, so beweise es, dass es unrecht sei! Habe ich aber recht geredet, warum schlägst du mich?
Annas. Du willst auch jetzt noch trotzen, da dein Leben und Tod in unserer Gewalt ist? Ich bin dieses Bösewichtes müde.
Balbus. [*Zu* CHRISTUS *der abgeführt wird.*] Warte nur, dein Trotz wird weichen!
Annas. Ich will mich noch eine Weile der Ruhe hingeben, oder vielmehr dem stillen Nachsinnen, wie das glücklich Begonnene zu Ende gebracht werden möge! Es wird schwerlich in früher Morgenstunde der Ruf in's Synedrium an mich kommen. [*Alle ab.*

VIERTE SZENE.

CHRISTUS *inmitten der* Rotte.

Rotte. [*Zu* SELPHA, *der* JESUM *bringt.*] Ha, ist ein Handel schon aus?
Selpha. Seine Vertheidigung ist schlecht ausgefallen.
Balbus. Sie hat ihm aber doch einen tüchtigen Backenstreich eingetragen.
Selpha. Nehmt ihn nun und fort mit ihm zu des Kaiphas Palast!
Rotte. Fort mit ihm! Hebe deine Füsse auf!
Balbus. Freue dich, bei Kaiphas wirst du noch einen besseren Empfang bekommen.
Rotte. Dort werden dir schon die Raben um die Ohren singen!

FUENFTE SZENE.

PETRUS *und* JOHANNES *vor dem Hause des* ANNAS. *Ein Priester.*

Petrus. Wie wird es hier dem besten Meister ergeh'n! O Johannes, wie ist mir so bange um ihn!

business." Repulsed on every side, Judas, striking his forehead with his hand, cried, "Woe is me! what have I done? Shall he die? No! that I did not wish. That I will not have." As he hurried into the street the Pharisees laughed at him and said, "Whether thou wilt have it or not, die he must."

Then said the priests to Annas, "High Priest, the prisoner is at the threshold." Annas said, "Let him be brought before me." Then was Jesus brought before Annas on the balcony in custody of Selpha, the leader of the Temple Watch, and the two servants of the Temple, Malchus and Balbus, holding the cords by which Jesus was bound. The rest of the watch remained in the street below. When Annas saw Jesus he said, "Have you brought him alone as a prisoner?" Balbus answered, "His disciples fled like timid sheep." Selpha said, "We did not find it worth the trouble to arrest them. Nevertheless, Malchus almost lost his life." "How did that happen?" asked Annas. "One of his followers," said Selpha, "with a drawn sword smote him and cut off his ear." "How could that be?" said Annas, looking first at one side of Malchus's head and then at the other. "It has left no mark: there is nothing to be seen." "Oh," said Balbus, mocking, "the magician has conjured it back again." "What sayest thou to that?" asked Annas. Malchus replied seriously, "I cannot explain it. It is a miracle that has happened to me." Annas frowned, "Has the deceiver also bewitched thee?" he asked, and then turning to Jesus said to him, "Say, by what power hast thou done this?" Jesus did not answer. "Speak," said Selpha, "when thy High Priest asks thee." "Speak," said Annas. "Give an account of thy disciples and thy teaching, which thou hast spread abroad over the whole land of Judea and with which thou hast corrupted the people."

Then Jesus answered and said unto him, "I spake openly to the world. I ever taught in the Synagogue and the Temple, and in secret I taught nothing. Why askest thou me? ask them that heard me what I have spoken. Behold, they know what I have said." Balbus, who was standing on the left hand of Jesus, holding one end of the cord by which his hands were bound, struck him over the face a resounding blow, saying, "Answerest thou the High Priest so?" Jesus answered, "If I have spoken evil, bear witness of the evil, but if I have spoken well, why smitest thou me?" Then Annas exclaimed, "Wilt thou even now defy us, when thy life and death is in our power? I am weary of this villain!" and gave the signal for Jesus to be removed.

"Oh," said Balbus, as he roughly thrust him forward, "wait a little. Thy obstinacy will vanish." As Jesus was being led down the steps, Annas said, "I will go in now for a little while to rest, or rather for quiet meditation as to how the work so happily begun may be brought to an end. In any case the summons to the Sanhedrin will reach me at an early hour in the morning." Annas then entered into his own house, leaving Jesus in the street below in the midst of the soldiers. As Selpha appeared bringing Jesus into the street the Watch cried out loudly, "Ha! is his business already over?" Selpha said, "His defence has turned out badly, it has only gained him a smart slap over the face." Selpha said, "Take him now and away with him to the Palace of Caiaphas." "Off with him," cried the soldiers, tumultuously. "Lift up thy feet!" "Cheer up," said Balbus, mocking. "Thou wilt have a still better reception from Caiaphas," and the soldiers shouted as they marched, "There will the ravens croak about thine ears!"

Hardly had the noisy soldiery passed with their prisoner out of the street than Peter and John appeared before the house of Annas. Then said Peter, "How will it fare here with our good Master? O John, how anxious I am about

Johannes. Gewiss wird er hier Spott und Misshandlungen zu erdulden haben! Ich habe grosse Angst, mich dem Hause zu nahern.
Petrus. Es ist aber Alles so stille umher.
Johannes. Man hört keinen Laut im Palaste. Sollten sie ihn wieder weggeführt haben?
Priester. [*Heraustretend.*] Was wollt Ihr hier beim Palaste nächtlicher Weile?
Johannes. Vergieb, wir sahen eine Menge Leute von ferne durch das Kidronthor hieherzgehn und gingen ihnen nach, um zu sehen, was sich ereignet hat.
Priester. Man hat einen Gefangenen eingebracht, er ist aber bereits zu Kaiphas geschickt worden.
Johannes. Zu Kaiphas? So wollen wir gleich wieder gehen.
Priester. Das wird Euer Glück sein, sonst würde ich Euch als nächtliche Ruhestörer aufheben lassen.
Petrus. Wir wollen keine Unruhe erregen und still abgehen.
[*Ab.*
Priester. [*Den Beiden nach.*] Sind es etwa gar Anhänger des Galiläers? Wenn ich wüsste! Doch, sie entgehen unsern Leuten nicht, wenn sie zu des Kaiphas Palast gehen. Der ganze Anhang muss vertilgt werden, sonst wird das Volk nicht mehr zum Gehorsam gebracht. [*Ab.*

IX. VORSTELLUNG.
JESUS VOR KAIPHAS.
PROLOG.

Vor erbosten Feinden, nun seinen Richtern,
Steht der Herr in Schweigen gehullt; geduldig
Hört Er all die Klage und Lüge, selbst das
  Urtheil des Todes.

Wie einst Naboth schuldlos verfolgt, verurtheilt
Ward, durch falsches Zeugniss als Gotteslästerer,
So auch Er, dess einzige Schuld ist: Wahrheit,
  Liebe und Wohlthun.

Bald auch werdet ihr von entmenschten Knechten
Ihn umrungen seh'n, des Gespöttes Rohheit
Preisgegeben, höhnisch misshandelt unter
  Wildem Gelächter.

Im geduld'gen Job, dem in tiefster Trübsal
Selbst von seinen Freunden mit Spott Belad'nen,
Seht ihr vorgebildet des lieben Heilands
  Himmlische Sanftmuth.

Choragus.—*Recit.*

Wie blutet mir das Herz!
Der Heiligste steht vor Gericht!
Er muss der Sünder Bosheit tragen.
Verrathen und beschimpft, gebunden und geschlagen.
Wem zittert nicht im Auge eine Thräne?
Von Annas weg zu Kaiphas fortgerissen,
Was wird er da, ach! leiden müssen!
Seht hier im Bilde diese neue Leidensscene!

VORBILDER.

1. Der unschuldige Naboth wird durch falsche Zeugen zum Tode verurtheilt.—3. Kön. 21, 8.

[Wie Naboth, so wird auch der unschuldige Heiland vor dem Hohenpriester Kaiphas durch falsche Zeugschaft zu Tode verurtheilt. Wie dem geduldigen Job, so wird auch dem geduldigen Heiland aller erdenkliche Spott angethan.]

Es sterbe Naboth! — er erfrechte sich,
Zu lästern Gott, zu schmäh'n, o König, dich.
  Er sei vertilgt aus Israel!
So geifern feile Lügnerzungen,
Von jener bösen Jezabel
Zu einem falschen Eid gedungen.

Chor.

Ach! mit dem Tode rächet man,
  Was Naboth nie verbrochen.
Der Weinberg wird dem König dann
  Von Schurken zugesprochen.

CHAPTER IX.
PROLOGUE.—ACT IX.

'Fore embittered foes, who are now his judges,
Stands the Lord, in majestic silence shrouded,
Patiently listens to lying accusations—
  E'en the death-sentence.

And as Naboth of old, condemned, though guiltless,
By false witnesses charged with blasphemy, perished:
So, too, he, whose only guilt was truth-speaking,
  Love, and well-doing.

Soon, too soon, ye will see him allsurrounded
By scarce human soldiers, a sport for their cruelty,—
Mocked, and shamefully, scornfully outraged with peals of
  Savagest laughter.

In the patience of Job, who, in deepest sorrow,
Even by his own friends with scorn was laden,
Ye can see foreshadowed the dear Redeemer's
  Heavenly patience.

How bleeds my heart!
The Holiest stands before the judgment-seat.
The malice of sinners He must bear,
Betrayed and outraged, bound and beaten there.
Where is the eye that will not shed a tear?
From Annas dragged to Caiaphas away—
What must he bear before the end of day!
See this new scene of anguish in a picture here!

[The thirteenth and fourteenth tableaux represent the stoning of Naboth, a venerable old man, who is being crushed beneath the missiles of Jezebel's sons of Belial, and the sufferings of Job, who is shown on his dunghill, scoffed at, plagued, and derided by his friends, his servants, and even by his wife.]

Let Naboth die! — he feared not impiously
God to blaspheme, speak ill, O King, of thee.
  Yes, let him out of Israel
Perish—so lying tongues proclaim,
  By evil-minded Jezebel
Hired for a price, to compass deeds of shame.

Alas! by death shall be avenged
  Wrong Naboth never wrought;
The vineyard then by wicked men
  Into Ahab's hands is brought.

Solo.
Auch wider Jesus vor Gericht
Steht Hass und Trug zusammen,
Bis dass die Bosheit Urtheil spricht,
Die Unschuld zu verdammen.

Chor.
Ihr möcht'gen Götter dieser Welt,
Zum Wohl der Menschheit aufgestellt!
Vergesst bei Uebung eurer Pflicht
Des unsichtbaren Richters nicht!
Bei Ihm sind alle Menschen gleich,
Sie mögen dürftig oder reich,
Geadelt oder Bettler sein,
Gerechtigkeit gilt Ihm allein.

2. Der leidende Job erdultet von seinem Weibe und seinem Befreundeten viele Beschimpfungen.—Job, 2, 9.

HANDLUNG.

CHRISTUS *wird zu* KAIPHAS *geführt, von demselben verhört und des Todes schuldig erklärt, von* PETRUS *verläugnet, von den Dienern verspottet und misshandelt.*

ERSTE SZENE.
Die Rotte, CHRISTUM *durch die Gasse herverführend.*

Rotte. [*Lärmend.*] Da wirst zum Schauspiel werden, zum Schauspiel der ganzen Nation!
Balbus. Beeile dich! Deine Anhänger sind schon bereit! Sie wollen dich zum Könige Israels ausrufen.
Rotte. Nicht wahr, davon hast du schon oft geträumt?
Selpha. Diesen Traum wird ihm jetzt Kaiphas der Hohepriester auslegen.
Balbus. Hörst du! Kaiphas wird dir deine Erhöhung verkünden.
Rotte. [*Mit Gelächter.*] Ja, deine Erhöhung zwischen Himmel und Erde!
Selpha. Aufgemerkt, ihr Leute! Da, durch die Burg des Pilatus, führt uns der nächste Weg zum Schlosse des Kaiphas. Dort stellt euch bis auf weiteres im Vorhofe auf.
Rotte. Dein Befehl soll vollzogen werden. [*Ab.*

ZWEITE SZENE.

KAIPHAS *in seinem Schlafgemach. Die Priester und Pharisäer.*

Kaiphas. Der glückliche Anfang verspricht uns frohes Gelingen unserer Wünsche. Dank Euch, edle Glieder des Synedriums, für Eure eifrige und kluge Mitwirkung!
Priester. Des Dankes höchster Preis gebührt unserem Hohenpriester.
Kaiphas. Nun lasst uns unsere Wege ohne Verzug weiter verfolgen! Alles ist vorbereitet. Der Rath wird gleich versammelt sein, die nöthigen Zeugen sind mitgebracht. . . . . Ich werde nun unverweilt das Verhör mit dem Gefangenen vornehmen, dann soll das Urtheil gesprochen und für dessen Vollziehung gesorgt werden. Vertraut mir, meine Freunde! Ich habe mir einen Plan entworfen und hoffe ihn auszuführen. . . . .
Alle. Der Gott unserer Väter segne alle Schritte unseres Hohenpriesters!

DRITTE SZENE.

Die Vorigen. Die Rotte führt CHRISTUM *ein. Die falschen Zeugen.*

Selpha, der Rottenführer. Erhabener Hoherpriester, hier ist der Gefangene.
Kaiphas. Führt ihn näher, damit ich ihm in's Angesicht sehen kann.
Selpha. Tritt vor, und ehre hier das Haus des Hohen Rathes!
Kaiphas. Du bist also Derjenige, der sich einfallen liess, unserer Synagoge und dem Gesetz Mosis den Untergang bereiten zu wollen? Du bist angeklagt, dass du das Volk zum Ungehorsam aufgereizt, dass du die heilige Erblehre der Väter verachtet, dass du das göttliche Gebot der Sabbathheiligung oftmals verletzt, dass du sogar viele gotteslästerliche Reden und Handlungen dir erlaubt hast. Hier stehen ehrenwerthe Männer, welche bereit sind, die Wahrheit dieser Anklagen

'Gainst Christ, before the judgment-seat,
Deceit and hate are banded,
Till malice on the innocent
Hath sentence sharp demanded.

Ye rulers of this world, in might
Appointed for to do men right,
Forget not, as your office ye
Fulfil, the Judge ye cannot see.
All men are equal him before,
Whether that they be rich or poor,—
Be noble or of low degree,—
For justice only careth he.

JESUS BEFORE CAIAPHAS.

WHEN Jesus was taken from the house of Annas he was led through the streets, the band accompanying him, shouting as they went. On their way to the Sanhedrim they led Jesus down the street which passed Pilate's house, and as they went they cried to him with riotous laughter, "Thou shalt become a laughing-stock for the whole nation!" Balbus said unto him scoffingly, "Make haste! thy disciples are quite ready to proclaim thee King of Israel!" And the soldiers laughed as they said, "Thou hast often dreamed of this, is it not so?" Then said Selpha, "Caiaphas will soon explain this dream to him." And Balbus, seeing that Jesus opened not his mouth and was silent, shouted in his ear, "Dost thou hear? Caiaphas will announce to thee thy exaltation to a high position!" A great burst of hoarse laughter from the Watch followed as they shouted, "An exalted position between heaven and earth!" "Look out, you fellows!" cried Selpha; "there through the hall of Pilate lies our nearest way to the palace of Caiaphas. There station yourselves in the courtyard until further orders." The soldiers answered, "Thy command shall be fully obeyed."

Meantime, in his bedchamber, Caiaphas, wearing a dressing-gown, surrounded by priests and Pharisees, exulted over the news which had been brought him of the arrest of Jesus. "This happy capture," said he, "promises us a fortunate realisation of our wishes. I thank you, noble members of the Sanhedrim, for zealous and prudent co-operation." But the priests with one voice cried, "The greatest share of praise belongs to our High Priest!" "Now," said Caiaphas, "let us pursue our path without delay. Everything is ready. The Council will immediately be assembled. The necessary witnesses have already been brought along. I shall now, without losing a moment, at once begin the trial of the prisoner. Then judgment shall be pronounced, and provision made that it shall be executed. Trust ye, my friends, I have a plan of my own which I hope to carry out." Then cried they all, "The God of our Fathers bless all the measures of our High Priest!"

Then Selpha, the leader of the band, brought Jesus into the bedchamber of Caiaphas, the High Priest, Balbus and Malchus holding the cords by which his hands were bound. "Illustrious High Priest, here is the prisoner," said Selpha. "Bring him nearer," said Caiaphas, "so that I may look him in the face." "Step forward," said Selpha, "and show respect here to the house of the Sanhedrim." Then Caiaphas, having looked into the face of Jesus, said to him, disdainfully, "Thou art he, then, who dreamed of bringing about the destruction of our synagogue and the law of Moses?" Then, assuming a more judicial tone, he said, "Thou art accused that thou hast stirred up the people to disobedience, that thou despisest the holy traditions of the Fathers, that thou hast transgressed the divine command for the keeping of the Sabbath day, and that thou hast been guilty of many blasphemous speeches and acts. Here," Caiaphas continued, pointing to five Jews who had entered the chamber at the same time as Selpha brought in Jesus, and had taken their stand on the left of the High Priest confronting the accused, "Here stand trustworthy men who are

mit ihrem Zeugnisse zu bekräftigen. Höre sie, und dann magst du dich verantworten, wenn du kannst!

1. Zeuge. Ich kann vor Gott bezeugen, dass dieser Mensch das Volk aufgereizt hat, indem er öffentlich die Rathsälteren und Schriftlehrer Heuchler, reissende Wölfe in Schafskleidern, blinde Führer der Blinden geschölten, und ausgesprochen hat, dass man ihnen nicht folgen soll.

2. Zeuge. Auch ich bezeuge dieses und kann noch hinzufügen, dass er dem Volke verboten hat, dem Kaiser den Tribut zu bezahlen.

1. Zeuge. Ja, wenigstens hat er zweideutige Reden darüber fallen lassen.

Kaiphas. Was sagst du dazu? Du schweigest? . . .

3. Zeuge. Ich habe oft gesehen, wie er mit seinen Jüngern, dem Gesetz zum Trotz, mit ungewaschenen Händen zu Tische gegangen, wie er mit Zöllnern und Sündern freundlichen Umgang pflog und in ihre Häuser ging, mit ihnen zu essen. [Die anderen Zeugen: Das haben auch wir öfter gesehen.] Ich habe von glaubwürdigen Leuten gehört, dass er sogar mit Samaritern gezecht, ja selbst tag lang bei ihnen gewohnt hat.

1. Zeuge. Ich war auch Augenzeuge, wie er am Sabbath gethan, was durch Gottes Gesetz verboten ist, indem er ohne Schen Kranke heilte. Er hat andere zum Brechen des Sabbathes verleitet. So hat er einem Menschen geboten, sein Bett nach Hause zu tragen.

Kaiphas. Was hast du gegen diese Aussagen einzuwenden? Weisst du nichts darauf zu antworten?

3. Zeuge. Du hast -ich war dabei -dir angemasst, Sünden zu vergeben, was doch nur Gott zukommt. Du hast also Gott gelästert!

1. Zeuge. Du hast Gott deinen Vater genannt, und dich erfrecht, auszusprechen, dass du Eins mit dem Vater seist. Du hast dich also Gott gleich gemacht.

2. Zeuge. Du hast dich über unsern Vater Abraham erhoben; du sagtest, du seist schon gewesen, ehe Abraham war.

4. Zeuge. Du hast gesagt, ich kann den Tempel Gottes niederreissen und in drei Tagen wieder aufbauen.

5. Zeuge. Ich habe dich sagen hören: Ich will diesen von Menschenhänden gebauten Tempel niederreissen und in drei Tagen einen andern herstellen, der nicht von Menschenhänden gebaut ist.

Kaiphas. Du hast dich also einer übermenschlichen, göttlichen Gewalt gerühmt! Das sind schwere Beschuldigungen und sie sind gesetzlich bezeugt. Widersprich, wenn du kannst! Du glaubst durch Schweigen dich retten zu können, du getraust dich nicht, vor den Vatern des Volkes zu bekennen, was du vor dem Volke gelehrt hast. Oder getraust du dich? So höre: Ich, der Hohepriester, beschwöre dich bei dem lebendigen Gott! Sage, bist du der Messias, der Sohn Gottes, des Hochgelobten?

Christus. Du sagst es und ich bin es. Ich sage Euch aber: Von nun an werdet Ihr den Menschensohn zur Rechten der Kraft Gottes sitzen und auf den Wolken des Himmels kommen sehen!

Kaiphas. Er hat Gott gelästert! Was brauchen wir noch Zeugen? Ihr habt selbst die Lästerung mitangehört! Was dünkt Euch?

Alle. Er hat den Tod verdient!

Kaiphas. Er ist also einstimmig des Todes schuldig erklärt. Doch nicht ich, nicht der Hohe Rath, das göttliche Gesetz selbst spricht das Todesurtheil über ihn. Ihr Lehrer des Gesetzes! Ich fordere Euch auf, zu antworten. Was sagt das heilige Gesetz von dem, welcher der von Gott vorgeschriebenen Obrigkeit ungehorsam ist?

prepared to prove the truth of these accusations by their testimony. Hear them, and then thou mayest answer if thou canst."

Then stood forth the **first witness** and spoke, saying, "I can testify before God that this man has stirred up the people by openly denouncing the members of the Council and the Scribes as hypocrites, raging wolves in sheeps' clothing, blind leaders of the blind, and has declared that no one should follow them." At this the members of the Sanhedrim smiled approvingly one to another. The **second witness** said, "I can also testify this, and can still further declare that he has forbidden the people to pay tribute to Cæsar." "Yes," interrupted the **first witness**, "at any rate he has dropped words of double meaning about that."

Then **Caiaphas** turned to Jesus and said, "What sayest thou unto this?" He paused for a reply, but Jesus opened not his mouth. Then said **Caiaphas**, "Art thou silent?" But Jesus never answered a word.

The **third witness** took up his testimony. "I have often seen how he, with his disciples, in defiance of the law, has eaten with unwashed hands; how he has been accustomed to hold friendly intercourse with publicans and sinners and go into their homes to eat with them."

"That we have also seen," cried the **other witnesses** together. "I have heard very credible people say that he has even spoken with Samaritans, and, indeed, has lived with them for days together."

Then the **first witness** began to speak again. "I was a witness how he has done on the Sabbath what is forbidden by God's law, in that he healed a sick man on that day. He has seduced others to break the Sabbath: he ordered a man to take up his bed and carry it to his house." Again Caiaphas turned to Jesus and said, "What hast thou to say against this evidence?" And, after a pause, seeing that Jesus still spoke not, he said, "Hast thou nothing to say in reply?" But Jesus spoke not.

Then said the **third witness**, addressing himself to Jesus, "Thou hast, for I was present, taken upon thyself to forgive sins, which belongs to God alone. Thou hast therefore blasphemed God."

Then again spoke the **first witness**, "Thou hast called God thy Father, and has dared to declare that thou art one with the Father. Thou hast therefore made thyself equal to God." The **second witness** added, "Thou hast exalted thyself above our Father Abraham. Thou didst say, 'Before Abraham was, I am.'" Then spoke the **fourth witness**, who said, "Thou hast said, 'I can destroy the Temple of God, and in three days build it up again.'" The **fifth witness**, who had not hitherto spoken, stood forward and said, "I have heard thee say, 'I shall destroy this Temple which is made with hands, and in three days I will build another, made without hands.'" This concluded the testimony of the witnesses.

Then **Caiaphas**, turning to Jesus, spoke to him with indignation: "So thou hast claimed to possess a superhuman, divine authority? These are serious accusations and they are legally proved; answer if thou canst." Jesus remaining silent, Caiaphas resumed, "Thou thinkest that by silence thou canst save thyself. Thou darest not to admit before the fathers of the people what thou hast taught before the people. Or dost thou dare?" Then rising to his utmost height and stretching his hand on high, **Caiaphas** continued, "Hear thee! I, the High Priest, adjure thee by the living God, art thou the Messiah, the son of the Most High?" and as he uttered the sacred name Caiaphas crossed his arms and dropped his head on his breast.

For a moment there was silence, then **Jesus** answered and said, "Thou hast said it, and so I am! Nevertheless I say unto you, hereafter ye shall see the Son of Man sitting on the right hand of God in power and coming in the clouds of heaven."

As Jesus spoke these words, the members of the Council started in horror, and **Caiaphas**, rending his robe, exclaimed with a loud voice, "He has blasphemed God! What need have we of any further witnesses? you yourselves have heard the blasphemy. What think ye?" And all the **members of the Council** cried together, "He is guilty of death!"

Then said **Caiaphas**, "He is thus unanimously declared guilty of death. But not I, not the Council, but the law of God pronounces the death sentence upon him. You teachers of the law, I call upon you to answer: what does the holy law

JESUS BEFORE CAIAPHAS.—ACT IX, SC. 2.

JESUS BEFORE CAIAPHAS.

1. Priester. [*Liest.*] Wer hoffärtig ist und dem Gebote des Priesters nicht gehorchen will, noch auch dem Urtheile des Richters, der Mensch soll sterben und du sollst das Böse ausrotten aus Israel.
Kaiphas. Was verordnet das Gesetz über den, der den Sabbath entheiligt?
2. Priester. [*Liest.*] Haltet meinen Sabbath, denn er ist Euch heilig! Wer ihn entheiligt, der soll des Todes sein! Wer an demselben ein Werk thut, dessen Seele soll ausgetilgt werden aus dem Volke.
Kaiphas. Wie straft das Gesetz den Gotteslästerer?
Nathanael. [*Liest.*] Sage den Kindern Israels, ein Mensch, der seinem Gotte flucht, soll seine Missethat tragen und wer den Namen des Herrn lästert, soll des Todes sterben! Steinigen soll ihn die ganze Gemeinde, er sei Eingeborner oder Fremdling.
Kaiphas. Somit ist das Urtheil über diesen Jesus von Nazareth gesprochen, dem Gesetze gemäss gesprochen, und soll so bald als möglich vollzogen werden. Indessen will ich den Verurtheilten verwahren lassen. Fuhrt ihn fort! Bewacht ihn und beim Morgengrauen bringt ihn in's hohe Synedrium!
Selpha. So komm', Messias! Wir wollen dir deinen Palast anweisen.
Balbus. Dort wirst du die gebührenden Huldigungen empfangen. [*Führen ihn ab.*

VIERTE SZENE.

Kaiphas. Wir sind unserem Ziele nahe! Nun bedarf es aber entschlossenen Fortschreitens!
Alle. Wir werden nicht ruhen, bis er zum Tode gebracht ist.
Kaiphas. Mit anbrechendem Tage versammeln wir uns wieder. Dann soll das Urtheil von dem ganzen versammelten Rathe bestätigt, der Gefangene hierauf sogleich dem Pilatus vorgeführt werden, damit auch er es bekräftige und sodann vollziehen lasse.
Die Priester. Gott befreie uns bald von unserem Feinde! [*Alle ab.*

FUENFTE SZENE.

Judas allein.

Bange Ahnungen treiben mich umher. Das Wort bei Annas: Er soll sterben! O dieses Wort verfolgt mich überall! Nein! So weit werden sie es nicht treiben! Es ware schrecklich. Nein — und ich, ich — Schuld daran! Nein! In des Kaiphas Haus hier werde ich wohl erfragen, wie es steht. Soll ich hineingehen? Ich kann sie nicht mehr ertragen, diese Ungewissheit, und es graut mir davor, die Gewissheit zu erfahren. Aber es muss einmal sein! [*Geht hinein.*

SECHSTE SZENE.

Halle. — HAGAR, SARA, MELCHI ; *dann* PANTHER, ARPHAXAD, ABDIAS, LEVI ; *später* JOHANNES, PETRUS ; *zuletzt* CHRISTUS, *von* SELPHA, MALCHUS *und* BALBUS *geführt*.

Hagar. [*Im Hereingehen zu* MELCHI.] Ihr Männer! kommet hier herein!
Sara. Hier ist's gemächlicher.
Melchi. Wahrhaftig, gute Kinder! [*Ruft hinaus.*] He! Kameraden! da herein! Es ist uns besser, in der Halle uns zu lagern. [*Die Knechte kommen.*
Arphaxad. Hier lass ich mir's gefallen. Warum wir doch längst hereingeschlüpft! Wir dummern Wichte. Steh'n immer draussen unterm hellen Himmel und frieren. — Doch wo gibt es Feuer?
Panther. Sara! Geh' und bringe uns Gluth; auch Holz, um nachzulegen.
Hagar. Gerne!
Sara. Das sollt ihr haben. [*Geh'n Beide ab.*
Rotte. Wird das Verhör nicht bald zu Ende geh'n?
Melchi. Das währt noch lange, bis die Zeugen alle vernommen sind.
Panther. Und der Beklagte wird wohl auch die Redekunst nicht sparen, sich hinauszuwinden.
Arphaxad. Doch so wird nichts helfen; er hat zu sehr die Priesterschaft beleidigt. [HAGAR *und* SARA *kommen wieder.*
Hagar. Hier habt ihr Gluth.

sty of him who is guilty of disobedience to the constituted authorities?" Then stood up Josue, and unrolling the book of the law, read therefrom: "The man that will do presumptuously and will not hearken to the priest that standeth to minister there before the Lord thy God, or unto the judge, even that man shall die ; and thou shalt put away the evil from Israel."

Then again said Caiaphas, "What does the law decree concerning him who profaneth the Sabbath?" Then Ezekiel stood up and read, "Ye shall keep the Sabbath therefore, for it is holy unto you. Every one that defileth it shall surely be put to death ; for whosoever doeth any work therein, that soul shall be cut off from his people."

Then asked Caiaphas, "How does the law punish the blasphemer?" Then stood up Nathanael and, unrolling the book of the law, read : "Speak unto the children of Israel, saying, Whosoever curseth his God shall bear his sin. And he that blasphemeth the name of the Lord he shall surely be put to death ; all the congregation shall certainly stone him, as well the stranger as him that is born in the land."

"Thus," said Caiaphas, "is the judgment pronounced upon this Jesus of Nazareth,—pronounced according to law, and shall be carried out as speedily as possible. Meanwhile I will have the condemned placed under safe guard. Lead him forth, guard him, and by the dawn of the morning bring him to the Great Sanhedrim."

"Come then, Messiah," said Selpha, roughly, "we will show thee thy palace." "There thou shalt receive due homage," said Balbus, as he placed his hand on the shoulder of Jesus and marched him out of the chamber.

Then said Caiaphas exultingly, "We are approaching the goal. Now, however, resolute steps are necessary." The priests and Pharisees cried altogether, "We will not rest until he is brought to death." Then said Caiaphas, "With the break of day let us come together again. Then shall the sentence be confirmed by the whole assembled Council, and the prisoner will immediately be brought before Pilate in order that he may confirm it and have it executed." The priests then departed, crying as they went, "God deliver us soon from our enemy !"

When the Council had been dismissed and all was still, Judas, moving as one distracted, came down the street in front of the High Priest's palace : as he went he muttered to himself. "Fearful forebodings drive me hither and thither. That word of Annas's, 'He must die!' Oh, that word pursues me everywhere !" Then, as if he remembered all that had happened, Judas cried, "No, they will not carry things so far! that would be too terrible, and I—guilty of it?—No!—Here, in the house of Caiaphas, I will inquire how things stand. Shall I go in? I can no longer bear this uncertainty. Yet it terrifies me to ascertain the certainty. Yet it must come some time." And thereupon he went in unto the house of the High Priest.

Meanwhile in the hall of the house of Caiaphas the Temple Watch was standing, waiting the result of the examination of Jesus before Caiaphas. In the hall were the servant maids, Sarah and Hagar, who, seeing the soldiers standing outside, went to the door and said, "You may come in here." It was Hagar who spoke first and Sarah added, "It is more comfortable in here." "True for you, good people," said Melchi, one of the soldiers. Then calling out, "Ho, comrades, come in ! it is better for us to lie down in the hall." Then said a soldier named Arphaxad, "I like this—I wish we had come in long ago ; we stupid fellows are always standing outside in the open air and shivering. But where is there any fire?" "Sarah," added another soldier ; "go and bring us fire, also wood to lay thereon." "Willingly," said Hagar. "That you shall have," said Sarah. They went out together to comply with the soldier's wish. "Will the trial soon come to an end?" asked several of the soldiers. "It will last," said Melchi, "until all the witnesses are examined." "And," added Panther, "the accused will also not spare any of his eloquence to get himself out of the scrape." "That will help him nothing," said Arphaxad ; "he has offended the priests too much." Then returned the serving-maids with a brazier in which there was a little fire and some wood, which they placed thereon, making a great smoke. "Here is your fire," said Hagar, "wood and

JESUS BEFORE CAIAPHAS.—ACT IX., SC. 6.

Sara. Und Holz und Feuerzange.
Rotte. Habt Dank, ihr guten Mädchen!
Panther. So ist's gut. Nun lasst uns sogleich achten, dass das Feuer uns nicht erlösche:

[*Einige setzen sich um das Feuer; Andere stehen in Gruppen beieinander; Sara trägt ihnen Brod und Getränk zu.*]

Hagar. [*Zu Johannes der am Eingange steht.*] Johannes, du kommst auch hieher mitten in der Nacht? Tritt nur herein! Hier kannst du dich wärmen. Nicht wahr Männer, Ihr gönnt auch diesem jungen Manne hier ein Plätzchen?
Rotte. Ja wohl, komm nur näher!
Johannes. Gute Hagar! Es ist noch ein Gefährte bei mir, dürfte er nicht auch hereinkommen?
Hagar. Wo ist er? Lass' ihn hereintreten. Was soll er draussen stehen in der Kälte? [*Johannes geht zu dem weitwärts stehenden Petrus, kommt aber allein zurück.*] Nun, wo ist er?
Johannes. Er steht an der Schwelle, getraut sich aber nicht hereinzukommen.
Hagar. Komm herein, guter Freund, sei ohne Furcht.
Rotte. Freund, komme auch du her zu uns. Wärme dich!

[*Petrus naht sich scheu dem Feuer.*]

Knecht. Man sieht und hört noch immer nichts von dem Gefangenen.
Rotte. Wie lange werden wir hier noch warten müssen?
2. Knecht. Wahrscheinlich wird er als ein zum Tode Verurtheilter aus dem Verhör kommen.
1. Knecht. Ich bin neugierig, ob nicht auch seinen Jüngern nachgeforscht werden wird.
Rotte. [*Mit Gelächter.*] Das wäre ein schönes Stück Arbeit, wenn man die Alle einfangen wollte.
2. Knecht. Wird der Mühe nicht werth sein. Ist einmal der Meister weg, so werden die Galiläer Reissaus nehmen und sich in Jerusalem nicht mehr blicken lassen.
1. Knecht. Wenigstens sollte doch der eine derbe Züchtigung erhalten, der im Garten sich zur Wehre gesetzt und dem Malchus sein Ohr abgehauen hat.
Rotte. Ja, da sollte es heissen: Ohr um Ohr!
1. Knecht. Ha, ha, ha! Die Regel findet hier aber keine Anwendung, denn Malchus hat sein Ohr wieder.
Hagar. [*Zu Petrus.*] Ich habe dich schon lange betrachtet. Wenn ich nicht irre, so bist du einer von den Jüngern des Galiläers? Ja, ja, du bist es.
Petrus. Ich? Nein—ich bin es nicht! Frau, ich kenne ihn nicht, weiss auch gar nicht, was du sagst.

[*Er will sich fortschleichen und kommt bei Sara vorüber.*]

Sara. Seht, dieser war auch bei Jesus von Nazareth.
Mehrere. Bist du etwa auch einer von seinen Jüngern?
Petrus. Ich bin's nicht, bei meiner Seele! Ich kenne den Menschen nicht. [*Der Hahn kräht.*]
2. Knecht. Seht diesen Mann an, wahrlich, auch dieser war bei ihm!
Petrus. Ich weiss nicht, was ihr mit mir habt. Was geht dieser Mensch mich an?
Mehrere. Ja, ja, du bist einer von Jenen! Du bist ja auch ein Galiläer, deine Mundart verräth dich.
Petrus. Gott sei mein Zeuge, dass ich den Menschen nicht kenne, von dem ihr redet. [*Der Hahn kräht zum zweiten Male.*]
4. Knecht. Was, habe ich dich nicht bei ihm im Garten gesehn da? meinem Vetter Malchus das Ohr abgehauen wurde?
Rotte. [*Beim Feuer.*]. Macht Euch fertig, man bringt den Gefangenen! [*Selpha erscheint mit Carastus.*]

fire-tongs." Then cried the soldiers together, "You good girls!" "Yes," said Panther, stooping down over the brazier, "that is good. Now take care that the fire does not go out." Several of the soldiers stooped over the fire, piled on wool, and Sarah busied herself with bringing in meat and bread.

Peter and John, who had been wandering about the streets seeking for tidings, came to the door, John preceding Peter. Hagar, who saw John standing in the entrance of the door, said, "John, comest thou also hither in the middle of the night? Come in here then, thou must warm thyself. Would you make a little room for this young man here?" said Hagar, addressing the soldiers. "Yes, indeed," cried the band together. Then said John, "Good Hagar, I have a companion with me, can he not also come in?" "Where is he?" said Hagar; "let him come in; why does he stand out in the cold?" John goes to where Peter was standing, but comes back alone. "Where is he?" said Hagar. "He stands on the threshold, but does not trust himself to come in," replied John. Then Hagar went to the door and said, "Come in, good friend, do not be afraid." All the soldiers cried, "Friend, come also in here to us and warm thyself!" Peter, without saying a word, timidly drew near to the fire and warmed his hands in the smoke. The men went on talking round the fire, and Arphaxad said, after a pause, "We still see and hear nothing of the prisoner." Several then asked together, "How much longer must we wait here?" Then said Panther, "Probably he will come out from the trial as a man condemned to death." "I wonder," said Arphaxad, "whether his disciples will be sought after?"

Peter trembled as the band, with hoarse laughter, cried aloud, "That would be a fine piece of work if they all had to be captured!" Then said Panther, "It would not be worth the trouble. If the Master is once out of the way then the Galileans will fly and never let themselves be seen again in Jerusalem!" "But," said Panther, "one at least ought to receive sharp punishment, he who in the garden drew his sword and cut off Malchus's ear." "Yes, yes!" cried the band, laughing, "that should be as it is said. An ear for an ear!" "Ha, ha, ha!" laughed Panther, "that rule would here find no application, for Malchus has his ear back again."

During this time while the soldiers were laughing and talking, Hagar was curiously looking at Peter. Immediately a pause took place, Hagar said to Peter, "I have been observing thee for some time. Now, if I do not mistake, thou art one of the disciples of the Galilean. Yes, yes, thou art." Peter started up from the fire over which he had been warming his hands, and stammered out, "If so, I am not. Woman, I know him not, neither know I what thou sayest." When Hagar thus spoke all the soldiers looked at Peter, who, fearing his attack on Malchus might be resented, tried to slip through the land and escape unobserved. Passing the fire, he came close to the other waiting maid, Sarah, who, looking him full in the face, said in a shrill voice, "See, this man was also with Jesus of Nazareth." The attention of the whole band being aroused they all clustered round Peter, asking, "Art thou also one of his disciples?" Levi said. "Thou art one of them quite certainly!" Peter in the midst of armed and violent men looked confusedly from side to side, and declared, "Upon my soul I do not know the man." Even as he spoke the cock crew, but the rattle of the weapons of the soldiers and imminent menace of a violent death left him no leisure to attend to anything but his own safety, for Addus at the same moment exclaimed, "Look at this man. Of a truth he was also with him." Then said Peter, stoutly, "I know not what ye have to do with me. What does this man matter to me?" But the soldiers crowding round him, said, "Yes, yes, thou art one of them. Thou art also a Galilean; thy speech betrayeth thee." Then Peter, raising his hands on high, said with a troubled voice, "God be my witness that I do not know the man of whom ye speak;" and the cock crew a second time. Then Malchi pressing forward, looked Peter full in the face, and leaning on his spear, said, "Did I not see thee in the garden with him when my cousin Malchus had his ear cut off?" At this moment, when the situation was getting very serious for Peter, attention was called off from him by a cry from the soldiers round the fire. "Make ready, they are bringing in the prisoner." Selpha then brought in Jesus bound between Malchus and Balbus. "Now,

2. **Knecht.** Nun, wie hat es gegangen?
Selpha. Er ist zum Tode verurtheilt.
Rotte. [*Höhnend.*] Armer König!
  [CHRISTUS *sieht Petrus schmerzlich an.*]
Selpha. Vorwärts, Kameraden! Bis zum dämmernden Morgen müssen wir ihn bewachen!
2. **Knecht.** Kommt, er soll uns die Langeweile verkürzen.   [*Ab.*

SIEBENTE SZENE.

Auf dem Processions.—PETRUS, *später* JOHANNES.

Petrus. Mein Meister! ach! wie tief bin ich gefallen!—O weh! ich schwacher, ich armsel'ger Mensch! Verläugnet hab' ich dich—o war es möglich? Dreimal verläugnet!—Ich,—o Herr, Du weisst es,—entschlossen war ich, in den Tod mit Dir zu geh'n. Und jetzt—o Schande mir und Schmach—in feiger Furcht sagt' ich mich los von Dir! Als ein abtrünn'ger Flüchtling steh' ich da, nicht werth, mich Deinen Jünger noch zu nennen, vor Gott verachtungswerth und vor mir selbst!—O Herr!—o bester Herr!—hast Du für mich noch eine Gnade, eine Gnade noch für einen Treuvergess'nen,—o so sende sie mir! Ich fluche diesem Wankelmuthe. Mein Herz bereue ewig ihn! Ich will ihn ewig bereuen!—Lieber, lieber Meister! Nur diesmal höre noch die flehende Stimme des reuevollen Herzens! Nimmermehr will ich Dich lassen! Nimmermehr!—Ach, Herr! Kannst Du mir noch verzeihen?—Ja, Du wirst, O Gütigster!—ich kenne Dich,—Du wirst die bitt're Reue nicht verschmäh'n. Der sanfte, der mitleidsvolle Blick, mit dem Du mich ansahst, den armen, tiefgesunk'nen Jünger, verheisst es: Vergeben wirst Du mir! Vergeben!—Und von nun an, bester Lehrer, soll meines Herzens ganze Liebe Dir gehören, inniglicht an Dich mich schliessen! Und nichts, ja nichts vermöge je mich wieder von Dir zu trennen!—Herr!—ach Herr!—verzeihe!   [*Geht zur rechten Seite ab.*

Johannes. [*Von der linken Seite kommend.*] Wo mag denn Petrus hingekommen sein? Vergebens späht' mein Auge im Gedränge nach ihm. Es wird ihm wohl nichts Widriges begegnet sein. Vielleicht doch treffe ich ihn auf dem Wege.—Nach Bethania will ich jetzt gehen.—Aber, liebste Mutter, wenn ich die schmerzvollen Dinge dir berichte, ach! was wird dein Herz empfinden!—O Juda! Juda! welche entsetzliche That hast Du vollbracht!   [*Geht ab, dem* PETRUS *nach.*

ACHTE SZENE.

CHRISTUS *inmitten der Rotte auf einem Stuhl sitzend.*

Die Knechte abwechselnd. Ist dieser Thron dir nicht zu schlecht, grosser König?—Sei uns gegrusst, du neugeborner Herrscher! Aber setze dich fester, du möchtest sonst etwa herabfallen. [*Bringt* JESUS *wanken.*]—Du bist ja auch ein Prophet. So sage, grosser Elias, [*schlägt ihn*] wer hat dich geschlagen?—Bin ich es gewesen? [*Schlägt ihn ebenfalls.*]—Hörst du gar nicht? [*Schüttelt ihn.*] Schläfst du?—Er ist taub und stumm. Ein schöner Prophet! [*Stosst ihn vom Stuhle herab, so dass er der Länge nach hinfällt.*] O weh, o weh, unser König ist vom Throne gestürzt!—Was ist jetzt anzufangen? Wir haben keinen König mehr.—Du bist ja zum Erbarmen, du grosser Wunderinann!—Kommt, helfen wir ihm wieder auf seinen Thron! [*Erheben ihn.*] Erlebe dich, mächtiger König! Empfange uns're Neue unsere Huldigung!

Bote des Kaiphas. [*Eintretend.*] Nun, wie stehtes mit dem neuen König?
Rotte. Er redet und deutet nicht, wir können ihn nicht tauschen.
Bote. Der Hohepriester und Pilatus werden ihn schon beredt machen. Kaiphas sendet mich, ihn vorzuführen.
Selpha. Auf, Kameraden!
Knecht. [*Nimmt* JESU *die Bande ab.*] Steh' auf, du bist lange genug König gewesen!
Alle. Fort mit dir, dein Reich ist zu Ende!   [*Alle ab.*

how have things gone?" eagerly inquired **Arphaxad.** "He is condemned to death," said **Selpha.** The soldiers mocking, cried, "Poor king!" At this moment Jesus met Peter and looked upon him with a gaze full of sorrow. Peter smote his head with his hand and went out into the night. "Come," said **Arphaxad,** "he will help us to pass the time." "Forward, comrades!" said **Selpha,** "We must guard him till morning." Thereupon they all went out.

Peter, when he had left the hall of the High Priest, went out into the street, weeping bitterly and suffering bitter anguish of soul . . . "Oh, my Master," he cried, "how deeply have I fallen! Oh, woe unto me, weak and wretched man! I have denied thee. Oh, was it possible?—three times denied thee! Lord, thou knowest it! I was determined to go to death with thee; and now—oh shame to me and disgrace!—in cowardly fright I have cut myself loose from Him. As a cowardly deserter I stand here, not worthy any longer to be called his disciple—contemptible before God and before man. Lord, my dear Lord, hast thou still forgiveness for one so faithless? Oh, grant it, Lord, to me! I curse this inconstancy, my heart will lament it ever, never will I cease to repent it. Dear, dear Master, only for this time, yet this time, listen to the entreating voice of a sorrowful heart. Nevermore will I leave thee. O Lord, canst thou yet forgive me? Yes! thou wilt, thou kindest One, I know that thou wilt. Thou wilt not despise my bitter repentance. The gentle compassionate look which thou gavest to me, thy poor fallen disciple, promises it: Thou wilt forgive me. Forgive, and from now for evermore, O best of teachers, the whole love of my heart shall belong to thee, and bind me more closely to thee; and nothing, yes, nothing shall ever be able again to separate me from thee. Lord, O Lord, forgive!"

And with a face beaming with hope of forgiveness even for his threefold denial, he went away.

Hardly had he gone when John entered at the other end of the street, asking anxiously, looking on either side, "Where then can Peter have gone? In vain my eyes have sought him in the crowd. Surely nothing evil can have befallen him. Perhaps I still may meet him upon the road. I will now go to Bethany. Dearest mother, if I bring these terrible tidings to thee, what will thy heart feel? O Judas, Judas, what hast thou done?"

Now it came to pass that the soldiers, having taken Jesus into the guard-room of Caiaphas's palace, mocked him, and despitefully used him until it was day. They seated him on a stool with a bandage over his eyes, and surrounded him, mocking, saying, "Is not this throne too mean for thee, great king? Hail to thee, thou new-born sovereign." But sit more firmly," said one, seizing Jesus from behind and pressing him down on his chair, "thou mightest otherwise fall down. Thou art, verily, also a prophet. So say, O great Elias, say who it is who has struck thee," and with that he dealt Jesus a blow on the face. Others came in and also struck him, saying, "Was it I?" but Jesus answered nothing. Then one of the band went up to him and shouted, "Hearest thou nothing?" and shook him violently by the shoulders, "Art thou asleep?" Then, turning to his comrades, he exclaimed, "He is deaf and dumb, a fine prophet indeed." And thereupon he roughly pushed **Jesus** forward so that he fell from his stool on the ground upon his face. "Alas! alas!" they cried, "our king has fallen from his throne. What is to be done now? We have no longer any king. Thou art to be pitied, thou great magician! Come, help us to put him again upon his throne." And then they seized him and lifted him from the ground where he lay with his eyes bandaged and his hands tied and lifted him up again upon his seat. "Raise thyself, O mighty king, receive anew our homage." As they were kneeling round him in scorn, a messenger of Caiaphas entered saying, "How goes it now with the new king?" and the band shouted, "He speaks and prophesies not; we can do nothing with him." "Then," said the messenger, "the High Priest and Pilate will soon make him speak. Caiaphas sends me to bring him." "Up, comrades," said **Selpha.** Thereupon, taking Jesus again by the cords which bound his hands, they led him off, saying, "Stand up! thou hast been king long enough." And all shouted, "Away with thee. Thy kingdom has come to an end."

X. VORSTELLUNG.

Des Judas Verzweiflung.

PROLOG.

Warum irrt Judas sinneverwirrt umher?
Ihn martert, ach! des bösen Gewissens Qual.
Die Blutschuld lastet auf der Seele,
Wandelt in Feuer den Sold der Sünde.

Beweine, Juda, was du verbrochen hast!
O koche es mit Thränen der Busse aus!
Demuthig hoffend fleh' um Gnade:
Noch steht die Pforte des Heils dir offen.

O weh! wohl quält die bitterste Reue ihn:
Doch durch das Dunkel leuchtet kein Hoffnungsstrahl.
Zu gross, zu gross ist meine Sünde!
Ruft er mit Kain, dem Brudermörder.

Wie diesen, ungetröstet und ungebüsst,
Erfasst mit Schrecken irre Verzweiflung ihn.
Das ist der Endelohn der Sünde;
Solchem Geschicke treibt sie entgegen.

Solo.

O Weh' dem Menschen, sprach der Herr,
Der mich wird übergeben!
Es wäre besser ihm, wenn er
Erhalten nie das Leben.
Und dieses Weh, das Jesus sprach,
Folgt Judas auf dem Fusse nach.

Chor.

Der Unthat vollen Lohn soll er nicht missen;
Laut schreit um Rache das verkaufte Blut.
Zur Raserei getrieben vom Gewissen,
Gepeitscht von allen Furien der Wuth,
Rennt Judas ohne Rast umher
Und findet keine Ruhe mehr,
Bis er, ach, von Verzweiflung fortgerissen,
Hinwirft von sich in wilder Hast
Des Lebens unerträglich schwere Last.

VORBILD.

Der Brudermörder Kain, von Gewissensbissen gequält, irrt unstät und flüchtig auf der Erde umher.—1 Mos. 4, 10–17.

[Abel ist das Vorbild des sterbenden Messias. Abel, der Gerechte, wird von seinem Bruder Kain gehasst wie Christus von seinen Brüdern den Juden. Draussen in der Wildniss wird Abel, vor der Stadt wird auch Christus getödtet. Abel's Blut schreit um Rache zum Himmel gegen Kain, Christi Blut somit auf Verlangen seiner Mörder rächend über sie und ihre Kinder. Unstät und flüchtig irrt Kain umher, auch die jüdische Nation wird aus ihrem Reiche vertrieben und über die ganze Erde zerstreut.]

Solo.

So flieht auch Kain. Ach, wohin!
Du kannst dir selbst doch nicht entflieh'n.
In dir tragst Du die Höllenqual;
Und eilest du von Ort zu Ort,
Sie schwingt die Geissel fort und fort;
Wo du bist, ist sie überall,
Entrinnen wirst du nie der Pein.

Chor.

Dies soll der Sünder Spiegel sein.
Denn kommt die Rache heute nicht,
Will noch der Himmel borgen:
So fällt das doppelte Gericht
Auf ihre Häupter morgen.

HANDLUNG.

Der versammelte hohe Rath bestätigt das über Christus ausgesprochene Todesurtheil.—Judas kommt voll Reue in die Rathsversammlung, wirft die dreissig Silberlinge hin, geht von Verzweiflung getrieben davon und erhängt sich.

ERSTE SZENE.

Judas allein.

So ist meine bange Ahnung zur schrecklichen Gewissheit geworden! Kaiphas hat den Meister zum Tode verurtheilt

CHAPTER X.

PROLOGUE.—Act X.

Why wanders Judas about like one amazed?
Alas! the torments of conscience are strong upon him,—
On his soul the guilt of blood lies heavy,
And turns into fire the reward of sin.

Weep, O Judas, the sin which thou hast sinned!
Oh! wash it out with the bitter tears of repentance!
In lowly hope entreat forgiveness—
Still open to thee is salvation's gate.

Alas! the bitterest remorse indeed is his portion,
But through the darkness there shines no ray of hope.
Too great, too great is my sin!
Cries he, with Cain, the brother-slayer.

Like him, unpardoned and uncomforted,
Wandering despair seizes upon him in terror.
That is the wages of sin,
Towards such a fate does it hasten.

The Lord said, " He who me betrays!—
Woe to him!—is undone;
"Twere better far for him that he
Had never seen the sun!"
This woe, of which Christ spake, hath come,
And Judas cannot flee from it.

The guilty devil fails not to win its wages,
The guiltless blood he sold cries from the ground;
Driven to madness by the worm that rages,
And scourged by furies, Judas ranges round
Wildly, and finds no rest
From the fire in his breast;
Till, swept away by bitterest despair
He flings away in reckless haste,
The load of life he can no longer bear.

[The fifteenth tableau, prefacing the despair of Judas, represents the despair of Cain. Cain, a tall, dark, and stalwart man, clad in a leopard's skin, is dropping the heavy tree-branch with which he has slain his brother. Abel, in a lambskin, lies dead with an ugly wound on his right temple. Cain's right hand is pressed upon the brow upon which is to be set the brand of God. It is a fine scene, full of simple, tragic effect.]

So too flies Cain. Ah! whither, then?
For from thyself thou canst not flee.
In thee thou bearest hell's worst pain;
And though from place to place thou go,
The scourge is wielded over thee;
Where thou art, it will always be.

Never canst thou escape thy woe.
Now this the sinner's fate will show,
Though vengeance may not come to-day,
Yet Heaven still can borrow,
And double share of judgment may
Fall on his head to-morrow.

THE DESPAIR OF JUDAS.

While Jesus was being mocked and ill-treated by the soldiers in the guard-room of Caiaphas's Palace, Judas wandered to and fro in despair. "Now my fearful foreboding has become a terrible certainty. Caiaphas has sentenced the Master to death, and

und der Rath hat in sein Urtheil eingestimmt! Es ist vorbei, keine Hoffnung, keine Rettung mehr! Hatte der Meister selbst sich retten wollen, so hätte er im Oelgarten seine Macht sie zum zweiten Male fühlen lassen! Jetzt thut er es nicht mehr. Und was kann ich für ihn thun, ich Unseliger, der Ich ihn in ihre Hände geliefert habe? Das Geld sollen sie wieder haben, das Blutgeld, sie müssen mir meinen Meister wieder herausgeben! Doch,—wird er dadurch gerettet? O eitle Hoffnung! Sie werden meiner spotten, ich weiss es! Verfluchte Synagoge! Du hast mich durch deine Sendlinge verführt, hast mir deine blutigen Absichten verheimlicht, bis du ihn in deinen Klauen hattest! Keinen Antheil will ich haben an dem Blute des Unschuldigen!

O der Folterqualen! O der Höllenwehen, die mein Innerstes durchtoben. [*Ab auf* ANNAS' *Seite.*

ZWEITE SZENE.

Der Hohe Rath.

Kaiphas. Ich glaubte, Ihr Väter, den Morgen nicht erwarten zu können, um den Feind der Synagoge in den Tod zu senden.

Annas. Auch ich konnte keinen Augenblick Ruhe finden vor Begierde, das Urtheil sprechen zu hören.

Alle. Es ist gesprochen. Er soll und muss sterben!

Kaiphas. In der Nachtzeit wollte ich nicht alle Glieder des Synedriums hieher bemüh'n. Doch war die nöth'ge Zahl von Richtern hier, nach Vorschrift des Gesetzes das Urtheil auszusprechen. Den Beklagten erklärten Alle wie aus Einem Munde des Todes schuldig; denn sie alle hatten in ihre eig'nen Ohren es vernommen, wie Jener sich erfrecht, als Gottes Sohn sich auszugeben, also Gott zu lastern mit unerhörtem keckem Frevelmuthe.

Priester und Pharisäer. [*Die vorhin zugegen waren.*] Ja, wir bezeugen es. Wir haben selbst die freche Gotteslästerung gehört aus seinem Munde.

Kaiphas. Nochmal will ich nun vorführen lassen den Verbrecher hier, damit ihr alle selbst euch überzeuget von seiner todeswürd'gen Schuld. Dann möge der ganze Rath gerechtes Urtheil fällen.

DRITTE SZENE.

JUDAS, *hereineilend.*

Judas. Ist es wahr? Ihr habt meinen Meister zum Tode verurtheilt?

Rabbi. Was drängst du dich unberufen hier ein? Hinaus! Man wird dich rufen, wenn man deiner bedarf.

Judas. Ich muss es wissen. Habt Ihr ihn verurtheilt?

Alle. Er muss sterben!

Judas. Wehe, wehe, ich habe gesündigt! Ich habe den Gerechten verrathen! O Ihr, Ihr blutdürstigen Richter. Ihr verdammt und mordet die Unschuld!

Alle. Judas, Ruhe, oder—

Judas. Keine Ruhe mehr für mich! Keine für Euch! Das Blut der Unschuld schreit um Rache!

Kaiphas. Was verwirrt deine Seele? Rede, aber rede mit Ehrfurcht. Du stehest vor dem Hohen Rath.

Judas. Ihr wollt Jenen dem Tode überliefern, der rein ist von jeder Schuld. Das dürft Ihr nicht! Da habe ich Einsprache zu machen! Ihr habt mich zum Verräther gemacht. Eure verfluchten Silberlinge . . .

Annas. Du hast dich selbst angetragen und den Kauf geschlossen . . .

Priester. Besinne dich, Judas! Du hast erhalten, was du verlangt hast. Und wenn du dich ordentlich beträgst, so kannst du noch . . . .

Judas. Ich will nichts mehr! Ich zerreisse Euern schändlichen Vertrag! Gebt die Unschuld heraus!

Rabbi. Packe dich, Unsinniger!

Judas. Die Unschuld fordere ich zurück! Meine Hunde sollen rein sein von dem Blute . . . .

Rabbi. Was, du schändliche Verrätherseele, du willst dem Hohen Rathe Gesetze vorschreiben? Wisse! Dein Meister muss sterben und du hast ihn in den Tod geliefert!

Alle. Sterben muss er!

---

the Council has concurred in his sentence. All is over. There is no hope, no way of escape. Had the Master wished to save himself he would have made them feel his might a second time in the garden. Now he does so no more. What can I do for him, I, a miserable wretch who have delivered him into their hands? They shall have the money back, that bloodmoney. They must give me my Master back again. But oh, will he be saved by that? Oh, idle hope! They will mock me, I know it. O cursed synagogue, thou hast tempted me through thy messengers, thou hast hidden from me thy bloody designs until thou hadst him in thy clutches. I will have no share in the blood of this innocent. Oh, what tortures, what pains of hell, tear my inmost soul!" So saying he departed.

Now within the hall of the Sanhedrim were assembled the **High Priest**, the **Scribes**, and the leaders. **Caiaphas** and **Annas**, arrayed in their robes, sat in the high place of the Council, and all the seats were filled except those of **Joseph of Arimathea** and **Nicodemus**, which were empty. **Caiaphas** spoke, saying, " I thought, Fathers, that I could not wait till the morning to send the enemy of the Synagogue to death." And **Annas** said, " I could not get a moment's rest for eagerness to hear the sentence pronounced." Then cried they all, " It is pronounced. He shall and must die." **Caiaphas** said : " I did not wish to trouble all the members of the Sanhedrim to come hither in the night-time. But there was present the necessary number of judges to pronounce sentence as the Law prescribes. All as with one mouth declared the accused guilty of death, for all had heard with their own ears how this man was impious enough to call himself the Son of God, and, therefore, to blaspheme God with unheard-of daring." The **Priests** and **Pharisees** who had previously been present, answered, " Yea, we bear witness to it. We have ourselves heard the impious blasphemy from his lips." Then said **Caiaphas**, " I will have the criminal brought before you once more, so that you may be convinced of his being guilty of death. Then may the whole Council pronounce the just sentence." As he was speaking, **Judas**, looking haggard and distracted, rushed into the midst of the Council, crying wildly, " Is it true? have you condemned my Master to death?" Then said the **Rabbi** unto him, " Why dost thou force thyself in here unwanted? Be off! We will call thee if we have need of thee." But **Judas** took no heed. " I must know it," he said, " have you condemned him?" Then all in the Council cried aloud, " He must die." "Woe! woe!" said **Judas**, " I have sinned, I have betrayed innocent blood. Oh, you bloodthirsty judges, to condemn the innocent blood." " Peace, peace, **Judas**!" cried the **Council**. " There will never, never more be peace for me," said **Judas**, bitterly, "and none for you. The blood of the innocent cries aloud for vengeance." " What has driven you crazy? Speak, but speak with reverence—thou standest before the Sanhedrim," said **Caiaphas**. Then said **Judas**, passionately, " You are determined to deliver him up to death, him who is free from all guilt. You must not do it, I have a protest to make against it. You have made me a traitor. Your accursed pieces of silver!—" **Annas** interrupted him, saying, " Thou didst propose it thyself and close the bargain." Then said a **Priest** unto him, " Recollect thyself, **Judas**, thou hast received what thou didst desire; and if thou behavest thyself decently thou canst still—" **Judas** interrupted him : " I will have nothing more. I tear up your shameful bargain. Let the innocent go!" " Be off, madman," said the **Rabbi**, angrily. But **Judas** took no heed. " I demand the release of the innocent. My hands shall be free from his blood." " What!" said the **Rabbi**, " thou contemptible traitor, wilt thou dictate to the Sanhedrim? Know this, thy Master must die, and thou hast delivered him to death." And all the **Priests** and **Pharisees** cried aloud,

Judas. [*Stieren Blickes.*] Sterben! Ich bin eine Verratherseele! [*Ausbrechend.*] Dann zerreisst mich, zehntausend Teufel aus der Hölle! Zermalmt mich! Hier, Ihr Bluthunde, habt Ihr Euer Fluch-Euer Blutgeld! [*Wirft den Beutel hin.*]
Kaiphas. Was lassest du dich zu einer Handlung brauchen, die du nicht vorher überlegt hast?
Alle. Da sieh' du nur zu!
Judas. So soll meine Seele verderben, mein Leib zerbersten, und Ihr — —
Alle. Schweige und fort von hier!
Judas. Ihr sollt mit mir in die Hölle versinken!
[*Stürzt hinaus.*]

VIERTE SZENE.

Kaiphas. [*Nach einer Pause.*] Ein fürchterlicher Mensch!
Annas. Ich habe so etwas geahnt.
Priester. Est ist seine Schuld.
Kaiphas. Er hat seinen Freund verrathen, wir verfolgen unsern Feind. Ich bleibe fest bei meinem Entschluss und wenn einer hier sein sollte, der anderer Gesinnung ist, der stehe auf!
Alle. Nein! Was beschlossen ist, werde ausgeführt!
Kaiphas. Was thun wir nun mit diesem Geld? Als Blutgeld darf es nicht mehr in den Gotteskasten zurückgelegt werden.
Priester. Es mangelt an einem Begräbnissplatz für Fremdlinge. Mit diesem Gelde könnte ein Acker dafür angekauft werden.
Kaiphas. Ist ein solcher käuflich?
Priester. Ein Hafner in der Stadt hat ein Grundstück zum Verkauf ausgeboten, gerade für diesen Preis.
Kaiphas. So geht und kauft es. Nun aber wollen wir nicht länger säumen, das Endurtheil über den Gefangenen zu fällen.
Rabbi. Sogleich will ich ihn vorführen lassen.
Annas. Ich will sehen, ob ihn der Trotz, den er mir gezeigt, noch nicht vergangen ist. Eine wahre Genugthuung wird es mir sein, einzustimmen in den Urtheilsspruch: Er sterbe!

FUENFTE SZENE.

CHRISTUS *vor dem Hohen Rathe.*

Selpha. [JESUM *einführend.*] Ehre dem Hohen Rath besser als vorhin!
Kaiphas. Führt ihn in die Mitte!
Balbus. Tritt vor. [*Stösst den Gefangenen vorwärts.*]
Kaiphas. Jesus von Nazareth, bestehst du auf dem Worte, das du in dieser Nacht vor deinen Richtern ausgesprochen hast?
Annas. Wenn du der Gesalbte bist, so sage es uns!
Christus. Wenn ich es sage, so werdet Ihr mir nicht glauben, und stelle ich Euch eine Frage entgegen, so werdet ihr weder darauf antworten, noch mich loslassen. Aber von nun an wird der Menschensohn zur Rechten des allmächtigen Gottes sitzen.
Alle. Du bist also der Sohn Gottes?
Christus. Ihr sagt es und ich bin es!
Annas. Es ist genug. Was bedürfen wir noch eines Zeugnisses?
Priester *und* Pharisäer. [*Die der nächtlichen Sitzung nicht beigewohnt.*] Wir haben es nun aus seinem eigenen Munde gehört!
Kaiphas. Väter des Volkes Israel! Euch gebühret es nun, den endgültigen Ausspruch über die Schuld und Strafe dieses Menschen zu thun!
Alle. Er ist der Gotteslästerung schuldig! Er hat den Tod verdient!
Kaiphas. Wir wollen ihn demnach vor den Richterstuhl des Pilatus führen!
Alle. Ja, fort mit ihm! Er sterbe!
Kaiphas. Pilatus muss aber zuvor in Kenntniss gesetzt werden, damit er noch vor dem Feste das Urtheil ergehen lasse.
Rabbi. Dürften Einige vom Rathe etwa sich vorausbegeben, um schleunige Verhandlung nachzusuchen?
Kaiphas. Du selbst, dann Dariabbas und Rabiath,—ihr geht voraus! Wir kommen sogleich nach. Dieser Tag wird also die Religion unserer Väter retten und die Ehre der Synagoge erhöhen, so dass der Nachklang unseres Ruhmes zu den spätesten Enkeln sich fortpflanzen wird. Fuhrt ihn weg, wir folgen. [*Die drei gehen ab.*]
Alle. Tod dem Galiläer! [*Alle ab.*]

"He must die." And Judas, with staring eyes as one demented, repeated, "Die? Then I am a traitor!" And then breaking out into wild passion, he shouted aloud, "May ten thousand devils from hell tear me in pieces! Let them grind me to powder! Here, ye bloodhounds, take your accursed blood-money!" And with that he snatched the bag from his girdle and flung it violently before the seat of the High Priest. "Why didst thou let thyself be made the tool for a transaction which thou didst not weigh beforehand?" said Caiaphas. "Yes," cried several, "it is your own business." Then shouted Judas, wildly, "May my soul be damned, my body burst asunder, and ye—" "Silence, and out from here," cried all the priests together. "And you," shouted Judas above them all, "you will sink with me into hell!" He then rushed from the hall.

After a pause, during which the chief priests and rulers looked at each other in silence, the money lay unnoticed on the floor. Caiaphas said, "What a fearful man!" "I had some foreboding of this," said Annas. "It is his own fault," remarked a priest. Then said Caiaphas, "He has betrayed his friend; we pursue our enemy. I remain steadfast by my determination, and if any one here should be of another opinion, let him stand up." "No," cried they all with one voice; "what has been resolved upon, let it be carried out." Then said Caiaphas, "What shall we do with this money? It is blood-money, it cannot be any more put into the treasury of God." A Priest said, "A burying-place for strangers is much wanted. With this money a field may be purchased for that purpose." "Is there such a one in the market," said Caiaphas. "Yes," said a Priest; "a potter in the city has offered a piece of ground for sale for just this price." "Go and buy it," said Caiaphas. They then picked up the money which had lain untouched on the floor. "But now we will no longer delay to pronounce the capital sentence upon the prisoner," continued Caiaphas. Then said the Rabbi, "I will have him brought in at once." "I shall see," said Annas, "whether the scorn which he showed towards me has not yet left him. A real satisfaction will it be to me to share in the sentence. Let him die."

Jesus then was brought in a second time before Caiaphas. Selpha, as before, preceded him, and Balbus and Malchus led him bound by the hands with a cord. "Stand there," said Selpha, "and show more respect to the Council than thou didst before." Then said Caiaphas, "Lead him into the middle." Balbus, laying his hand on the shoulder of Jesus, thrust him forward, saying, "Step forward." Then Caiaphas spake unto Jesus, saying, "Jesus of Nazareth, dost thou stand by the words which thou hast pronounced this night before thy judges?" Annas added, "If thou to the Christ, tell us!" Then Jesus answered and said, "If I tell you, ye will not believe; if I also ask you, ye will not answer me nor let me go. But hereafter shall ye see the Son of Man sitting on the right hand of Almighty God." A shudder ran through the Sanhedrim, and all cried excitedly, "Art thou then the Son of God?" Jesus answered, "Ye say it, and so I am." Annas exclaimed, "It is enough: what need have we of any further witnesses?" The Priests and Pharisees who had not attended the night Council said, "We have now heard it out of his own mouth." Then said Caiaphas, "Fathers of the people of Israel, it is now our duty to come to a final decision as to the punishment of this man." Then cried they all, "He is guilty of blasphemy. He hath deserved death." Caiaphas said, "We will therefore lead him before the judgment-seat of Pilate." And they all answered and said, "Yes, away with him. Let him die." "Pilate," said Caiaphas, "must first be informed, in order that he may proclaim the sentence before the feast." The Rabbi said, "Could someone be sent before from the Council in order to give him timely information?" "Thou thyself," said Caiaphas, "together with Dariabbas and Rabiath, shalt go before. We will speedily come after." When these three had departed Caiaphas said, "This day then will save the religion of our fathers and exalt the honour of the Synagogue, so that the echo of our fame shall reach our latest descendants. Lead the way! we follow." Once more they cried, "Down with the Galilean," and departed.

SECHSTE SZENE.

Die drei Abgesandten des Hohen Rathes vor dem Hause des PILATUS.

Rabbi. Endlich athmen wir wieder freier. Lange genug wurden wir beschimpft.

Rabinth. Es war höchste Zeit, der Synagoge hätte die letzte Stunde bald geschlagen, sein Anhang war schon sehr gross.

Rabbi. Jetzt ist von ihm nichts mehr zu fürchten. Die Händler haben in diesen Tagen die rühmlichste Thätigkeit entwickelt, eine Menge entschlossener Leute für uns zu gewinnen. Ihr werdet sehen: Wenn es zu etwas kommt, so werden diese kräftig den Ton angeben, die Wankelmüthigen werden mit einstimmen und die Anhänger des Nazareners werden es für gut finden, zu schweigen und sich zurückzuziehen.

Rabinth. Wie werden wir unser Gesuch bei Pilatus anbringen? Wir dürfen das Haus des Heiden heute nicht betreten, sonst werden wir unrein, das Osterlamm zu essen.

Rabbi. Wir werden das Gesuch durch seine Leute vortragen lassen.

(Pocht am Thore.)
Quintus. *[Oeffnet.]* Willkommen, Rabbi! Tretet nur herein!

Rabbi. Es ist nach Vorschrift des Gesetzes heute uns nicht gestattet.

Quintus. So? — Kann etwa ich den Auftrag auch vollziehn?

Rabbi. Der Hohepriester sendet uns, die Bitte an den erhabenen Statthalter des Kaisers zu stellen, er wolle erlauben, dass der Hohe Rath vor ihm erscheine, und ihm einen Missethäter zur Bestätigung des Urtheils vorführe.

Diener. Ich will es sogleich melden. *[Ab.]*

1. Priester. Es ist doch traurig, dass wir bei einem Heiden anklopfen müssen, um die Ansprüche des heiligen Gesetzes vollziehen zu lassen.

Rabbi. Sei getrost! Wenn einmal der einheimische Feind aus dem Wege geräumt ist — wer weiss, ob wir uns nicht bald auch dieser Fremdlinge entledigen?

2. Priester. O möchte ich den Tag noch erleben, der den Kindern Israels die Freiheit bringen wird!

Diener. *[Zurückkommend.]* Der Statthalter grüsst euch. Ihr sollt dem Hohenpriester melden, dass Pilatus bereit sei, das Anliegen des Hohen Rathes zu vernehmen.

Rabbi. Empfangt unsern Dank!

2. Priester. *[Beim Abgehn.]* Pilatus wird wohl in die Forderung des Hohen Rathes einwilligen?

Rabbi. Er muss! Wie könnte er widerstehn, wenn der Hohe Rath und das ganze Volk den Tod dieses Menschen fordern?

THE DESPAIR OF JUDAS.

The three messengers sent by the Sanhedrim drew near to the house of Pilate, and as they went they spoke among themselves. The Rabbi said, "At last we can breathe more freely again; we have been insulted enough." Dariabbas replied, "It was indeed high time; his following was becoming very large." "Now," said the Rabbi, "there is nothing more to be feared from him. The traders have in these days displayed the most creditable activity, to have gained for us a crowd of determined people. You will see if it comes to anything, they will effectively take the lead. The waverers will concur with them and the followers of the Nazarene will find it well to be silent and take themselves off."

Then said Rabinth, seeing that they had approached the palace of Pilate, "How shall we bring our message to Pilate? We dare not enter the house of the Gentile to-day, as in that case we should become unclean and could not eat the Passover." "We will send a message through one of his own people," said the Rabbi, and going up the stairs to the balcony of Pilate's house, he knocked gently at the door.

A servant of Pilate's opened it. "We come from the Sanhedrim," said the Rabbi. "Will you not come in?" said the servant. "No, that we cannot do," said the Rabbi. "The High Priest sends us to bring a petition to the illustrious Viceroy of Cæsar to ask if he will allow the Council to appear before him, and to bring before him a malefactor for the confirmation of his sentence." "I will deliver the message at once," said the servant, and went in to Pilate. The Rabbi, returning down the steps, joined Dariabbas and Rabinth, who stood below. "It is very sad," said Dariabbas, "that we must knock at the door of a Gentile in order to have executed the behests of our holy law." "Take courage," said the Rabbi; "when once this domestic enemy is removed out of the way, who knows whether we might not soon free ourselves from the foreign foe?" Rabinth exclaimed, "Oh, may I live to see the day which will bring freedom to the children of Israel!" Pilate's servant returned and spoke unto them, saying, "The Governor greets you. You are to inform the High Priest that Pilate is ready to receive the petition of the Sanhedrim." "Accept our thanks," said the Rabbi. The servant then returned and closed the door behind him. The three messengers then returned. Rabinth remarked anxiously, "Pilate will surely agree to the demand of the Council." "He must," said the Rabbi; "how could he resist, it when the Sanhedrim

1. Priester. Was liegt dem Statthalter an dem Leben eines Galiläers? Schon dem Hohenpriester zu gefallen, der bei ihm viel gilt, wird er keinen Anstand nehmen, die Hinrichtung zu genehmigen. [Alle drei ab.

SIEBENTE SZENE.

Des Judas Ende. Waldgegend.

Judas. Wo gehe ich hin, meine Schande zu verbergen! Kein Waldesdunkel ist versteckt, keine Felsenhöhle tief genug! Verschlinge mich, Erde! Ach meinen Meister, den besten aller Menschen, habe ich verkauft, ihn der Misshandlung, dem schmerzvollsten Tode überliefert! Zum schmerzenvollsten Martertode! — Ich abscheulichster Verräther! — O wo ist ein Mensch, auf dem noch solche Blutschuld liegt! — — wie gütig war er immer gegen mich! Wie tröstete er mich, wenn manchmal finsterer Unmuth mir auf der Seele lag. Wie liebreich mahnte und warnte er mich noch, da ich schon über Verrath brütete! Vermaledeiter Geiz, nur du hast mich verleitet! Ach! nun kein Jünger mehr, darf ich nie wieder einem der Brüder vor die Augen treten. Ein Ausgestossener — überall verhasst und verabscheut, von Jenen selbst, die mich verführt, irre ich einsam umher mit dieser Feuerglut in meinem Innern! Ach, dürfte ich sein Antlitz nochmals sehn! Ich möchte mich anklammern an ihn, den einzigen Rettungsanker! Doch er liegt im Kerker, ist vielleicht schon getödtet durch die Wuth seiner Feinde — ach nein! Durch meine Schuld! Weh' mir, mir Auswurf der Menschheit! Für mich ist keine Hoffnung. Mein Verbrechen ist durch keine Busse mehr gut zu machen; Er ist todt und ich bin sein Mörder! Unglückseligo Stunde, da meine Mutter mich geboren! Soll ich noch länger diese Qualen tragen? Nein, keinen Schritt mehr weiter! Hier will ich, verfluchtes Leben, dich aushauchen! An diesem Baume hange die unglückseligste aller Früchte! [*Reisst sich den Gürtel ab.*] Ha, komm', du Schlange, umstricke mich! Erwürge den Verräther!

[*Macht Anstalt zum Selbstmord. Der Vorhang fällt.*]

XI. VORSTELLUNG.

CHRISTUS VOR PILATUS.
PROLOG.

Kaum ertönte das Wort: Tod ihm, des Moses Feind!
Tönt es vielstimmig nach. Dürstend mit Tigerdurst
    Nach dem Blute der Unschuld
    Eilen sie zu Pilatus hin.

Vor des Heiden Gericht häufet ihr Ungestüm,
Unerschöpflich beredt, Klagen auf Klagen an,
    Ungeduldig erharrend
    Den verdammenden Urtheilsspruch.

So ertönte auch einst wider den Daniel
Tausendstimmiger Ruf: Er hat den Bel zerstört!
    Fort zur Grube der Löwen!
    Diesen werde zum Frasse er!

Ach! wenn trugvoller Wahn sich in die Menschenbrust
Hat den Eingang gebahnt, kennt sich der Mensch nicht mehr.
    Unrecht wird ihm zur Tugend;
    Tugend hasst und befeindet er.

and the whole people demand the death of this man?" "And besides," said Dariabbas "what does the Governor care about the life of a single Galilean? Were it merely in order to please the High Priest, who is of great importance to him, he would not hesitate to permit the execution."

Now Judas, being distracted by remorse, found himself, after wandering to and fro, in the potter's field purchased with the thirty pieces of silver, in the midst of which stood a blasted tree. Then, after looking wildly round to see if anyone was near, he said: "Oh! where, where can I go to hide my shame? How escape the torments of conscience? No forest fastness is there dark enough! No rocky cavern deep enough! O earth, open and swallow me up! I can no longer exist. O my dear Master! Him, best of all men, have I basely sold, giving him up to treatment vile and rude, yea, perhaps to martyrdom and torture—I, detestable betrayer! —Oh! where is there another man on whom such guilt of blood doth rest? How good the Master ever was to me! How did he comfort me with kindly words, when gloomy thoughts lay on my soul! How wondrously happy did I feel when I sat with the brethren at his feet, and heard sweet, heavenly teachings proceed from his mouth! How, full of love, did he admonish me, even while my soul was brooding over shameful treachery,—the good Lord; and all his goodness have I thus repaid! Accursed avarice! Thou alone didst lead my heart astray; didst make me deaf and blind! Thou wast the ring by which foul Satan held my soul and dragged me down the dread abyss! No more his follower shall I ever dare show my face again before the brethren! Shut out from them and hated everywhere, despised and jeered at, indeed, by those vile men who led me on. As a betrayer now, branded with shame, I wander on, bearing this glowing fire within my breast! Oh, were the Master there! Oh, could I see his face once more! I would cast myself at his feet, and cling to him, my only saving hope! But now he lies in prison,—is perhaps already murdered by his raging foe—alas, no—through my own guilt! through my own guilt! I am the outcast villain who hath brought my benefactor to these bonds and death! The scum of men! there is no help for me! no hope! My crime is much too great! The fearful crime no penance can make good. Too late! Too late! For he is dead, and I—I am his murderer! Thrice unhappy hour, in which my mother gave me to the world! How long must I drag on this life of shame, and bear these tortures about with me?—as one pest-stricken, fire from men, and be despised and shunned by all the world! Not one step further! Here, O life accursed, here will I end thee! On these branches let the most disastrous fruit hang. (*loosens his girdle and prepares to hang himself.*) Ha! come, thou serpent, entwine my neck, and strangle the betrayer!"

As Judas spoke the last words he tied with convulsive and feverish energy the long girdle round his neck and fastened it to the branch of the tree and swung himself off; but it was not sufficient to support his weight, and falling headlong he burst asunder in the midst, and his bowels gushed out.

CHAPTER XI.

PROLOGUE.—Act XI.

Scarce was uttered the word, "Death to him, Moses' foe!"
When on all sides it was echoed. Thirsting with tigers' thirst
    For the blood of the guiltless,
    Haste they away to Pilate.

'Fore the judgment-seat of the heathen, their fierce impatience
Heaps, untiringly eloquent, accusation
    On accusation, awaiting
    Tidings of doom, athirst for blood.

Thus of old arose the cry against Daniel,
Thousand-voiced: "This man hath destroyed Bel's image!
    Away to the den of the lions,
    Let him become their food."

When deceitful Error has found an entrance
Into man's heart, he knows himself no longer;
    Wrong becomes his virtue,
    Virtue he hates and seeks to destroy.

Choragus.
Gelästert hat er Gott!
Wir brauchen keinen Zeugen mehr.
Verdammt zum Tod
Durch das Gesetz ist er.
So lärmt die Priesterrotte hier.
Auf! zu Pilatus wollen wir,
Ihm unsre Klagen vorzubringen,
Das Todesurtheil zu erzwingen!

Vorbild.

Die Landvögte verklagen den Daniel vor dem Könige Darius und dringen darauf, dass er in die Löwengrube geworfen werde.—Dan. 6, 4.

[Wie Daniel ohne allen Grund verklagt wird, so bringen auch die Hohenpriester bei Pilatus die ungerwissesten Klagen gegen Jesus vor und begehren, dass er ihn zum Kreuzestode verdammen soll.]

Chor.
In diesem stummen Bilde sehet ihr:
    Verklagt wird fälschlich Gottes Sohn,
    Wie Daniel zu Babylon.
Der Götter Feind ist Daniel!
O König! höre deiner Völker Klagen!
Zerstört hat er den grossen Bel,
Die Priester und den Drachen todtgeschlagen!
Ergrimmt vor deinem Throne
Erscheint ganz Babylon.
Willst du dich retten vom Verderben,
So muss der Feind der Götter sterben.
Der grosse Gott, den er gehöhnt,
Wird nur durch seinen Tod versöhnt.

Solo.
So dem Pilatus Stuhl sich naht
Voll Leidenschaft der hohe Rath
Und fordert heftig Jesu Blut.

Was hat sie also blind gemacht?
Was hat in ihnen angefacht
So wilden Rasens dust're Gluth?
Der Neid, der kein Erbarmen kennt,
In dem der Hölle Feuer brennt,
    Hat diesen Brand entzündet.
Er opfert Alles seiner Wuth!
Nichts ist ihm heilig, Nichts zu gut,
Um seinen Groll zu stillen.
Weh' denen, die die Leidenschaft
In Schlangenketten mit sich rafft!

Chor.
Vor neidischen Gelüsten,
O Brüder! bleibet auf der Hut!
Nie lasset diese Natterbrut
In eurem Busen nisten!

HANDLUNG.

CHRISTUS *wird zu* PILATUS *abgeführt und von den Priestern vor demselben verklagt. Dieser erklärt ihn für unschuldig und lässt ihn zu* HERODES *führen.*

ERSTE SZENE.

Vor dem Hause des PILATUS. *Links der Hohe Rath, die Händler und Zeugen, rechts die Rotte mit* JESUS.

Rotte. [JESUM *herausführend.*] Fort mit dir zum Tode, falscher Prophet!—Ha, grauet es dir, dass du nicht vorwärts willst?
Selpha. Treibt ihn an!
Rotte. Soll man dich auf den Händen tragen?—Gehe nur! Deine Reise dauert ohnehin nicht mehr lang! Nur nach Kalvarien hinaus! Dort am Kreuze kannst du gemächlich ausruhn!
Kaiphas. Bleibt ruhig, wir wollen uns melden lassen.
                        [*Es geschieht.*]
Rabbi. Geht zum Thore und pocht.

Chorus.
"He hath spoken blasphemy!
    No witness more we need.
    Condemned to death is He—
    So hath the Law decreed,"—
So clamours loud the murderous crew:
"Come, let us now to Pilate sue!
Bring our complaint to him, that we
May force from him the death-decree."

[The sixteenth tableau, which precedes the appearance of Christ before the tribunal of Pilate, the foreign ruler, is devoted to the scene in which Daniel was denounced before Darius immediately before his consignment to the den of lions. Daniel stands forth before the king undismayed by his accusers, a much more vigorous and rugged specimen of persecuted virtue than the Man of Sorrows, who immediately afterwards was led before Pilate.]

Chorus.
In this dumb picture here you see
    How falsely is accused God's Son—
    As Daniel once in Babylon.
"Foe of the gods is Daniel!—
Hear thou, O king, thy folk complain—
He has destroyed the mighty Bel,
The priests, moreover, and the Dragon slain—
In wrath before thy throne
    Appears all Babylon.
If thou wilt from destruction fly,
This enemy of the gods must die.
The god he mocked can only be
By his death reconciled to thee."

Solo.
Thus before Pilate's judgment-seat,
The Council full of passion's heat
Come to demand Messiah's blood.

Oh! what has made them mad and blind?
And what has kindled in their mind
Of fury such a fiery flood?
'Tis envy—which no mercy knows,
In which hell's flame most fiercely glows—
    Lights this devouring fire.
All's sacrificed unto its lust—
Nothing too sacred, good, or just
    To fall to its desire.
Oh! woe to those whom passion sweeps
Helpless and bound into the deeps!

Chorus.
From envious thoughts depart!
O brethren mine! beware! beware!
And let this brood of vipers ne'er
    Be nested in your heart!

JESUS BEFORE PILATE.

THEN went the **High Priests** and the **Scribes**, together with the rulers and traders of the Temple, and the witnesses, to the house of **Pilate**. Jesus was led forth in front of them by **Balbus** and **Malchus** as before, Selpha being in command of the band of soldiers. As they went the soldiers shouted aloud, "Away with thee to death, thou false prophet! Ha! doth it dismay thee? that thou wilt not go forward?" "Drive him on," said Selpha. But Jesus, being weary, walked with slow footsteps. Then the soldiers thrust him forward, crying, "Shall we have to carry thee in our arms? Go on: thou hast not far to go, only to Calvary; there upon the cross thou canst rest in comfort!"

By this time they had approached the precincts of Pilate's house. Then said Caiaphas to the soldiers, "Be still; we have to announce our coming." And they were still. The **Rabbi** said, "Go to the door, and knock." It was done, and

JESUS BEFORE PILATE.—ACT XI., SC. 1. 83

RABBI ARCHELAUS.

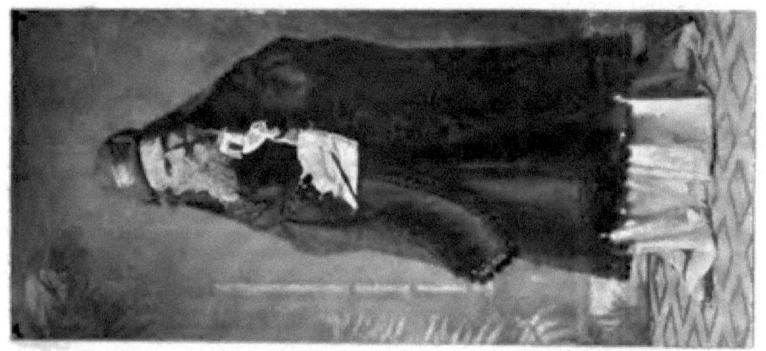

SAMUEL.

RABINTH.

MEMBERS OF THE SANHEDRIM.

Quintus. [*Tritt heraus.*] Was will denn diese Menge Leute hier?
Rabbi. Der hohe Rath hat sich allhier versammelt.
Quintus. Ich will sogleich es melden.
Rabbi. [*Zu den Rathsgliedern.*] Hört! er wird nicht säumen, unsere Gegenwart zu melden.
Kaiphas. Ihr Glieder des Hohen Rathes! Liegt euch unsere heilige Erblehre, unsere Ehre, die Ruhe des ganzen Landes, noch am Herzen, so bedenkt diesen Augenblick! Er entscheidet zwischen uns und jenem Verführer! Seid ihr Männer, in deren Adern noch der Vater Blut wallt, so hört uns! Ein unvergängliches Denkmal werdet ihr euch setzen! Seid fest in eurem Entschlusse!
Der Hohe Rath. Es leben unsere Väter, es sterbe der Feind unseres Volkes!
Kaiphas. Ruhet nicht, bis er aus dem Kreise der Lebenden hinausgetilgt ist!
Alle. Wir werden nicht ruhen!
Rotte. Hörst du, König, Prophet?

ZWEITE SZENE.

PILATUS *erscheint mit Gefolge auf seinem Balkon.*

Kaiphas. [*Sich verbeugend.*] Statthalter des grossen Kaisers zu Rom!
Alle. Heil und Segen dir!
Kaiphas. Wir haben einen Menschen, Namens Jesus, hieher vor deinen Richterstuhl gebracht, dass du das von dem Hohen Rathe über ihn gefällte Todesurtheil vollziehen lassen mögest.
Pilatus. Führt ihn vor! Welche Anklage habt ihr wider diesen Mann?
Kaiphas. Wenn er nicht ein grosser Uebelthäter wäre, so würden wir ihn dir nicht überliefert, sondern selbst ihn nach Vorschrift unseres Gesetzes abgestraft haben.
Pilatus. Nun—welcher Uebelthaten hat er sich schuldig gemacht?
Kaiphas. Er hat in vielfacher Weise das heilige Gesetz Israels schwer verletzt.
Pilatus. So nehmt ihn hin und richtet ihn nach eurem Gesetze!
Annas. Er ist bereits vom Synedrium gerichtet und des Todes schuldig erklärt worden.
Alle Priester. Denn nach unserem Gesetze hat er den Tod verdient.
Kaiphas. Es ist uns aber nicht erlaubt, das Todesurtheil an Jemandem zu vollziehen. Darum bringen wir die Bitte um Vollstreckung des Urtheils an den Statthalter des Kaisers.
Pilatus. Wie kann ich einen Menschen in den Tod hingeben, ohne dass ich sein Verbrechen kenne und ehe ich mich von der Todeswürdigkeit des Verbrechens überzeugt habe? Was hat er gethan?
Rabbi. Das Urtheil des Rathes wider diesen Menschen ward einstimmig ausgesprochen und auf genaue Untersuchung seiner Verbrechen gegründet. Es scheint daher nicht nothwendig, dass der erhabene Statthalter die Mühe einer nochmaligen Untersuchung auf sich nehme.
Pilatus. Wie? ihr wagt es, mir, dem Stellvertreter des Kaisers, zuzumuthen, dass ich euch ein blindes Werkzeug zur Vollführung eurer Beschlüsse sei? Das sei ferne von mir! Ich muss wissen, welches Gesetz, und in welcher Weise er es übertreten habe.
Kaiphas. Wir haben ein Gesetz und nach diesem Gesetz muss er sterben, denn er hat sich selbst zum Sohne Gottes gemacht.
Annas. Darum müssen wir darauf bestehen, dass er die gesetzliche Strafe des Todes erleide.
Pilatus. Um einer solchen Rede willen, die höchstens die Frucht einer schwärmerischen Einbildungskraft ist, kann ein Römer Niemanden des Todes schuldig finden. Wer weiss auch, ob nicht dieser Mann der Sohn irgend eines Gottes ist?—Habt ihr ihm kein anderes Verbrechen zur Last zu legen, so denket nicht daran, dass ich euer Verlangen erfüllen werde!
Kaiphas. Nicht bloss gegen unser heiliges Gesetz, sondern auch gegen den Kaiser selbst hat sich dieser Mensch schwerer Verbrechen schuldig gemacht. Wir haben ihn als einen Aufrührer und Volksverführer befunden.
Alle. Er ist ein Volksaufwiegler, ein Empörer!

Quintus came out, saying, "What does this crowd of people want here?" The Rabbi replied that the Council had assembled there. Quintus promised to announce them at once, and the Rabbi, turning to the members of the Sanhedrim, said, "Do you hear? He will announce our presence without delay." Caiaphas addressed those who were following him: "Ye members of the Sanhedrim, if you have at heart the holy traditions, our honour, the tranquillity of the whole land, then consider well this moment. It decides between us and that deceiver. If you are men in whom flows the blood of your fathers, then listen to us. An imperishable monument you will set up for yourselves. Be firm in your resolve." Then cried the priests, "Our fathers for ever! death to the enemy of the nation!" "Do not rest then," said Caiaphas, "until he is blotted out of the number of the living!" And they cried again, "We will not rest." Then the soldiers turned to Jesus and said, "Hearest thou that, O king and prophet?"

Then came Pilate out with his attendants upon the balcony of his house; three spearmen on either side advanced to the foot of the steps of the balcony, and stood spear in hand whilst the audience listed. Then Caiaphas stepped forward in front of the crowd, and, bowing low, thus began, "Governor and representative of the great Cæsar, health and blessing to thee." Then Caiaphas continued : "We have brought here before thy judgment-seat a man of the name of Jesus, that thou mayest consent to the execution of the death sentence pronounced against him by the Sanhedrim." Pilate answered, "Bring him forth!" And the soldiers led Jesus out before Pilate, so that he stood on the right hand of the judgment-seat. Pilate having looked upon him, asked, "What accusations have ye to bring against this man?" Caiaphas, speaking with some surprise, said, "If he were not a great malefactor, we would not have delivered him over to thee, but have dealt with him ourselves according to the direction of our holy law." "Well, of what evil deeds has he been guilty?" asked Pilate. Caiaphas answered, "He has in many ways grievously offended against the holy law of Israel." Pilate answered, "Then take him away and judge him according to your law." Then said Annas, "He has already been judged by the Sanhedrim, and has been declared to be guilty of death." Then all the priests cried aloud, "For according to our law he has deserved death." But Caiaphas explained, "It is not lawful for us to execute the sentence of death on anyone; therefore we bring the application for the execution of the sentence to the representative of Cæsar." Then Pilate, having looked upon Jesus and upon Caiaphas, asked with indignation, "How can I deliver a man over to death unless I know his crime, and before I have satisfied myself that the crime is worthy of death? What has he done?" Then said the Rabbi, "The sentence of the Council upon this man was unanimously pronounced, and grounded upon a careful investigation into his crimes. It seems therefore unnecessary that the illustrious Governor should take upon himself the trouble of a second investigation." "What!" said Pilate hotly, "do you dare to suggest to me, the representative of Cæsar, that I should be a blind instrument for the execution of your orders? Be that far from me! I must know what law he has broken, and in what way."

Caiaphas, Annas, and the members of the Sanhedrim waxed wroth and spoke warmly among themselves on hearing the words of Pilate. Caiaphas answered and said, "We have a law and by our law he ought to die because he made himself the Son of God;" and Annas added, "And upon that account we must insist that he suffers the legal punishment." Then Pilate said scornfully unto them, "On account of such a speech, which at the most is only the outcome of an enthusiastic imagination, a Roman can find no one guilty of death. Who knows also," he added, with a glance at Jesus, "whether this man may not be the son of some god! If you have no other crime to lay to his charge you need not think that I will fulfil your desire." Caiaphas answered and said, "Not only against our holy law but also against Cæsar himself has this man been guilty of serious offences. We have found him to be an insurgent and deceiver of the people." Then cried all the Priests and Pharisees, together tumultuously, "He is an agitator and a rebel." Pilate answered, "I have heard of one Jesus,"

JESUS BEFORE PILATE.—ACT XI., SC. 2.

HEROD.

PILATE.

Pilatus. Ich habe wohl von einem Jesus gehört, der im Lande herumziehe und lehre und ausserordentliche Thaten verrichte. Aber nie habe ich etwas von einem durch ihn erregten Aufruhr vernommen. Wäre etwas dergleichen vorgefallen, so würde ich es vor euch erfahren haben, der ich zur Handhabung der Ruhe im Lande aufgestellt und von Thun und Treiben der Juden ganz gut unterrichtet bin. Oder sagt: Wann und wo hat er einen Aufruhr erregt?

Nathanael. Er versammelt Volkeschaaren zu Tausenden um sich, und erst vor Kurzem hat er, von einer solchen Schaar umgeben, feierlichen Einzug in Jerusalem selbst gehalten.

Pilatus. Ich weiss es, aber es ist nichts Aufrührerisches dabei vorgefallen.

Kaiphas. Ist es nicht Aufruhr, wenn er dem Volke verbietet, dem Kaiser den Tribut zu entrichten.

Pilatus. Wo habt ihr Beweise?

Kaiphas. Beweise genug, da er sich für den Messias, den König Israels ausgiebt! Ist das nicht Aufforderung zum Abfall vom Kaiser?

Pilatus. Ich bewundere euren plötzlich erwachten Eifer für das Ansehen des Kaisers. [Zu Christus]: Hörst du, welche schwere Anklagen diese gegen dich vorbringen? Was antwortest du?

Christus. [Schweigt.]

Kaiphas. Sieh, er kann es nicht laugnen.

Priester. Sein Schweigen ist Eingeständniss seiner Verbrechen.

Alle. [Lärmend.] Verurtheile ihn also!

Pilatus. Geduld! Dazu ist noch Zeit. Ich will ihn allein in besonderes Verhör nehmen. [Zum Gefolge]: Vielleicht, wenn er nicht mehr durch die Menge und Hitze seiner Ankläger eingeschüchtert ist, giebt er mir Rede und Antwort. Man führe ihn in den Vorhof! [Zum Dienr.]: Gehe, mein Kriegsvolk soll ihn übernehmen. [Zu den Rathsgliedern]: Ihr aber überlegt nochmal den Grund oder Ungrund eurer Klagen und prüfet wohl, ob sie nicht etwa aus unlauterer Quelle kommen! Lasset mich dann eure Gesinnungen wissen. [Kehrt sich von ihnen.]

Rabbi. [Abziehend.] Das giebt eine verdriessliche Zögerung.

Kaiphas. Verliert den Muth nicht! Dem Standhaften gehört der Sieg. [Alle ab.

DRITTE SZENE.

Pilatus und Gefolge. Christus wird auf den Balkon gebracht.

Pilatus. [Zu Christus.] Du hast also die Klagen des Rathes über dich vernommen. Gieb mir hierüber Antwort! Du habest dich, sagen sie, einen Gottessohn genannt. Woher last du? [Christus schweigt.] Auch mit mir redest du nicht? Weisst du nicht, dass ich Macht habe, dich zu kreuzigen und Macht habe, dich loszugeben?

Christus. Du hättest keine Macht über mich, wenn sie dir nicht von oben herab gegeben wäre. Darum hat der, welcher mich dir überliefert, eine grössere Sünde.

Pilatus. [Für sich.] Ein freimüthiges Wort! [Zu Christus.] Bist du der König der Juden?

Christus. Fragst du mich dieses aus dir selbst, oder nur desshalb, weil es andere von mir gesagt haben?

Pilatus. Bin ich denn ein Jude? Dein Volk und die Priester haben dich mir überliefert. Sie beschuldigen dich, dass du habest der König Israels sein wollen. Was ist an der Sache?

Christus. Mein Reich ist nicht von dieser Welt. Wenn mein Reich von dieser Welt wäre, so würden ja meine Diener für mich gestritten haben, dass ich nicht in die Hände der Juden gekommen wäre. So aber ist mein Reich nicht von hier.

Pilatus. Du bist also doch ein König?

Christus. Du sagst es. Ich bin ein König. Ich bin dazu geboren und dazu in die Welt gekommen, dass ich der Wahrheit Zeugniss gebe. Wer immer aus der Wahrheit ist, der gehorchet meiner Stimme.

Pilatus. Was ist Wahrheit?

who was said to go about the country and teach and do extraordinary works, but I have never heard of any sedition stirred up by him. Were anything of that kind to happen I should have heard of it before you, who am appointed for the maintenance of peace in the land, and am perfectly well informed concerning the words and deeds of the Jews. But tell me, where and where has he stirred up any commotion?" Then **Nathanael** stood forward, and said unto **Pilate**, "He brings together multitudes by thousands around him, and he has, quite recently, surrounded by such a crowd, made a solemn entry into Jerusalem itself." "I know that," said **Pilate**, contemptuously, "but nothing took place on that occasion to disturb the public peace!"

By this time **Caiaphas** and the **Priests** were in a state of indignation which they did not care to conceal, and **Caiaphas** asked angrily, "Is it not sedition if he forbids the people to pay tribute to Cæsar?" **Pilate** asked, "Where have you proof of that?" "Proof enough," retorted **Caiaphas**, "for he gives himself out as the Messiah, the King of Israel. Is not that to challenge the imperial authority?" **Pilate** replied, sarcastically, "I admire your suddenly awakened zeal for the authority of Cæsar."

Then turning to **Jesus**, who had stood silent during the altercation, he asked him, saying, "Hearest thou what serious accusations these bring against thee? What answerest thou?" **Jesus** remained silent. "See," said **Caiaphas**, eagerly, "He cannot deny it. His silence is an admission of his crime." Then cried all the multitude, stretching out their hands towards **Pilate**, "Sentence him then!" "Patience," said **Pilate**, "There is time enough for that. I will take him apart for a private hearing."

Caiaphas turned his back upon **Pilate** and looked with indignation upon his followers, who showed the liveliest manifestations of disgust. **Pilate**, speaking to his attendants, said, "Perhaps, when he is no longer confused by the crowd and the fury of his accusers, he will answer me." Then speaking to his servants, he said, "Lead him into the court." And turning to **Caiaphas** and the Sanhedrim, he said, "Go! my guard shall take charge of him, but do you examine the justice or injustice of your complaints, and be careful to investigate whether they do not come from a somewhat polluted source. Then let me know the result of your reflection." The Jews, turning to go, angrily discussed this reverse. "This is a troublesome delay," said the **Rabbi**. But **Caiaphas** encouraged them, saying, "Do not lose heart, victory belongs to the steadfast."

Then was **Jesus** brought before Pilate's judgment seat, and **Pilate** said unto him, "Thou hast heard the complaint of the Council against thee. Give me an answer thereto. Thou hast, they say, called thyself a Son of God. Whence art thou?" But **Jesus** made no answer. Then **Pilate** said unto him with some surprise, "Dost thou not speak unto me? Knowest thou not that I have power to crucify thee and to release thee?"

Then **Jesus** turned to him and said, "Thou couldest have no power at all against me except it were given unto thee from above. Therefore he that delivereth me unto thee hath the greater sin." "Frankly spoken," said **Pilate** aside. Then speaking to Jesus, he said, "Art thou the King of the Jews?" **Jesus** answered, "Sayest thou this thing of thyself, or only because others have told it to thee?" **Pilate** answered, "Am I a Jew? Thine own nation and the chief priests have delivered thee unto me. They accuse thee that thou hast desired to be the King of Israel. What is it all about?"

Then answered **Jesus** unto him, and said, "My kingdom is not of this world. If my kingdom were of this world, then would my servants fight, so that I should not be delivered into the hands of the Jews; but now is my kingdom not from hence." Then said **Pilate**, "Art thou a king then?" **Jesus** answered, "Thou sayest it, I am a king. To this end was I born, and for this cause I came into the world, that I might bear witness unto the truth. Everyone that is of the truth heareth my voice." When **Pilate** heard this he said, "What is truth?"

VIERTE SZENE.

Ein Diener des Pilatus *tritt auf.*

Quintus. [*Schnell eintretend.*] Dein Diener Klaudius, o Herr, ist da. Er habe Dringendes dir mitzutheilen von deiner Ehegemahlin.

Pilatus. Lass ihn kommen! Den Mann hier führt einstweilen in die Halle! [*Zu* Klaudius, *der hereintritt, nachdem* Christus *abgeführt worden.*] Was bringst du von meiner lieben Gemahlin?

Diener. Herr, deine Gemahlin grüsst dich, und lasst dich an deines und ihres Wohles wegen herzlich bitten, du wolltest nichts zu schaffen haben mit jenem Gerechten, der vor deinem Richterstuhle angeklagt worden ist. Sie hat seinetwillen in verflossener Nacht durch ein furchtbares Traumbild Angst und Schrecken gelitten.

Pilatus. Gehe hin und melde ihr, sie möge ohne Kummer sein. Ich werde mich auf die Anträge der Juden nicht einlassen, sondern Alles aufbieten, ihn zu retten.

FÜNFTE SZENE.

Pilatus. [*Zu seinem Gefolge.*] Ich wollte, dass ich von diesem Handel nichts wüsste. Was haltet ihr, meine Freunde, von der Klage der Judenpriester?

1. **Hofherr.** Mir scheint, dass nur Neid und Eifersucht sie dazu getrieben haben. Der leidenschaftlichste Hass spricht aus ihren Worten, ihren Mienen.

2. **Hofherr.** Die Heuchler stellen sich, als ob ihnen das Ansehen des Kaisers am Herzen lage, während es ihnen nur um ihr eigenes Ansehen zu thun ist, welches sie durch diesen berühmten Volkslehrer gefährdet glauben.

Pilatus. Ich denke wie ihr. Ich kann nicht glauben, dass dieser Mann verbrecherische Pläne im Sinne führe. Er hat so viel Edles in seinen Gesichtszügen, in seinem Benehmen; auch seine Rede zeugt von so edlem Freimuthe und höherer Begabung, dass er mir vielmehr ein sehr weiser Mann zu sein scheint, vielleicht nur zu weise, als dass diese finstern Menschen das Licht seiner Weisheit ertragen könnten. — Und der schwere Traum meiner Gemahlin um seinetwillen? — Wenn er etwa wirklich höherer Abkunft wäre? — Nein! ich werde mich durchaus nicht herbeilassen, den Wünschen der Priesterschaft entgegen zu kommen. (*Zum Diener*); Lasse die Oberpriester nochmal hier erscheinen, — und der Beklagte werde wieder aus dem Richthause geführt. [*Diener ab.*

SECHSTE SZENE.

Vorige. Der Hohe Rath unter dem Balkon.

Pilatus. Hier habt ihr euren Gefangenen wieder. Er ist ohne Schuld.

Annas. Wir haben das Wort des Kaisers, dass unser Gesetz aufrecht erhalten werden soll. Wie kann Der ohne Schuld befunden werden, der dieses nämliche Gesetz mit Füssen tritt?

Alle. Des Todes ist er schuldig!

Kaiphas. Ist er nicht auch vor dem Kaiser strafbar, wenn er frevelnd das verletzt, was des Kaisers Wille uns gewährleistet hat?

Pilatus. Ich habe es euch gesagt. Hat er sich gegen euer Gesetz vergangen, so bestrafet ihn nach eurem Gesetze, in soweit ihr dazu befugt seid. Ich kann das Todesurtheil über ihn nicht aussprechen, weil ich nichts an ihm finde, was nach den Gesetzen, nach denen ich zu richten habe, den Tod verdiente.

Kaiphas. Wenn sich jemand zum Könige aufwirft, ist er nicht ein Empörer? Verdient er nicht die Strafe des Hochverrathes, die Todesstrafe?

Pilatus. Wenn dieser Mann sich einen König genannt hat, so berechtigt mich dieses vieldeutige Wort noch lange nicht, ihn zu verurtheilen. Bei uns wird öffentlich gelehrt, dass jeder Weise ein König sei. Thatsachen aber, dass er sich königliche Macht angemaßt habe, habt ihr nicht vorgebracht.

Nathanael. Ist es nicht Thatsache genug, wenn durch ihn das ganze Volk in Unruhe kommt, wenn er ganz Judäa mit seiner Lehre erfüllt von Galiläa an, wo er zuerst Anhänger gesammelt, bis hieher nach Jerusalem?

Pilatus. Ist er aus Galiläa gekommen?

Alle. Ja, ein Galiläer ist er.

Rabbi. Seine Heimath ist Nazareth, im Gebiete des Königs Herodes.

Hardly had he asked this question when the servant Quintus entered hastily from the door behind. "Lord! thy servant Claudius is here; he has to bring to thee a pressing message from thy wife." Pilate said, "Let him come in. Lead the man hence for a moment into the hall." The attendants having led Jesus out, Claudius entered. Pilate asked him, "What bringest thou from my dear spouse?" "My lord!" said Claudius, "thy wife greeteth thee and prays thee from her heart, for thine own sake and for hers, that thou wouldst have nothing to do with this just man who has been accused before thy judgment seat! She has suffered anguish and terror on his account last night owing to a fearful dream." Pilate answered, "Go back and tell her that she need not disturb herself. I will have nothing to do with the proposals of the Jews, but do all that I can to save him." Saluting Pilate, the messenger departed.

Pilate then said to his attendants, "Would that I had nothing to do with this business. What do you think, my friends, of the complaint of the Jewish priests?" Then said the courtier Mela, "It seems to me that they are only inspired by envy and jealousy. The most passionate hatred appears in their words and countenances." And the courtier Silvius added, "The hypocrites pretend that they have the authority of Cæsar at heart, whereas the matter only concerns their own authority, which they believe endangered by this famous teacher of the people." Pilate answered, "I agree with you. I cannot believe that this man entertains any criminal schemes in his mind. There is so much that is noble in his features and in his demeanour. His speech displays so noble a candour and such high natural gifts that he seemed much more to be a very wise man, perhaps only too wise for this benighted people to be able to bear the light of his countenance. And then the dream which troubled my wife on his account!—If he were really of higher origin? No," said Pilate, decidedly, arriving at a resolution, "I will not let myself be induced to comply with the wishes of the priests." Then ordered his servants saying, "Let the Chief Priests appear here again, and let the accused be led out again from the judgment hall."

Then came Caiaphas, Annas, and the chief priests, and the scribes and rulers of the people once more before Pilate to receive his decision. Then Pilate spoke unto them as follows, "Here you have your prisoner again, he is without guilt." Consternation and fury were displayed on the faces of all the Jews. Then Annas said, "We have Cæsar's word that our law shall be upheld. How can he be without guilt who treads this very law beneath his feet?" Then cried all the Council saying, "He is guilty of death." Caiaphas, who stood before the Council asked, "Is he not punishable by Cæsar when he maliciously injures that which Cæsar's will has guaranteed us?" Pilate said, "I have told you already, if he hath done anything against your law, then punish him according to your law, in so far as you are authorised so to do. I cannot pronounce the death sentence upon him, because I find nothing in him which, according to the laws upon which I have to act, is deserving of death."

Then were the Jews sorely troubled and muttered among themselves in hot displeasure, but Caiaphas replied, "If anyone proclaims himself as king is he not a rebel? Does he not deserve the death punishment of high treason?" "If," said Pilate, "this man has called himself a king it seems to me that so ambiguous a word is not sufficient to condemn him. For it is openly taught among the Romans that every wise man is a king. But you have brought forward no facts to prove that he has usurped kingly authority." Then said Nathanael, "Is it not a sufficient fact that through him the whole people is stirred up, when he fills the whole of Judea with his teaching, beginning from Galilee, where he first assembled his disciples, until here in Jerusalem." Then asked Pilate in surprise, "Has he come out of Galilee?" Then cried they all "Yes, he is a Galilean," and the Rabbi added, "His home is in Nazareth, in the juris-

Pilatus. Wenn das ist, so bin ich des Richteramtes überhoben. Herodes, der König von Galiläa ist auf das Fest hierher gekommen; er mag nun über seinen Unterthan richten. Nehmt ihn also fort und bringet ihn zu seinem Könige. Von meiner Leibwache soll er geführt werden!

[*Ab mit seinem Gefolge.*

Kaiphas. Auf denn zu Herodes! Bei ihm, der selbst sich zum Glauben unserer Väter bekennt, werden wir bessern Schutz finden für unser heiliges Gesetz.

Alle. (*Zu Christus.*) Eine Stunde früher oder später! Du musst doch d'ran! Heute noch!
[*Alle ab.*

XII. VORSTELLUNG.

Christus vor Herodes.

PROLOG.

Neue Schmach begegnet dem Liebevollsten
Vor Herodes, weil Er dem eitlen Fürsten
Nicht die Schergabe, nicht Wunderkräfte
  Schmeichelnd zur Schau tragt.

Deshalb wird der Weiseste von den Thoren
Als ein Thor behandelt, im weissen Kleide
Ausgestellt zur Schau für der Fürstenknechte
  Höhnende Kurzweil.

Samson, der gefürchtete Heldenjüngling,
Jetzt des Augenlichtes beraubt, gefesselt,
Steht, verlacht, verachtet ob seiner Schwäche,
  Vor den Philistern.

Doch, der schwach jetzt scheint, wird die Stärke zeigen;
Der erniedrigt steht, wird in Hoheit glänzen.
Ueber der Nichtswürdigen Spott erhalten
  Thronet die Tugend.

Chor.

Vergebens vor des Heidenrichters Schranken
  Der Hohepriester Hass die Flamme schürt,
Des Römers Sinn sie bringen nicht zum Wanken,
  Der Leidenschaft Getose ihn nicht rührt.

Solo.

Ein Wort — und man schleppt Jesum weiter
  Hin zu Herodes, ach!
Dem dünkt des Heilands Anblick heiter —
  Betrachtet diese neue Schmach!

Vorbild.

Der gefangene Samson muss den Philisterfürsten zu höhnender Kurzweil dienen.—Richt. 16, 25.

[Dieses Bild soll die Beschimpfung und Verspottung Christi vor Herodes vorstellen.]

Chor.

Seht Samson! Seht! die starke Hand —
Sie muss der Knechtschaft Fessel tragen!
Der Held, der Tausende geschlagen —
Er trägt des Sklaven Spottgewand!
Den Feinden einst so furchterlich
Dient er zu ihres Hohnes Ziele;
Philister brauchen ihn zum Spiele
Und freuen seiner Schwäche sich.

So steht auch Jesus, Gottes Sohn,
Zu stolzer Thoren Augenweide,
Geschmäht, verlacht im weissen Kleide,
Und überhauft mit Spott und Hohn.

HANDLUNG.

Herodes *behandelt* Christum *mit Spott und Hohn und sendet ihn zu* Pilatus *zurück.*

ERSTE SZENE.

Saal des Herodes.—Herodes. Naasson, Manasses, *Hofleute.* Zabulon, *Diener.*

Herodes. (*Im Herrintreten.*) Wie? den berühmten Mann von Nazareth, den bringen sie gefangen her zu mir?

diction of King Herod." "If that be so, then am I relieved of the jurisdiction. Herod, King of Galilee, has come hither for the feast; he can now judge his own subject. Take him away and bring him unto his own king. He shall be conducted thither by my body guard." Then Pilate, with his attendants, left the judgment hall. Caiaphas exclaimed, "Off then to Herod. With Herod, who professeth the faith of our fathers, we shall find better protection for our holy law." Then they cried to Christ, as they went off to the palace of Herod, "One hour sooner or later—what matters it?—thou must come to die! and this very day."

CHAPTER XII.

PROLOGUE.—Act XII.

Outrage now awaiteth the One most loving
In the presence of Herod, because He will not
Flatter kings vainglorious by displays of
  Signs and of wonders.

Thus the Wisest of all by fools is treated
As a fool, and mocked in white robes of honour—
Made a spectacle for the slaves of princes,—
  Evil-entreated.

Samson, in his young strength, the dread of the heathen—
Blinded now and weak, stands helpless and fettered,
Laughed at and despised and shorn of his glory
  'Fore the Philistines.

But He who now seems weak, will in strength be revealed;
He who stands abased will be raised in glory.
Goodness ever above the scorn of sinners
  Rises triumphant.

Chorus.

Before the Heathen's judgment-seat, in blind
  Fury, the priests stir up their passions hot.
They cannot change the Roman's steadfast mind,
  The din of stormy clamour moves him not.

Solo.

One word—they drag the Christ away
  To stand 'fore Herod's face,
Who thinks the sight a merry jest:—
  Behold this new disgrace!

[Tableau the seventeenth, which prefigures the contemptuous mockery of Christ by Herod, represents Samson avenging himself upon the Philistines by pulling down the temple upon their heads. The blinded giant strains at one of the two pillars on which the roof rests, breaking it asunder, and the company, arrested in their mirth, wait in horror to see their impending doom. The parallel in this case is between the mocking of Samson and the jeers to which Christ was subjected, and does not refer to the vengeance of the former upon the Philistines.]

Chorus.

Behold, how mighty Samson brave
  Is fettered by a coward crew.
The hero, who his thousands slew,
  Wears now the garments of a slave.
So dreadful, erst unto the foe,
  He makes Philistines sport to-day—
Serves them as pastime rare — and they
  Exult, for they his weakness know.

So Jesus, Son of God, doth stand,
  A mark for proud fools' scorn and spite,
Mocked in a royal robe of white,—
  Despised, abused, on every hand.

JESUS BEFORE HEROD.

King Herod stood beside his throne arrayed in scarlet robes, wearing a golden crown upon his head, and holding a golden sceptre in his hand. On either side were his courtiers. He said unto them, "What? have they the famous man from Nazareth?

JESUS BEFORE HEROD.—ACT XII., SC. 1.

Zabulon. Gewiss, o Herr! Ich habe ihn gesehen und auf den ersten Blick erkannt.
Herodes. Schon lange sehnte ich mich diesem Mann zu sehen, über dessen Thaten das ganze Land so laut spricht, dem das Volk, wie durch einen Zauberschlag gewonnen, zu Tausenden nachströmt. [Setzt sich.] Er wird wohl nicht der vom Tode erstandene Johannes sein?
Naasson. O nein! Johannes wirkte keine Wunder; von dem erzählt man aber Thaten sich, in Wahrheit wunderbar, wenn nicht die Sage vergrössert.
Herodes. Da ich ihn so unerwartet zu sehen bekomme, bin ich begierig seine Wunderkraft zu erproben.
Manasses. Sehr gerne wird er dich damit vergnügen, um Gunst und Schutz bei dir sich zu erwirken.
Herodes. [Zu Zabulon.] Sage der Priesterschaft sie möge nun mit dem Gefangenen herauf kommen. [Zabulon ab.
Manasses. Sie werden wohl mit Klagen kommen wider diesen Mann, da sie verlassen sind von allem Volke.
Herodes. In ihre frommen Zaukereien lasse ich mich nicht ein; nur sehen will ich ihn und seine angebliche Wundergabe prüfen.

ZWEITE SZENE.

Vorige. KAIPHAS, ANNAS, *Rabbi. Die vier Priester.*
CHRISTUS *von Soldaten des* HERODES *geführt.*

Kaiphas. O mächt'ger König!
Alle Priester. Heil und Segen dir von dem Allmächtigen!
Kaiphas. Vom hohen Rathe wird ein Verbrecher hier dir vorgeführt, dass du an ihm die Strafe des Gesetzes vollziehest.
Nathanael. Das Gesetz will seinen Tod.
Annas. Dem Könige gefalle es, das Urtheil der Synagoge zu genehmigen.
Herodes. Wie kann im fremden Land ich Richter sein? Geht zu eurem Statthalter! Der wird euch Recht sprechen.
Kaiphas. Pilatus schickt ihn hierher, weil er ein Galiläer, dein Unterg'b'ner ist.
Herodes. Ist dieser Mann aus meinem Gebiete? Wer ist er?
Priester. Jesus ist's, von Nazareth.
Kaiphas. D'rum sprach Pilatus selbst: Es möge der Gebieter Galiläa's das Urtheil sprechen seinem Unterthan.
Herodes. Dies sprach Pilatus? Sonderbar. [Zu den Hofherrn.] Pilatus sendet ihn zu mir? räumt mir das Richteramt in seinem Gebiete ein.
Naasson. Er will, so scheint es, dir sich wieder nahern.
Herodes. Es soll mir als Beweis seiner neuen Freundschaft gelten. [Zu Christus.] Vieles, sehr vieles habe ich von dir durch die Sage vernommen und lange so einen Mann, über den die Länder staunen, zu sehen gewunscht.
Rabbi. Ein Verführer ist er, ein Feind des heiligen Gesetzes.
Herodes. Ich habe gehört, dass du die Geheimnisse der Menschen durchschauest und Thaten verrichtest, welche die Grenzen der Natur überschreiten. Lass uns eine Probe, einen Beweis deiner Wissenschaft und hohen Kraft sehen,—wir wollen mit dem Volke dich ehren und an dich glauben.
Sadok. [Ironistisch.] O König! lass dich doch nicht irre führen! Er steht mit Belzebub im Einverständnisse!
Herodes. Das gilt mir gleich! How! Ich habe in vergangener Nacht einen sonderbaren Traum gehabt. Kunnst du mir sagen was mir getraumt hat so will ich dich als einen grundlichen Herzenskenner preisen. [CHRISTUS *schweigt.*] Sowrit blet du also nicht. Vielleicht aber verstehst du meinen Traum mir auszulegen wenn ich ihn dir offenbare. Mir träumte: Ich stand auf den Zinnen meines Palastes zu Machaerus und sah die Sonne untergehen. Da stand plötzlich ein Mann vor mir, der streckte seine Hand aus, und zeigte gegen Abend und sprach: Sieh dorthin! Dort in Hesperia ist dein Schlafgemach! Kaum hatte ers gesagt, nothm seine Gestalt in Nebel. Ich erschrack und erwachte.—Wenn du erleuchtet bist wie Joseph als er vor Aegypten König stand, so deute auch du deinem Könige diesen Traum. [CHRISTUS *sieht schweigend und wehmütigen Blicke ihn an.*] Bist du in diesem Fache nicht bewandert? Nun, so zeige uns deine viel gerühmte Wunderkraft. Mache, das es plötzlich finster werde in diesem Saale!—oder—erhebe dich und wandle von uns, ohne dass du den Boden berührest—oder—verwandle die Rolle

and are they bringing him a prisoner here to me?" "Yes, my lord," said Zabulon. "I saw him, and recognised him at the first glance." Then said Herod, "I have already for a long time desired to see this man, with whose wondrous works the whole land rings; to whom, as if by magic, people run in crowds. Can he be John, risen from the dead?" "Oh, no," said Naasson, "John worked no miracles; whereas they relate deeds done by this man which in truth are wonderful if they are not exaggerated." "As I have," said Herod, "so unexpected an opportunity of seeing him, I am impatient to put his magic skill to the proof." "He will be very willing," said Manasses, "to oblige you in that respect, in order to obtain your favour and protection." Then said Herod, who had seated himself, to Zabulon. "Tell the priesthood they may bring their prisoner in." "They are probably coming with complaints against this man," said Manasses, "as they are forsaken by all the people." Herod replied, "I do not enter into their pious quarrels. I will see him for myself, and test his alleged miraculous powers."

Then came into the presence of Herod, Caiaphas, Annas, the Rabbi, Nathanael, and four priests, bringing Jesus with them, led by the soldiers of Herod. Caiaphas bowed before King Herod, saying, "Most mighty king"; and all the priests cried. "Prosperity and blessing upon thee!" Then said Caiaphas, "A criminal is brought before thee here from the Sanhedrim, that thou mayest execute on him the judgment of the law." "The law," said Nathanael, "decrees his death;" and Annas added, "May it please the king to confirm the sentence of the Synagogue." But said Herod, "How can I be a judge in a foreign territory? Go to your own Governor; he will do justice." Then said Caiaphas, "Pilate sent him hither, because being a Galilean he is thy subject." "Then this man belongeth to my jurisdiction? Who is he?" The priests said, "Jesus of Nazareth." Caiaphas added, "Pilate said that the ruler of Galilee must himself pronounce sentence upon his own subject." "Did Pilate say that? Wonderful!" said Herod. And turning to his courtiers he remarked, "Pilate sends him to me! Allows me to act as judge in his own province!" A courtier replied "It seems as if he wished to make approaches to thee again." Herod replied, "I will accept it as a proof of his friendly feeling." Then turning to Jesus Herod said, "I have heard very much of thee by common report, and have longed to see the man who has created such a sensation in the country." "He is a deceiver," said the Rabbi; "an enemy of the holy law." "I have heard," said Herod, taking no notice of the interruption, "that thou canst interpret all mysteries and achieve feats which set at defiance the laws of nature. Let us have an example of the skill and mighty power, then we will honour thee like the people, and believe on thee." "O king," said Zadok, "do not let him lead thee astray, for he is in league with Beelzebub!" "That is all the same to me," said Herod. Then, addressing Jesus, he said, "I have had last night a wonderful dream. If thou canst tell me what I have dreamed I will esteem thee as a first-class reader of hearts." Herod paused, but Christ remained motionless and silent. "Thou canst not do so much as that," continued Herod, "but, perhaps thou understandest how to explain the dream if I tell thee what it was. I dreamt I stood upon the battlements of my palace at Machaerus and saw the sun go down. There stood suddenly a man, who stretched out his hand and pointed to the setting sun and said, 'See there, there in Hesperia is thy bedchamber.' Hardly had he said this when he vanished away in a cloud. I started and woke up. If thou desirest to be like Joseph when he stood before the king of Egypt, interpret to thy king this dream." Christ remained silent looking sadly at Herod. "Art thou not experienced in this branch of the business? Well then, show some of thy famous magic art. Cause it suddenly to become dark in this hall, or raise thyself and depart from us without touching the ground, or convert the roll on which thy death sentence is written, into a

dort, die dein Todesurtheil enthält, in eine Schlange!—Du willst nicht? Oder du kannst nicht? das sollte dir ein Leichtes sein; man erzählt sich ja viel grössere Wunderwerke von dir: [Zu den Hofherrn.] Er regt sich nicht. Ei! ich sehe wohl: die Sage die von ihm so viel Rühmens macht, ist eitler Volksgeschwätz. Er weiss und kann nichts.

Naasson. Leicht ist's, dem Volke etwas vorzuspiegeln. Ein Anderes ist, zu stehen vor dem weisen, dem mächt'gen Könige.

Manasses. Ist an Dir etwas? Warum verstummst denn Deine Weisheit hier? Warum zerrinnt vor Deines Königs Augen, wie eine Seifenblase, deine Macht?

Herodes. Es ist nichts an ihm. Er ist ein thörichter Mensch, den des Volkes Beifall toll gemacht hat. [Zu den Priestern.] Den lasst ihr laufen? Er ist nicht werth, dass ihr um seinetwillen euch Mühe macht.

Kaiphas. O König! traue nicht! Er ist ein Schalk, schlau und verschlagen. Ja, er stellt sich nur als einen Thoren, um ein milderes Urtheil von dir zu erschleichen.

Annas. Wird er nicht hinweggeschafft, so steht auch die Person des Königs in Gefahr; denn dieser hat sich erfrecht, zum Könige sich aufzuwerfen.

Herodes. Dieser zu einem König?—zum Narrenkönig.—Das ist glaubwürdiger.—Als solcher verdient er, anerkannt zu werden. Drum will ich ihm einen Königsmantel zum Geschenk machen und selbst ihn formlich zum König aller Thoren einsetzen. [Winkt einem Diener.

Alle Priester. Nicht dies, den Tod hat er verdient!

Kaiphas. O König! Beschützer unsrer heiligen Gesetze! Gedenke deiner Pflicht, den Uebertreter zu strafen, wie es das Gesetz verordnet.

Herodes. Was habt ihr denn eigentlich wider ihn?

Rabbi. Den Tag des Herrn hat er verletzt.

Nathanael. Er ist ein Gotteslästerer.

Alle Priester. Als solchen spricht ihn also das Gesetz des Todes schuldig.

Ezechiel. Er hat verächtungsvoll auch von dem Tempel gesprochen, den dein Vater uns so herrlich erneuerte; er hat erklärt, er wolle an dessen Statt wohl einen schöner bauen und in drei Tagen!

Herodes. [Lachend.] Nun, da hat er sich ganz ausgewiesen als der Narrenkönig.

Josue. Von dir auch selbst hat schmählich er gesprochen. O frecher Wort! Er hat sich unterstanden, dich, seinen Herrn und König, einen Fuchs zu schelten!

Herodes. Da hat er mir eine Eigenschaft beigelegt, die ihm selbst gänzlich abgeht. [Diener kommt mit dem Mantel.] Bekleidet ihn! So soll er vor dem Volke seine Rolle spielen.

Zabulon. [Nachdem er Christus bekleidet hat.] Jetzt wirst Du erst ein rechtes Aufseh'n machen, du grosser Wunderthäter!

Priester. Sterben soll er!

Herodes. Nein, das Blut eines so erhabenen Königs will ich mich nicht schuldig machen. In diesem seiner würdigen Anzuge führt ihn dem Volke vor, dass es ihn nach Herzenslust bewundere, bis es sich an ihm satt gesehen hat.

Erster Soldat. So komme, Du Wunderkönig, und erlaube uns, dich zu begleiten!

Zweiter Soldat. Welches Glück für mich, dem hohen Herrn zur Seite hinzuschreiten! [Sie führen Christus ab.

DRITTE SZENE.

Die Vorigen—ohne CHRISTUS *und die Soldaten.*

Kaiphas. Du hast nun selbst dich überzeugt, o König, dass seine Werke Lug und Trug nur sind, wodurch das Volk von ihm bethöret wird. Thu' also deinen Ausspruch!

Alle Priester. Sprich das Urtheil des Todes über ihn, wie das Gesetz verlangt!

Herodes. Mein Ausspruch ist. Er ist ein einfältiger Mensch und der Verbrechen gar nicht fähig, deren ihr ihn anklagt. Hat er vielleicht etwas Gesetzwidriges gethan oder gesprochen, so ist das seiner Einfalt zuzurechnen.

Kaiphas. O König! habe Acht, dass du nicht irrest!

Annas. Ich fürchte, du wirst selbst es noch bereuen, wenn du so ungestraft ihn jetzt entlassest.

Herodes. Ich fürchte nichts. Einen Thoren muss man nur als einen Thoren behandeln. Er hat jetzt seine Thorheiten

snake. Thou wilt not, or thou canst not? Any of these things ought to be easy to thee; they relate much more wondrous miracles of thine." Then turning to his courtiers Herod said, "He does not stir. Ah! I see well that what has made him so notorious was only idle tittle tattle. He knows nothing and can do nothing." "It is easy," said Naasson, "to make believe before the people; it is another thing to stand before a wise and powerful king." Then said Manasses to Jesus. "Why should you not display your wisdom here? Why should your power vanish before the eyes of the king, even as a soap bubble?" Then said Herod scornfully, "There is nothing remarkable about him. He is a foolish fellow, whom the applause of the people hath made crazy. Let him go. It is not worth while making so much trouble on his account." "O king!" said Caiaphas, "deceive thyself not; he is a sly and crafty rogue. Indeed, he only makes himself out to be a fool in order to obtain a milder sentence from thee." Annas said, "If he be not put away then would the peace of the kingdom also stand in danger, for he has presumed to exalt himself to be king." "What!" said Herod, "to be a king! To be a king of fools, that is more credible. As such he deserves to receive homage, therefore will I give him as a present a king's mantle, and so formally install him as the king of all fools." Then cried the priests aloud, "Not this: he has deserved death." Caiaphas said, "O king, preserver of our holy law, remember thy duty to punish the transgressor as the law ordains." Then said Herod, "What have you really against him?" "He hath profaned the Sabbath," said the Rabbi. Nathanael added, "He is a blasphemer." And all the priests cried, "And as such the law declares him guilty of death." Then said Ezekiel, "He has also spoken contemptuously of the Temple, which thy father so gloriously rebuilt; he has declared that he would build a more beautiful one in three days." Then Herod laughed and said, "Now, that proves indeed that he is a king of fools." Then said Josue, "He has also spoken insultingly of thee. He has presumed to call thee, his lord and king, a fox." "Then he has attributed to me a quality which he cannot certainly claim himself," replied Herod. "Clothe him, so that he may play his part before the people."

Then came in a servant bringing a white robe, which he put on the shoulders of Jesus, and after Jesus had been robed, Zabulon said to him, "Now, for the first time, thou wilt create a real sensation, thou great wonder worker." The priests cried, "He must die!" Herod said, "No, I will not be guilty of the blood of so exalted a king; rather lead him forth before the people in this his proper apparel, that they may admire him to their heart's content." Then said the first soldier to Jesus, "Come, thou miraculous king, and allow us to accompany thee." The second soldier said, "What good luck for me to walk by the side of so illustrious a lord," and so saying they led away Jesus wearing the white robe which Herod had put upon him.

Then said Caiaphas, "Thou hast convinced thyself that his works were nothing but lies and deceit, whereby the people were defrauded by him. Give them thy sentence." And all the priests cried, "Pronounce the sentence of death upon him, as the law demands." Herod replied, "My opinion is, he is a simple fellow, and not capable of the crime of which you accuse him. If he has, perchance, done or spoken anything against the law it is to be attributed to his simplicity." "O king," said Caiaphas, "take care that thou dost not err!"

"I fear," said Annas, "thou wilt repent if thou allowest him to escape punishment." "I fear nothing of the kind,"

geblüst und wird sie sich für die Zukunft vergehen lassen. Somit ist das Gericht zu Ende.
 Rabbi. Ach! So ist es um Gesetz, Religion, um Moses und Propheten ganz geschehen!
 Herodes. Es bleibt bei meinem Spruch. Ich bin ermüdet und will mich mit der Gewissheit nicht weiter befassen. Pilatus mag nach seiner Amtspflicht entscheiden. Entbietet ihm Gruss und Freundschaft vom König Herodes. [*Die Priester ab.*

VIERTE SZENE.
HERODES. NAAMON. MANASSES.

Herodes. (*Von seinem Sitze heraltretend.*) Diessmal hat der Erfolg unseren Erwartungen durchaus nicht entsprochen. Ich versprach mir den angenehmsten Genuss von weiss Gott was für Wunderstücken und Redekünsten; und wir sehen einen ganz gewöhnlichen Menschen, und hören keinen Laut aus seinem Munde.
 Manasses. Wie doch die Sage auszumalen weiss, was in der Nähe als ein Nichts erscheint!
 Herodes. Freunde! dieser ist Johannes nicht. Johannes redete doch und redete mit einer Weisheit und Kunst, die man achten musste. Dieser aber ist noch stumm wie ein Fisch. Ich denke um so weniger daran ihn aus dem Wege zu schaffen, da ich ihn nun selbst gesehen habe. Pilatus würde ihm mir auch nicht zugesendet haben, wenn man ihn eines gegründeten Staatsverbrechens schuldig befunden hätte. Sich an einem solchen Menschen . . . . wäre die grösste Thorheit. Doch haben wir uns lange genug mit diesem lästigen Handel abgegeben. Lasst uns gehen! Wir wollen uns für die verlorene Zeit durch eine angenehme Unterhaltung zu entschädigen suchen.

XIII. VORSTELLUNG.
Die Geisslung und Dornenkrönung.
PROLOG.

Ach, welcher Anblick, ewig beweinenswerth
Dem Jünger Christi, stellt sich den Augen dar!
   Der Leib des Herrn ringsum verwundet
    Von den unzähligen Geisselstreichen!
Sein Haupt umhüllt vom spitzigen Stachelkranz!
Blutriefend, kaum noch kenntlich, sein Angesicht!
   Wem sollte da nicht eine Thräne
    Innigen Mitleids vom Auge quellen?
Als Vater Jakob sah seines Lieblings
Von Blut getränktes Kleid, wie erbebte er!
   Wie weinte er, voll Schmerz ausrufend
    Herzendurchdringende Jammerlaute!
Lasst uns auch weinen, da wir den göttlichen
Freund unserer Seele Solches erdulden seh'n!
   Denn leider! unsre, unsre Sünden
    Haben sein liebendes Herz verwundet.

Solo.

Sie haben noch nicht ausgewüthet;
   Nicht ist der Rache Durst gestillt.
Nur über Mordgedanken brütet,
   Die Schaar, von Satans Grimm erfüllt.

Chor.

Kann diese harten Herzen nichts erweichen?
Auch nicht ein Leib, zerfleischt von Geisselstreichen?
   Mit Wunden ohne Zahl bedeckt?
   Ist nichts, was noch ihr Mitleid weckt?

VORBILD.

1. Josephs Rock mit Blut besprengt.—1 Mos 37, 31.

[Christus wird am ganzen Leibe grausam durch die Geisselstreiche zugerichtet und mit Blut gefärbt. Isaak ist das Vorbild des leidenden und sterbenden Messias. Isaak ein Kind der Verheissung, der einzige Sohn Abrahams, trägt selbst das Holz, auf dem er geopfert werden sollte, den Berg Moria hinauf. Jesus, gleichfalls das Kind so vieler Verheissungen und der einzige Sohn Gottes, trägt das Kreuz den Kalvarienberg hinauf, der nach einer alten Ueberlieferung der Berg Moria, oder doch ein Theil desselben Höhenzuges war. An Isaaks Statt wird ein Widder geopfert, um anzudeuten, dass Christus wirklich sein Blut vergiessen solle, nachdem ihm die schmerzliche Krone von Dornen aufgesetzt.]

said Herod. "A fool one must treat as a fool. He has already suffered for his follies, and will avoid them in the future. With that, the trial is at an end."
 Then said the Rabbi, "Then it is all over with our law, our religion, Moses and the prophets!" Herod said, "I abide by my decision. I am weary, and will not concern myself further about the affair. Pilate may decide according to his official duty. Offer to him greeting and friendship from king Herod."
 Then went the priests out sorely dissatisfied with the decision of the king. Then Herod rose from his seat and said, "This time the result has not corresponded to our expectations. I expected to find a great wonder worker and eloquent orator, and behold, there is only quite an ordinary man with never a word to say for himself." "Ah!" said Manasses, "how lying rumour exaggerates, that which, when more closely examined, is shown to be nothing." "Friends," said Herod, "that is not John; John at least spoke, and spoke with wisdom, and an eloquence which one must esteem, but this one is as dumb as a fish. I am less than ever purposed to put him out of the way, now that I have seen him for myself. Pilate would not have sent him to me if he had been found guilty of any serious crime against the state. To make a to-do about such a man would be the greatest folly. We have occupied ourselves about this wearisome business long enough. Let us now go, and make up for lost time by seeking more agreeable amusement."

CHAPTER XIII.
PROLOGUE.—ACT XIII.

Oh! what a sight, for ever to be mourned
By Christ's disciples, here doth meet our eyes!
   The body of the Lord is wounded
    All over with countless strokes of scourges.

His head, surrounded by the sharp crown of thorns;
His face we scarcely know, sprinkled with drops of blood.
   Where is the eye that would not
    Shed a tear of compassion?

When father Jacob his dear one's raiment beheld,
All torn and stained with blood, how trembled he then!
   How wept he, uttering in his anguish
    Cries that might pierce the hardest heart.

Let us also weep, when we see the Divine One,
Friend of our souls, enduring such cruel torment.
   Alas! 'tis our own transgressions
    That have wounded His loving heart.

Solo.

Not yet the host have raged their fill,
   Not yet for vengeance slaked their thirst,—
On thoughts of murder brooding still,
   And full of Satan's wrath accursed.

Chorus.

Can nothing melt their hearts for evermore?
The body, marred with stripes and bruises sore—
   With wounds unnumbered—
   Is all compassion dead?

[The eighteenth and nineteenth tableaux precede the Scourging. The former represents the bringing of Joseph's coat, all steeped in blood, to the patriarch Jacob; the latter the sacrifice of Isaac. Joseph's coat is not very bloody. His father's distress is very vividly expressed. Isaac lies on Mount Moriah, a black-haired, curly-headed youth—boy or girl it was difficult to make out—while Abraham, who is just about to slay him with a bright falchion, is restrained by an angel, who points to a ram in a thicket.]

THE SCOURGING AND CROWN OF THORNS.—ACT XIII., SC. 2.

O welche schauderrolle Scene!
Seht Josephs Rock mit Blut besprengt!
Und an den Wangen Jakobs hängt
Der tiefsten Leides heisse Thräne.

Wo ist mein Joseph, meine Freude,
Auf dem des Alter's Hoffnung ruht?
Ach wehe! Es klebet Josephs Blut,
Des Kindes, an diesem Kleide!

Solo.

Ein wildes Thier hat ihn zerrissen,
Zerrissen meinen Liebling! Ach!
Dir will ich nach, dir, Joseph, nach!
Hier kann kein Trost mein Leid versüssen.
So jammert er, so klaget er.
Und Joseph, Joseph ist nicht mehr.

Chor.

So wird auch Jesu Leib zerrissen
Mit wilder Wuth.
So wird sein kostbar Blut
In Strömen aus den Wunden fliessen.

1. Der zum Opfer bestimmte Widder im Dornengesträuche verwickelt.
1 Mos. 22, 13.

Choragus.—*Recit.*

Abraham! Abraham! tödt ihn nicht!
Dein Glaube hat—so spricht
Jehova—ihn, den einzigen, gegeben,
Er soll nun wieder dir zum Volksglücke leben.

Solo.

Und Abram sah im Dorngesträuch
Verwickelt einen Widder steh'n;
Er nahm und opferte sogleich
Ihn, von Jehova auserseh'n.

Tenor.

Ein gross Geheimniss zeigt das Bild,
Im heil'gen Dunkel noch verhüllt.
Wie dieses Opfer einst auf Moria,
Steht Jesus bald gekrönt mit Dornen da.
Der Dornbekrönte wird für uns sein Leben,
Wie es der Vater will, zum Opfer geben.

Chor.

Wo trifft man eine Liebe an,
Die dieser Liebe gleichen kann?

HANDLUNG.

CHRISTUS *wird nochmal dem* PILATUS *vorgeführt; dieser schlägt die Auswahl zwischen* CHRISTUS *und* BARABBAS *vor und lässt* JESUM *geisseln.*

ERSTE SZENE.

KAIPHAS, ANNAS, *der Hohe Rath, die Händler und Zeugen erscheinen mit dem von Soldaten geführten* CHRISTUS *abermals vor* PILATUS' *Hause.*

Kaiphas. Nun müssen wir desto ungestümer den Pilatus auffordern, und wenn er nicht nach unserem Willen richtet, so soll ihm des Kaisers Ansehn den Ausspruch abzwingen.

Annas. Sollte ich noch in meinem grauen Alter die Synagoge stürzen sehen? Aber nein! Mit stammelnder Zunge will ich Blut und Tod über diesen Verbrecher ausrufen, und dann in die Gruft der Väter herabsteigen, wenn ich dieses Bösewicht am Kreuz erblasst gesehen.

Rabbi. Eher wollen wir uns unter den Ruinen des Tempels begraben lassen, als von unserem Beschluss abgehen.

Pharisäer. Man lasse nicht nach, bis er des Todes ist.

Kaiphas. Wer nicht bei diesem Entschluss verharrt, der sei aus der Synagoge verstossen!

Annas. Den treffe der Fluch der Väter!

Kaiphas. Die Zeit drängt, der Tag rückt vor. Jetzt müssen alle Hebel in Bewegung gesetzt werden, damit heute noch, vor dem Feste, unser Wille geschehe.

ZWEITE SZENE.

PILATUS *erscheint mit Gefolge auf dem Balkon.*

Kaiphas. Den Gefangenen bringen wir nochmals vor deinen Richterstuhl, und fordern nun mit Ernst seinen Tod.

Oh! what a scene of horror here!
See Joseph's coat, with blood besprent!
Down Jacob's cheek, with suffering spent,
Flows deepest sorrow's bitter tear.

Where is my Joseph—all my joy—
On whom the old man's hope did rest?
Alas! there's blood upon this vest,
The life-blood of my boy!

Solo.

Ah me! a raging beast has slain,
Has torn my dearest one.
After thee, Joseph, I will run!
No comfort here can ease my pain.
So mourns the father o'er and o'er,
And Joseph, Joseph is no more!

Chorus.

Thus, too, these fiends Christ's body tear,
In raging mood:—
His precious blood
Flows streaming from the deep wounds there.

Choragus.

Abraham! Abraham! do not slay!
Thy faith was great enough to-day,
To God thy son, thine only son to give,
For joy of all the nations he shall live.

Solo.

And Abraham saw a ram
Caught in a thicket there,
He took and sacrificed the same,
As did the Lord declare.

Tenor.

This picture shows a mystery great,
In sacred darkness shrouded yet.
Like to this offering on Moriah found,
Even so, the Christ shall soon with thorns be crowned.
The Thorn-crowned One, as wills the Father, thus
Shall yield His life a ransom up for us.

Chorus.

Where can we find a love that is
As great as this dear love of His?

THE SCOURGING AND CROWN OF THORNS.

CAIAPHAS and ANNAS and the chief priests and the rulers and the Council and the traders of the Temple and the witnesses accompanied the soldiers who once more led Jesus to Pilate's house. Then said Caiaphas, "Now Pilate must be challenged more imperiously; and if he does not do according to our will, then shall the authority of Cæsar extort the sentence from him." "Shall I now," said Annas, "in my grey old age see the Synagogue overthrown? No! with stammering tongue I will call for the blood and death of this criminal, and then descend to the bosom of my fathers, when I have seen this evildoer die upon the cross." "We would sooner," cried the Rabbi, speaking with great animation, "be buried in the ruins of the Temple than go back upon our resolution. We shall never leave off until he is dead." Then proclaimed Caiaphas. "Whoever goes back upon this decision, let him be cast out of the Synagogue." And Annas added, "Let the curse of the Fathers fall upon him." Then said Caiaphas, "Time presses, the day is advancing; now we must employ all the means at our disposal in order to carry out our will b fore the Feast." All this time the Jews and the soldiers leading Jesus, stood once more before the house of Pilate.

Pilate, attended by his servants, soon appeared on the balcony. "We bring the prisoner once more before thee and earnestly desire his death," said Caiaphas. All the Priests cried aloud,

Die Priester und Pharisäer. Wir beharren darauf! Er soll sterben.
Pilatus. Ihr brachtet mir diesen Menschen als einen Volksaufwiegler. Und sehet! Ich habe eure Klagen vernommen; ich habe ihn selbst verhört und an ihm nichts von dem gefunden, weswegen ihr ihn anklagt.
Kaiphas. Wir bleiben bei unserer Anklage. Er ist ein des Todes würdiger Verbrecher!
Die Priester. Ein Verbrecher gegen unser Gesetz und gegen den Kaiser.
Pilatus. Ich habe ihn, weil er ein Galiläer ist, zu Herodes geschickt. Habt ihr eure Klagen dort vorgebracht?
Kaiphas. Ja. Herodes wollte aber nicht richten, weil du hier zu befehlen hast.
Pilatus. Auch er hat nichts an ihm gefunden, was den Tod verdiente. Ich will also diesen Mann, um doch eurem Verlangen entgegen zu kommen, mit Geisselstreichen züchtigen lassen, dann aber ihn losgeben.
Annas. Das genügt nicht!
Kaiphas. Das Gesetz spricht über solche Verbrecher nicht die Strafe der Geisselung aus, sondern die Strafe des Todes.
Die Priester. In den Tod mit ihm!
Pilatus. Ist euer Hass gegen diesen Mann so tief und bitter, dass er selbst durch das Blut aus seinen Wunden nicht ersättigt werden kann? Ihr zwingt mich, euch offen zu sagen, was ich denke. Von unedler Leidenschaft getrieben, verfolgt ihr ihn, weil das Volk ihm mehr zugethan ist als euch. Ich habe eurer gehässigen Klagen genug gehört, ich will nun die Stimme des Volkes hören! Es wird ohnehin bald zahlreiches Volk sich hier versammeln, um nach altem Herkommen einen der Gefangenen zur Feier des Osterfestes loszubitten. Da wird es sich zeigen, ob eure Klagen der Ausdruck der Volksgesinnung oder nur eurer persönlichen Rache seien.
Kaiphas. [Sich verbeugend.] Es wird sich zeigen, o Statthalter, dass du mit Unrecht Böses von uns denkst.
Priester. Wahrlich, nicht Rachsucht, sondern der heilige Eifer für Gottes Gesetz ist es, was uns antreibt, seinen Tod zu begehren.
Pilatus. Ihr wisset von dem Mörder Barabbas, der in Ketten liegt, und von seinen Schandthaten. Zwischen dem und zwischen Jesus von Nazareth werde ich dem Volke die Wahl lassen. Welchen es freibitten wird, den werde ich freigeben.
Alle. Den Barabbas gieb los, und diesen da an's Kreuz!
Pilatus. Ihr seid nicht das Volk, das Volk wird sich aussprechen. Indessen will ich diesen zuchtigen lassen. [Zum Diener.] Die Soldaten sollen ihn fortführen, und nach römischem Gesetze geisseln. [Zu seiner Umgebung.] Was er etwa gefehlt hat, wird dadurch hinlänglich gebüsst, und vielleicht mildert der Anblick des Gegeisselten die blinde Wuth seiner Feinde! [Mit dem Gefolge ab.

DRITTE SZENE.
Die Priesterschaft, &c., unter dem leeren Balkon.

Kaiphas. Pilatus beruft sich auf die Stimme des Volkes. Wohlan, auch wir berufen uns darauf! [Zu den Händlern und Zeugen]. Jetzt wackere Israeliten, ist eure Zeit gekommen! Gehet hin in die Gassen Jerusalems, fordert eure Freunde auf, herbeizukommen. Vereinigt sie zu geschlossenen Schaaren! Entzündet sie zum glühendsten Hasse gegen den Feind Mosis! Die Wankelmüthigen sucht zu gewinnen durch die Kraft eures Wortes, durch Versprechungen. Die Anhänger des Galiläers aber schüchtert ein durch verdutes Geschrei wider sie, durch Schimpf und Spott, durch Drohungen, und wenn es sein muss, durch Misshandlungen, dass keiner es wage, sich hier blicken zu lassen, viel weniger seinen Mund zu öffnen!
Händler und Zeugen. Wir eilen hin und kommen bald wieder, jeder an der Spitze einer begeisterten Schaar.
Kaiphas. In der Synedriumsgasse kommen wir alle zusammen. [Die Händler ab. Die Priester rufen ihnen nach:] Heil euch, treue Jünger Mosis!"]
Kaiphas. Lasst uns nun keinen Augenblick säumen! Gehen wir den Schaaren entgegen, sie zu ermuntern, zu entflammen!
Annas. Aus allen Gassen Jerusalems wollen wir dann das aufgebrachte Volk vor das Richthaus führen.

"We insist upon it, he must die." Then said Pilate, "Ye brought me this man as an agitator; and see! I have heard your complaints, and I have myself examined him, and have not found anything in him touching those things whereof you accuse him." Then said Caiaphas, angrily, "We abide by our accusation; he is a criminal worthy of death." And the Priests cried, clamorously, "He is an offender against our law and against Cæsar." Then said Pilate, "I have sent him, because he is a Galilean, to Herod. Have you brought forward your complaints before him?" "Yes," said Caiaphas, "but Herod would not judge the case because thou art in authority here." Then said Pilate, "He has found nothing in the man that deserves death, but in order to meet your desire I will have this man scourged and let him go." But Annas said, "That sufficeth not," and Caiaphas said, "The law prescribes for such a criminal not the punishment of scourging, but the punishment of death." The Priests cried again, "To death with him!"

Then Pilate, hearing the clamour of the Jews, and seeing how bitter they were against Jesus, said unto them, "Is your hate so deep and bitter unto this man that it can not even be satisfied by the blood from his wounds? You compel me to tell you frankly what I think. Driven by ignoble passion ye persecute him because the people follow him more than they do you. I have heard enough of your hateful accusations. I will now hear the voice of the people. An innumerable number will soon assemble here in order to demand, according to old custom, the release of one prisoner at the Passover Festival. Then it will be seen whether your complaint is the outcome of popular sentiment or only of your personal revenge." Caiaphas, smiling to himself, bowed low before Pilate and said, "The result will show, O Governor, that thou thinkest evil of us unjustly." Then the Priests cried, "It is not vengeance but zeal for the holy law of God which compels us to demand his death." Pilate said, "You know of the murderer, Barabbas, who lies in chains, and of his evil deeds. Between him and Jesus of Nazareth I will let the people choose. The one whom they ask for, him will I release." Then cried all with one voice, "Release Barabbas, and to the cross with the other!" "You are not the people," said Pilate, haughtily, "the people will speak for themselves. Meanwhile I will have this one scourged." Then, speaking to his servants, he said, "The soldiers will lead him hence and scourge him according to the Roman law." Then turning to his courtiers, he said, "Whatever he has done amiss will be sufficiently atoned for, and perhaps the spectacle of the scourging may soften the blind wrath of his enemies."

When Pilate quitted the balcony and entered his house, Caiaphas addressed a stirring speech to the Jews. His opportunity had come. "Pilate," said Caiaphas, "appeals to the voice of the people. All right; we appeal to it also. Now," said he, turning to the Traders and Witnesses, "now, true-hearted Israelites, your opportunity has arrived. Go hence into the streets of Jerusalem, summon your friends to come hither, unite them in masses, kindle in them the most glowing hatred against the enemy of Moses. The waverers seek to win by the strength of your words and by promises, but terrify the followers of the Galilean by an overwhelming outcry against them, by insult and mockery, by threats, and if necessary by ill-treatment, so that none of them may dare to let himself be seen here, much less to open his mouth." Then cried the traders and witnesses together, "We will go hence and soon return again, everyone at the head of an excited mob." Caiaphas said, "Let us all meet in the street of the Sanhedrim." The traders bowed, and as they went the priests cried after them, "Hail to you, faithful disciples of Moses." Then said Caiaphas, "Let us not lose a single moment. Let us go together to the crowds to encourage them, to inflame them." Annas added, "From all the streets of Jerusalem will we lead the exasperated

THE SCOURGING AND CROWN OF THORNS.—ACT XIII., SC. 3.

THE CROWN OF THORNS.

Rabbi. Weil Pilatus die Stimme des Volkes hören will, so höre er sie!
Kaiphas. Er höre den einstimmigen Ruf der Nation: Den Barabbas los, den Galiläer an's Kreuz!
Alle. Barabbas los, den Galiläer an's Kreuz!   [Ab.

VIERTE SCENE.

CHRISTUS *entkleidet und die Hände an eine niedere Säule gebunden, um ihn her die Kriegsknechte.*

Die Kriegsknechte. [*Abwechselnd.*] Jetzt hat er genug; er ist ganz mit Blut überronnen.—Du erbarmungswerther Judenkönig!—Aber was ist das für ein König? Führt kein Scepter in der Hand, keine Krone auf dem Haupte?—Da lässt sich helfen. Ich will sogleich die Insignien des Judenreiches herbeiholen. [*Kommt mit einem rothen Mantel, der Dornenkrone und dem Schilfrohr.*] Hier! Das ist gewiss ein allerliebster Schmuck für einen Judenkönig! Nicht wahr, eine solche Ehre hattest du nicht erwartet?—Komm, lass' dir den Purpurmantel umhängen, aber setze dich, ein König soll nicht stehn. Und hier, eine herrliche, ausgezackte Krone! [*Setzen sie ihm auf.*] Lass' dich anseh'n! [*Gelächter.*] Damit sie ihm aber nicht vom Haupte falle, muss man sie ihm fest aufsetzen. Nehmt Brüder, helft mir! [*Vier Knechte fassen an den Enden von zwei Stäben an und drücken die Krone fest.* CHRISTUS *zuckt schmerzlich.*] Hier das Scepter!—Jetzt geht dir nichts mehr ab.—Welch ein König! [*Knieen vor ihm nieder.*] Sei gegrüsst, grossmächtigster König der Juden!

Diener des Pilatus. [*Eintretend.*] Der Gefangene soll sogleich in's Richthaus gebracht werden.

Kriegsknechte. Du kommst zur Unzeit. Du hast uns mitten in unsern Ehrfurchtsbezeugungen gestört. Erhebe dich! Man wird dich zur Schau herumführen. Das wird ein Jubel unter dem Judenvolke sein, wenn sein König in vollster Pracht vor ihm erscheint!   [*Ab mit* JESUS.

XIV. VORSTELLUNG.

JESUS zum Kreuzestode verurtheilt.
PROLOG.

Eine Jammergestalt steht der Erlöser da.
Selbst vom Mitleid gerührt stellt ihn Pilatus vor.
　Hast denn du kein Erbarmen,
　O betörtes, verführtes Volk?

Nein! von Wahnsinn erfasst, ruft es: An's Kreuz mit ihm!
Schreit nach Marter und Tod über den Heiligsten.
　Für Barabbas, den Mörder,
　Fordert es die Begnadigung!

O wie anders stand einst vor dem Aegyptervolk
Joseph! Freudengesang, Jubel umtönte ihn;
　Als der Heiland Aegyptens
　Ward er feierlich vorgestellt.

Ihn, den Heiland der Welt, aber umtobt mit Wuth
Ein verblendetes Volk, ruhet und rastet nicht.
　Bis unwillig der Richter
　Spricht: so nehmt ihn und kreuzigt ihn!

VORBILDER.
Solo.

Ach! seht den König! seht zum Hohne
Gekrönt ihn, ach! mit welcher Krone!
Und welch ein Scepter in der Hand!
Mit Purpur seht ihr ihn behangen.
Zu Henkers Lust in Fetzen prang'n.
　Ist das des Königs Festgewand?
Wo ist an ihm der Gottheit Spur?
　Ach! welch ein Mensch!
　Ein Spiel der rohen Henker nur.

---

people before the judgment seat." The Rabbi said, complacently, "Since Pilate wishes to hear the voice of the people, let him hear it!" "Let him hear," said Caiaphas, "the unanimous cry of the nation: Release Barabbas; the Galilean to the cross!" Then all the Jews cried aloud, with an exceeding loud voice, "Release Barabbas, the Galilean to the cross!"

Then the soldiers led Jesus away to the pretorium, and took off his robe, and tied his hands to a low pillar and scourged him. When they were weary with scourging they said, "He has had enough, he is all running down with blood." "Thou pitiable King of the Jews!" said one of the soldiers, "what kind of a king can this be? he has no sceptre in his hand, no crown upon his head. That can be mended, I will at once bring the insignia of the Jewish sovereignty!" And then, going out, he brought a scarlet mantle, a crown of thorns, and a reed. They were laid upon a cushion, and together with these were laid iron gloves so that they might handle the crown of thorns without suffering therefrom. "Here," cried they, "this is certainly the most lovely attire for a King of the Jews. Is it not true that thou hast never expected such an honour? Come, let us hang this purple robe about thee! But sit down, a king should not stand. Here is a beautiful, pointed crown." And a soldier taking the crown of thorns with the iron gloves placed it upon the head of Jesus. "Let us look at you!" Then they laughed aloud for joy. "But," said one, "if it is not to fall off your head thou must we set it on firmly. Come brother-help me." Then four of the soldiers seized in their hands two staves, and crossing them over his head, pressed the crown heavily down upon the brow of Jesus. Jesus shuddered in agony. "Here," cried the soldiers, "is the sceptre!" And taking the reed they placed it in his hands. "Now nothing more is wanted. What a king!" Then all knelt before him, crying, "Hail to thee, most mighty king of the Jews!" When they were mocking him a servant entered from Pilate, saying that the prisoner must be brought immediately into the judgment hall. Then said the soldiers, "Thou comest at the wrong time. Thou hast disturbed us in the middle of our demonstrations of reverence." Then they said to Jesus, "Stand up, we will lend thee about us a spectacle. There will be rejoicing among the Jewish people when their king appears before them in full splendour!"

CHAPTER XIV.

PROLOGUE.—ACT XIV.

See! what form of woe standeth the Saviour there.
Even Pilate himself's touched with compassion now.
　Foolish people and blinded,
　Have ye no hearts to pity him?

No! for, seized with madness, they cry, "To the Cross with Him!"
Cry for torture and death upon the Holiest,
　For Barabbas, the murderer,
　Pardon asking, and liberty.

Oh! how otherwise once 'fore the Egyptian folk
Joseph!—Around him shouts echoed, and songs of joy,
　As the saviour of Egypt
　He was solemnly shown to them.

But round the World's Deliverer rages a nation in wrath,
Blinded, maddened with hate, no man among them will rest
　Till the judge, all unwilling,
　Says, "Then take ye, and crucify Him!"

Solo.

Ah! see the king that's crowned in scorn!
What monarch such a crown has worn,
　Or sceptre borne—and He so great?
Ye see Him decked with purple shreds;
They laugh and jeer and shake their heads:
　Is this the royal robe of state?
Where is the trace of Deity?
　Ah! what a man,—
　The sport of the rude hangmen he.

1. Joseph wird als Landesvater dem Volke vorgestellt.—1 Mos. 41, 41.

[Wie Josef aus dem Kerker befreit und auf den Thron Aegyptens erhöht wird als der Retter seines Landes, so entsteigt Jesus dem Grabe und bewahrt sich als Heiland der ganzen Welt. Oder auch: Christus in der Gestalt eines schmerzhaften Königs wird allem Volke vorgestellt. Das Bild erinnert daran wie die Juden den Mörder Barabbas dem Heilande vorzogen.]

Chor.
Seht! welch ein Mensch!
Pilatus ruft mitleidig aus:
  "Seht, welch ein Mensch!"
Vor Joseph tönt's im Jubelbrans.
Laut soll es durch Aegypten schallen:
  "Es lebe Joseph—ihm sei Ehr!"
Und tausendfach soll's widerhallen!
Aegyptens Vater, Schirm und Wehr!
Und alles stimme, gross und klein,
In unsern frohen Jubel ein!

Solo.
Die Augen alle auf dich schauen,
  Als Retter dich Aegypten preist.
Auf dir ruht Hoffnung und Vertrauen,
  Dir Huldigung das Land erweist.
Laut soll es durch Aegypten schallen (wie oben).

2. Loosung über die zwei Böcke, von denen der eine entlassen, der andere für die Sünden des Volkes geschlachtet wird.—3. Mos. 16, 7.

Solo.
Des alten Bundes Opfer dies,
Wie es Jehova bringen hiess,
Zwei Böcke werden vorgestellt,
Darüber dann das Loos gefällt,
Wen sich Jehova auserwählt.

Chor.
Jehova, durch das Opferblut
Sei Deinem Volke wieder gut!

Solo.
Das Blut der Böcke will der Herr
Im neuen Bunde nimmermehr.
Ein Lamm, von aller Makel rein,

Chor.
Muss dieses Bundes Opfer sein;
Den Eingebornen will der Herr;
Bald kommt, bald fällt, bald blutet er.
Ich höre schon das Mordgeschrei:

Volk [hinter dem Vorhang].
"Barabbas sei
Von Banden frei!"

Chor.
Nein! Jesus sei
Von Banden frei!
Wild tönt, ach! der Mörder Stimm':

Volk.
"An's Kreuz mit ihm!
An's Kreuz mit ihm!"

Chor.
Ach, seht ihn an!
Ach, seht ihn an!
Was hat denn Böses Er gethan?

Volk.
Entlässest du den Bösewicht,
So bist des Kaisers Freund du nicht.

Chor.
Jerusalem! Jerusalem!
Das Blut des Sohnes rächet noch an euch der Herr!

Volk.
"Es falle über uns und unsre Kinder her!"

Chor.
Es komme über euch und eure Kinder!

[The scene in which Christ is sentenced to death is prefaced by two tableaux. The first represents Joseph acclaimed as Grand Vizier of Pharaoh. The stage is filled with a bright spirited multitude of acclaiming beholders. The tableau is unquestionably vivid, but as a preface to the Death Sentence it is somewhat out of place. More appropriate, although scenically less telling, is the Choice of the Scapegoat, which is represented as taking place in the Temple, before an interested crowd of spectators.]

Chorus.
See! what a man!
  Cries Pilate, pitying,
See! what a man!
The joyous shouts 'fore Joseph ring,
Through Egypt's realms loud let them sound,
  "May Joseph live! be he adored!"
And thousand-fold re-echo round,
O Egypt's father, shield and lord!
And let all folk both great and small
Join in our joyous festival.

Solo.
The eyes of Egypt rest upon thee,
  As saviour thee shall Egypt praise;
The people's hope and trust hast won thee,
  The land her grateful homage pays.

Through Egypt's realms, &c.

Solo.
This is the covenant-sacrifice
Jehovah hath ordained of old:
Two goats are chosen from the fold,
And 'twixt those two, the priest, by voice
Of lot, decides Jehovah's choice.

Chorus.
O Lord! through this our Victim's blood,
Forgive Thy people—Thou art good!

Solo.
The blood of goats no more will He.
In this new cov'nant there shall be
A lamb from every blemish pure.

Chorus.
And that shall be the Victim sure,
  The Lord hath called His only-born—
Soon He shall come, fall, bleed forlorn;
I hear the shouts of cruelty.

People.
Barabbas be
From fetters free!

Chorus.
May Jesus be
From fetters free!
How fiercely sounds the murderers' voice!

People.
To the cross with Him!
To the cross with Him!

Chorus.
Ah! look on Him!
Ah! look on Him!
What evil hath He done?

People.
If thou dost let this wretch depart,
Cæsar's friend no more thou art.

Chorus.
Jerusalem! Jerusalem!
The Lord will yet avenge Messiah's blood on thee!

People.
Upon us and upon our children let it be!

Chorus.
Yes! let it come upon you and your children!

HANDLUNG.

PILATUS *stellt den geguisselten und gekrönten* CHRISTUS *dem Volke vor; — dieses verlangt die Freilassung des* BARABBAS *und den Tod Christi.* — *Die Standhaftigkeit des* PILATUS *wird durch Drohungen erschüttert; — er gibt die Unschuld* JESU *nochmal Zeugniss, und spricht* BARABBAS *frei und über* JESUS *das Todesurtheil.*

ERSTE SZENE.

Nathanael. Moses, euer Prophet, fordert euch auf! Zur Rache ruft euch sein heiliges Gesetz!

Volk I. Wir gehören Moses an! Wir sind und bleiben Bekenner Mosis und seiner Lehre!

Volk III. Wir halten uns an unsere Priester und Lehrer. Fort mit ihm, der sich gegen sie erhebt!

Volk IV. Ihr seid unsere Väter! Für eure Ehre stehen wir ein.

Annas. Kommt, Kinder, werft euch in die Arme des heiligen Synedriums! Es wird euch retten.

Ezechiel. Schüttelt es ab, schüttelt es ab, das Joch des Verführers!

Volk II. Wir wollen nichts mehr wissen von ihm! Euch folgen wir!

Volk III. Das ganze Volk ruft euch Beifall zu!

Volk IV. Wir wollen frei sein von dem falschen Lehrer, dem Nazarener!

Die vier Anführer. Eurer Väter Gott wird euch wieder aufnehmen, ihr seid ihm wieder ein heiliges Volk!

Alles Volk. Ihr seid unsere wahren Freunde. Es lebe das hohe Synedrium! Es leben unsere Lehrer und Priester!

Annas. Und der Galiläer sterbe!

Kaiphas. Auf, lasst uns hineilen zu Pilatus!

Ezechiel *und* Nathanael. Seinen Tod, sein Blut lasst uns fordern!

Alles Volk. Fort zu Pilatus! Der Nazarener soll sterben!

Die Führer. Er hat das Gesetz verfälscht! Er hat Moses und die Propheten verachtet. Er hat Gott gelästert!

Alles Volk. In den Tod mit dem falschen Propheten!

Volk II. In den Kreuzestod!

Volk II *und* III. Pilatus muss ihn kreuzigen lassen!

Die Führer. Am Kreuze soll er seine Frevel büssen!

Volk III *und* IV. Wir ruhen nicht, bis das Urtheil gesprochen ist. [*Die ganze Masse ist jetzt in Vordergrunde.*]

Kaiphas. [*Das Volk mit Blick und Geberde beherrschend.*] Heil euch, Kinder Israels! Ja, ihr seid noch die echten Nachkommen eures Vaters Abraham! O frohlocket, dass ihr dem namenlosen Verderben entronnen seid, dass dieser Betrüger über euch und eure Kinder bringen wollte!

Annas. [KAIPHAS *zur seite.*] Nur das rastlose Bestreben eurer Väter hat die Nation vor dem Abgrunde bewahrt!

Alles Volk. Es lebe der Hohe Rath, es sterbe der Nazarener!

Priester *und* Pharisäer. Fluch ihm, der zu seinem Tode nicht stimmt!

Volk. Wir fordern seinen Tod.

Kaiphas. Ausgestossen aus dem Erbrechte unserer Väter sei er!

"JESUS OR BARABBAS?"

THEN was Jerusalem in an uproar; the traders and the priests ran everywhere hither and thither, stirring up the people against Jesus. On all sides mustered the crowds, and, directed by the priests to assemble in the street of the Sanhedrim, and from this to proceed to Pilate's house to demand the release of Barabbas and the crucifixion of Jesus, from four sides the tumultuous mobs came pouring down to the place of assembly. Their hoarse cries of "To the cross with him! to the cross with him!" were heard in the distance before the foremost leaders came in sight. At the head of one mob came Nathanael, fervently exhorting the multitude to demand the death of Jesus. "Moses and the prophets," said he, "call upon you. His holy law demands that you should avenge it." And the multitude cried together, "We belong to Moses. We are and remain followers of Moses and of his teaching. We hold fast by our priests and teachers. Away with him who would rise against them!" The multitude poured down from the right into the central thoroughfare. Caiaphas was leading them, proudly exulting in the manifestations of their zeal. Into the same central place came a third band, led by Annas, whose followers shouted aloud, "Ye are our fathers, we will answer for your honour!" Annas answered, "Come, children, throw yourselves into the arms of the holy Sanhedrim. It will save you." While the clamorous multitudes from these three quarters were pouring down confusedly into the main street, the shouting of a fourth mob was heard down Pilate's street. Ezekiel marched at the head of this new company, crying "Shake it off; the yoke of the deceiver!" and they cried in answer, "We will have nothing more to do with him; we follow you!" As the four contingents of the populace collected thus in the open space it could be seen how successfully they had been organized. Each of the four divisions was led by a ruler of the people, and had in its ranks a number of the traders of the Temple, the witnesses and the priests whose violent zeal gave movement and direction to the whole crowd. Various cries burst forth from the multitude, and each section as it saw the strength of the others exulted and greeted their leaders with shouts of joy. "The whole people applauds you!" "We will be free from that false teacher the Nazarene!" answered another section of the crowd. Then Caiaphas, Annas, Nathanael and Ezekiel, meeting together, cried with a loud voice, "Your fathers' God will receive you again! You are again to him a holy people!" The crowd, now massed together in the main street, cried, "You are our true friends! Long live the great Sanhedrim! Long live our teachers and priests!" and Annas answered, "Death to the Galilean!" "Up!" said Caiaphas, "let us now hasten to Pilate," and Nathanael and Ezekiel added, "Let us demand his death, his blood!" Then all the people answered, "On to Pilate; the Nazarene shall die!" As they came trooping forward their leaders addressed them from time to time to incite their zeal. "He hath falsified the law!" cried the leaders. "He has contemned Moses and the prophets! He hath blasphemed God!" Then all the people cried again, "To death with the false prophet!" The section led by Ezekiel shouted, "Death by the cross!" and the other sections took it up: "Pilate must let him be crucified!" Then said the leaders, "On the cross he shall atone for his crimes!" "We will not rest," cried the crowd, "until his sentence is pronounced." The whole multitude had now arrayed themselves before the judgment seat of Pilate. Caiaphas, who lorded it over the whole assemblage with look and gesture, thus addressed them: "Hail to you, children of Israel! You are indeed still true descendants of your father Abraham! Oh, rejoice that you have escaped the nameless destruction which this deceiver would bring upon you and your children!" "Only," said Annas, "by the untiring efforts of your fathers has the nation escaped the abyss." Then cried the people, "Long live the Council! Death to the Nazarene!" and the priests and Pharisees cried out, "Curse him who does not vote for his death!" The people responded, "We demand his death!"

Then for some time there was nothing heard but a confused clamour, but the voice of Caiaphas rang out notwithstanding, while the people responded to his appeals. It sounded from afar in this wise: Caiaphas: "Let him be cast out from

JESUS OR BARABBAS?—ACT. XIV., SC. 1.

99

BARABBAS.

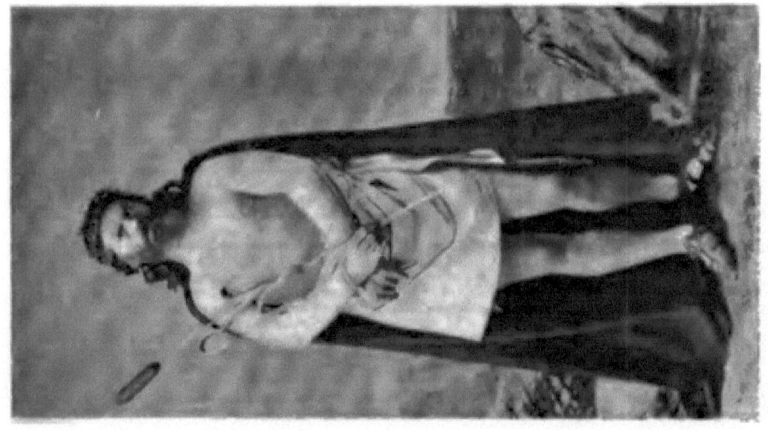

"ECCE HOMO."

Volk. Er sei ausgestossen!
Kaiphas. Der Statthalter wird euch die Wahl geben zwischen diesem Gotteslästerer und dem Barabbas. Lasst uns auf der Loslassung des Barabbas bestehen!
Volk. Barabbas werde frei, der Nazarener gehe zu Grunde!
Annas. Seid gepriesen, ihr Väter, ihr habt unsere Wünsche erhört.
Alle. Pilatus muss einwilligen. Die ganze Nation fordert ihn auf.
Kaiphas. Schönster Tag des Volkes Israel! Kinder, seid standhaft!
Priester und Pharisäer. Dieser Tag giebt der Synagoge die Ehre, dem Volk die Freiheit zurück.
Kaiphas. [Dem Hause des Pilatus näherstretend.] Fordert mit Ungestüm das Urtheil, droht mit einer allgemeinen Empörung!
Alle. [Tumultuarisch.] Das Blut unseres Feindes fordern wir!
Diener des Pilatus. [Aus dem Hause stürzend.] Aufruhr, Empörung!
Volk. Der Nazarener soll sterben!
Kaiphas. Zeiget Muth! Unerschrocken harret aus, die gerechte Sache schützet uns.
Alle. Pilatus, spreche das Todesurtheil!
Diener. [Vom Balkon.] Stille, Ruhe!
Alle. Nein, wir ruhen nicht, bis Pilatus einwilligt!
Diener. Pilatus wird sogleich erscheinen. [Ab.
Alle. Den Tod des Nazareners fordern wir.
Kaiphas. [Zu den Priestern.] Nun möge Pilatus, wie er es gewünscht, die Gesinnung des Volkes kennen lernen!

ZWEITE SZENE.

Die Vorigen. PILATUS *mit Gefolge und mit dem dornengekrönten* CHRISTUS, *den zwei Soldaten führen, auf dem Balkon.*

Alle. Richte! Urtheile über ihn!
Pilatus. [Auf JESUM hinweisend.] Seht, welch ein Mensch!
Priester und Pharisäer. An's Kreuz mit ihm!
Pilatus. Kann selbst dieser bedauernswerthe Anblick eurem Herzen kein Mitleid abgewinnen?
Alle. Er sterbe! An's Kreuz mit ihm!
Kiaphas. Herr, o Statthalter, die Stimme des Volkes! Sich, es stimmt in unsere Klagen ein und fordert seinen Tod.
Volk. Ja, wir verlangen seinen Tod!
Pilatus. [Zu den Soldaten.] Führt ihn hinab. Und Barabbas werde aus dem Gefängnisse hieher gebracht! Der Kerkermeister soll ihn sogleich an den Oberlictor ausliefern.
Annas. Barabbas lebe! Ueber den Nazarener sprich das Todesurtheil!
Volk. Zum Tode mit dem Nazarener!
Pilatus. Ich verstehe dieses Volk nicht. Vor wenigen Tagen habt ihr, jubelnd und Beifall zujauchzend, diesen Mann durch die Gassen Jerusalems begleitet. Ist es möglich, dass heute dasselbe Volk Tod und Verderben über ihn rufe? Das ist verachtungswürdiger Wankelmuth!
Kaiphas. Das gute Volk hat es endlich einsehen gelernt, dass es von einem Abenteurer betrogen worden, der sich angemasst hat, sich den Messias, den König Israels zu nennen.
Nathanael. Jetzt sind diesem Volke die Augen vollends aufgegangen, da es sieht, wie er sich selbst nicht helfen kann, er, der Freiheit und Heil der Nation zu bringen versprach!
Ezechiel. Israel will keinen Messias, der sich fangen und binden und allen Spott mit sich treiben lässt!
Volk. Er sterbe, der falsche Messias, der Betrüger!
Pilatus. Männer des Judenvolkes! Es ist Gewohnheit, dass ich euch auf das Fest einen Gefangenen losgebe. Seht nun diese Beiden an! Der Eine — sanften Blickes, würdevollen Benehmens, das Bild eines weisen Lehrers, als den ihr ihn lange verehrt habt, keiner einzigen bösen That überwiesen, und bereits durch die empfindlichste Züchtigung gedemüthigt! Der Andere — ein hässlicher, verwilderter Mensch, ein überwiesener Räuber und Mörder, das gräuliche Bild eines vollendeten Bösewichtes! Ich berufe mich auf eure Vernunft, auf euer Menschengefühl! Wählet! Welchen wollt ihr, dass ich euch losgeben soll, den Barabbas oder Jesum, der Christus genannt wird?
Priester und Volk. Barabbas werde frei!

---

the heritage of our fathers," and all the people cried, "Let him be cast out." Caiaphas said, "The Governor will give you the choice between this blasphemer and Barabbas. Let us insist upon the release of Barabbas." Then the people cried, "Let Barabbas go free, and down with the Nazarene." Then said Annas, "Let the fathers be praised who have heard our wishes." Then all cried out, "Pilate must consent, the whole nation demands it of him." Caiaphas, walking backwards and forwards with excited mien but proud and triumphant step, said, "Oh, most glorious day of the people of Israel! Children, be steadfast!" The priests and Pharisees: "This day brings back honour to the Synagogue and freedom to the people." "Now," said Caiaphas, as they approached the house of Pilate, "let us demand the sentence with uproar and threaten him with universal revolt!" Then cried the whole multitude tumultuously, "We demand the blood of our enemy!" So loud was the cry, so savage its emphasis, that two servants of Pilate started out of the house, and, looking down on the turbulent throng, cried out, "Uproar! insurrection!" And the people answered, "The Nazarene shall die!" Caiaphas hastening hither and thither in the crowd to excite them to still further violence, said, "Show courage. Stand out undismayed. A righteous cause defends us." Then the people called out clamorously, "Pilate! pronounce the sentence of death!" Pilate's servants from the balcony said, "Silence! be quiet," but the crowd shouted at him louder than before. "No, we will not be quiet until Pilate consents." Then said the servant, "Pilate will come out immediately." Then cried all once more, "We demand the death of the Nazarene." And Caiaphas, listening to the shouts of the people, said to the priests, "Now let Pilate, as he wished, learn the opinion of the people!"

Then came Pilate with his followers out upon the balcony, and with them came Jesus led by two soldiers, with the crown of thorns upon his head and the scarlet robe about him. The crowd, instead of shouting, "Hail, all hail," as before, shouted violently, "Give judgment! Pass sentence upon him!"

Then Pilate spoke, pointing to Jesus, who, with bound hands and the scarlet robe upon his bleeding shoulders, stood between the soldiers, "Behold the man." The priests and Pharisees answered, "To the cross with him." Pilate pleaded, "Cannot even this pitiful sight awaken any compassion in your hearts?" But the multitude answered, "Let him die! To the cross with him!"

Then Caiaphas said with a loud voice, "Hear, O governor, the voice of the people. It concurs in our complaint, and demands his death." "Yes," shouted the crowd again, "we demand his death." Then said Pilate to his soldiers: "Lead him down, and let Barabbas be brought out of prison. The gaoler must at once deliver him up to the chief lictor." When Annas heard Pilate's command, he cried: "Let Barabbas live! Pronounce the death sentence on the Nazarene!" Then the people cried again: "To death with the Nazarene!" Then said Pilate: "I do not understand this people. Only a few days ago, with rejoicing and joyful clamour, you accompanied this man through the streets of Jerusalem. Is it possible that the same people this day call for death and destruction upon him? That is indeed contemptible fickleness." "The good people," said Caiaphas, "have at last learned that they have been deceived by an adventurer, who pretended to be the Messiah, the king of Israel!" "And now," said Nathanael, "the eyes of this people are fully opened, and they see that he cannot help himself—he who promised to bring freedom and blessing to the nation." "Israel," said Ezekiel, "will recognise no Messiah who allowshimself to be taken and bound and treated with scorn." "Let him die, the false Messiah, the deceiver!" cried the crowd.

Then Pilate spoke unto the people, and said: "Men of Judea! it is customary that I liberate to you a prisoner at the feast. Look upon these two. One with mild countenance and dignified demeanour, the ideal of a wise teacher, whom you have long honoured as such, convicted of no single evil deed and already humiliated by the severest chastisement. The other, a vicious, savage man, convicted of robbery and murder, a horrible image of a perfect scoundrel. I appeal to your reason, to your human feelings—choose! Which will ye that I shall release unto you, Barabbas or Jesus, who is called the Christ?" Then the priests and people cried out together:

Pilatus. Wollt ihr nicht, dass ich euch den König der Juden losgebe?

Priester und Volk. Hinweg mit diesem, den Barabbas gieb uns los!

Kaiphas. Du hast versprochen, Den frei zu geben, den das Volk verlangen würde.

Pilatus. [Zu KAIPHAS.] Ich bin gewohnt, mein Versprechen zu halten, ohne einer Mahnung zu bedürfen. [Zum Volke.] Was soll ich denn mit dem Könige der Juden thun?

Priester und Volk. Kreuzige ihn!

Pilatus. Wie? Euren König soll ich an's Kreuz schlagen?

Volk. Wir haben keinen König, als allein den Kaiser.

Pilatus. Ich kann diesen Mann nicht verurtheilen, denn ich finde kein Verbrechen an ihm. Er ist gezüchtigt genug, ich will ihn loslassen.

Priester. Wenn du diesen loslässest, so bist du nicht der Freund des Kaisers.

Kaiphas. Er hat sich zum König aufgeworfen.

Priester. Und wer sich zum Könige aufwirft, ist ein Rebell gegen den Kaiser.

Nathanael. Und dieser Rebell soll ungestraft bleiben, um noch fernerhin den Samen der Empörung auszutreten?

Volk. Es ist die Pflicht des Statthalters, ihn aus dem Wege zu schaffen.

Kaiphas. Wir haben unsere Pflicht als Unterthanen des Kaisers gethan, und diesen Empörer dir überliefert. Wenn du unsere Anklage und des Volkes Verlangen nicht beachtest, so sind wir frei von Schuld. Du allein, o Statthalter, bist dann dem Kaiser für die Folgen verantwortlich.

Annas. Wenn um dieses Menschen willen allgemeine Unruhe und Empörung entsteht, so wissen wir, wer die Schuld daran trägt, und auch der Kaiser wird es erfahren.

Volk. Die Sache muss vor den Kaiser gebracht werden.

Ezechiel. Mit Staunen wird man es in Rom vernehmen, dass des Kaisers Statthalter einen Hochverräther in Schutz genommen, dessen Tod das ganze Volk verlangte.

Volk. Du musst ihn hinrichten lassen, sonst wird keine Ruhe im Lande.

Pilatus. Was hat er denn Böses gethan? Ich kann und darf den Schuldlosen nicht zum Tode verdammen!

Kaiphas. Es sei mir eine Frage erlaubt. Warum richtest du diesen so ängstlich, da du doch neulich Hunderte wegen einigen aufrührerischen Geschreies ohne Gericht und Urtheil hast durch deine Soldaten hinmorden lassen. [PILATUS bestürzt.]

Volk. Du darfst auch diesen nicht begünstigen, wenn du ein treuer Diener des Kaisers sein willst.

Pilatus. Man bringe Wasser!

Kaiphas. Das Volk wird nicht eher von der Stelle gehen, bis du das Todesurtheil über den Feind des Kaisers ausgesprochen hast.

Volk. Ja, wir gehen nicht mehr von der Stelle, bis das Urtheil gesprochen ist.

Pilatus. So zwingt mich denn euer Ungestüm, in euer Verlangen zu willigen. Nehmet ihn hin zur Kreuzigung! Aber seht! [Wäscht sich die Hände.] Ich wasche meine Hände; ich bin unschuldig an dem Blute des Gerechten. Ihr möget es verantworten!

Priester und Volk. Wir nehmen es auf uns. Sein Blut komme über uns und unsere Kinder!

Pilatus. Barabbas sei auf Forderung des Volkes frei. Führt ihn fort—zum Stadtthore hinaus, dass er nie mehr diesen Boden betrete. [Die Soldaten führen den BARABBAS ab.]

Priester und Volk. Nun hast du gerecht gerichtet!

Pilatus. Ich habe eurem ungestümen Andrängen nachgegeben, um grösseres Uebel zu verhüten. Aber an der Blutschuld will ich keinen Theil haben. Es geschehe, was ihr mit lärmender Stimme gerufen habt: sie falle auf euch und eure Kinder!

Priester und Volk. Wohl, sie falle auf uns und unsere Kinder!

Annas. Wir und unsere Kinder werden den heutigen Tag segnen, und mit dankbarer Freude den Namen Pontius Pilatus aussprechen.

Volk. Es lebe unser Statthalter, es lebe Pontius Pilatus!

Pilatus. Man bringe die im Gefängnisse aufbewahrten zwei Mörder herbei! Der Oberlictor gebe sie ungesäumt an die Bewaffneten ab! Sie haben den Tod verdient—viel mehr als der Angeklagte.

Priester und Volk. Dieser hat den Tod vor Allen verdient!

"Let Barabbas go free." "Will ye not that I release unto you the King of the Jews?" asked Pilate. Then the priests and people cried: "Away with him, release unto us Barabbas!" Then said Caiaphas: "Thou hast promised to release him whom the people demand." Pilate answered shortly to Caiaphas: "I am accustomed to keep my promise without needing a reminder." Then said he to the people: "What shall I do with the King of the Jews?" And the priests and people cried: "Crucify him!" "What," said Pilate, "shall I crucify your king?" And the people cried: "We have no king but Cæsar." Pilate said: "I cannot condemn this man, for I find no fault in him. He has been sufficiently chastised; I will let him go free." Then said the priests: "If thou let him go free thou art no friend of Cæsar's." Caiaphas added: "He has proclaimed himself king;" and the priests said: "Who proclaims himself king is a rebel against Cæsar." And Nathanael said: "If this rebel still remains unpunished, he will still scatter abroad the seed of revolt." Then cried the people: "It is the duty of the governor to put him out of the way."

Caiaphas, seeing that Pilate hesitated, pressed more vehemently upon him, saying: "We have done our duty as subjects of Cæsar, and delivered this rebel to thee. If thou payest no attention to our accusation and the desire of the people, then are we free from guilt. Thou alone, O governor! art responsible to Cæsar for the consequences." And Annas said: "If on account of this man universal disorder and revolt ensues, then we know who must bear the guilt, and," he added significantly, "Cæsar will know it also." Then cried the people again: "The matter must be brought before Cæsar!" Then Ezekiel said to Pilate: "They will be astonished when they hear at Rome that Cæsar's viceroy has taken under his protection a traitor whose death the whole people desired." And the crowd cried: "Thou must execute him, or otherwise there will be no peace in the land." Then said Pilate: "Why, what evil hath he done? I cannot, I dare not, condemn the innocent to death."

Then said Caiaphas: "Permit me to ask one question. Why shouldest thou judge this man so carefully when quite recently thou hast allowed thy soldiers to massacre hundreds without judgment or sentence, merely on account of a rebellious outcry?" As Pilate heard the question of Caiaphas he was dismayed, and the crowd shouted: "Thou canst not show favour to this man, if thou wilt be a faithful servant of Cæsar."

Then Pilate's resolution forsook him, and turning to his servants, he said: "Bring water." Caiaphas said unto him: "The people will not go away from this place until thou hast pronounced sentence of death upon the enemy of Cæsar." "Yes," cried the multitude, "we will not go from this place till sentence is pronounced." Then said Pilate sorrowfully: "Your violence compels me to yield to your desire. Take him hence and crucify him! But see," said he, as he washed his hands in the basin which had been brought at his command: "I wash my hands; I am innocent of the blood of this just man. See ye to it."

Then arose from the excited multitude a great and awful cry, in which priests and people joined, speaking as with one voice, "We take it upon ourselves. His blood be upon us and our children!" Then said Pilate: "Let Barabbas be set free at the demand of the people. Lead him outside the city gate and let him never tread this ground again." The soldiers then led Barabbas away. The priests and the people cried, "Now hast thou justly judged." Pilate said unto them: "I have given way to your violent demands in order to avoid a greater evil. But in the blood-guiltiness I will have no share. Let it fall upon you and your children as you have so loudly cried." Then again the priests and people cried: "It is good; let it fall upon us and upon our children." Annas said: "We and our children will bless this day and with thankful joy pronounce the name of Pontius Pilate." "Long live our governor," cried the crowd: "Long live Pontius Pilate!"

Then said Pilate: "Bring hither the two murderers who are kept in gaol. Let the chief lictor give them over without delay to the guard. They have deserved death much more than the accused." But the priests and people cried: "He has deserved death more than any." Pilate said: "The sentence

Pilatus. Das Todesurtheil soll schriftlich abgefasst und öffentlich vor allem Volke verkündet werden. [*Der Schreiber beginnt zu schreiben.* Aus der Tiefe der Strasse hört man die Soldaten, welche die Schächer führen, diese antreiben:] "Wollt ihr gehn, ihr Ruchlosen! Habt ihr es nicht schon lange verdient? Stosst sie fort, die Auswürflinge der Menschheit!"]

Rabbi. [*Auf die Schächer zeigend.*] Das giebt eine würdige Gesellschaft für den Lügenmessias auf seinem letzten Wege!

Pilatus. [*Zu den Schächern.*] Von euch und euren Schandthaten soll heute die Erde rein werden. Ihr sollt am Kreuze sterben. Das Todesurtheil werde nun laut gemacht.

Schreiber. [*Erhebt sich und liest*]: Ich, Pontius Pilatus, des mächtigen Kaisers Claudius Tiberius Landpfleger in Judäa, spreche, auf zudringliches Verlangen der Hohenpriester, des Synedriums und des gesammten Volkes der Juden, das Todesurtheil über einen gewissen Jesus von Nazareth, welcher angeklagt ist, dass er das Volk zur Empörung aufgereizt, dem Kaiser die Steuer zu entrichten verboten und sich selbst zum Könige der Juden aufgeworfen habe. Derselbe soll ausserhalb der Stadt zwischen zwei Missethätern, die wegen mehrerer Raubanfälle und Mordthaten gleichfalls zum Tode verurtheilt sind, an das Kreuz geschlagen und vom Leben zum Tode gebracht werden. Geschehen zu Jerusalem, am Vorabende des Osterfestes.

Pilatus. [*Bricht den Stab.*] Nun nehmt ihn hin, und kreuziget ihn! [*Geht rasch in das Innere des Hauses.*

Kaiphas. Triumph! Der Sieg ist unser! Der Feind der Synagoge ist vernichtet.

Priester und Volk. Fort mit ihm zur Schädelstätte!

Volk. Es lebe die Synagoge!

Priester und Pharisäer. Es lebe die Nation!

Annas. Eilt, dass wir zur rechten Zeit nach Hause kommen, das Osterlamm zu essen!

Priester und Pharisäer. Mit Freuden werden wir dieses Osterlamm halten, wie unsere Väter in Aegypten!

Kaiphas. Mitten durch Jerusalem gehe unser Triumphzug!

Rabbi. Wo sind seine Anhänger? Sie sind eingeladen, Hosannah zu rufen.

Volk. [*Abgehend.*] Auf und fort! Nach Golgatha hinaus! Kommt, ihr zu seh'n, wie er am Kreuze erblasst! O Freudentag, der Feind des Moses ist gestürzt! So gehe es Jedem, der das Gesetz verachtet! Er verdient den Kreuzestod! Glückseliges Osterfest! Jetzt kehrt die Freude ein in Israel! Zu Ende ist es mit dem Galiläer!

[*Ab in tumultuarischem Zuge.*

[*Schluss der zweiten Abtheilung.*]

DRITTE ABTHEILUNG.

Von der Verurtheilung durch Pilatus bis zur glorreichen Auferstehung des Herrn.

XV. VORSTELLUNG.

Der Kreuzweg.

PROLOG.

Der errungene Urtheilspruch ist gesprochen.
Schon hinaus zum Berge der Schädelstätte
Seh'n wir Jesum wanken, belastet mit dem
Balken des Kreuzes.

Einst trug Isaak willig auf seinem Rücken
Jenes Opferholz auf die Bergeshöhe,
Wo er selbst als Opfer bestimmt war nach dem
Willen Jehova's.

Jesus auch trägt willig die Last des Kreuzes,
Welches durch das Opfer des heil'gen Leibes
Bald nun werden sollte zum segensreichen
Baume des Lebens.

Denn wie, aufgerichtet dort in der Wüste,
Heilung brachte der eh'rnen Schlange Anblick,
So geht Trost und Segen und Heil auch aus vom
Stamme des Kreuzes.

THIRD DIVISION.

From the Condemnation by Pilate to the Resurrection.

PROLOGUE.—Act XV.

The condemnation won by force has been uttered;—
Even now, out to the place of skulls we see Him
Staggering under the weight of the cross He beareth,
On His last journey.

Once did Isaac willingly bear on his shoulders
Wood for sacrifice up to Mount Moriah,
Where himself was destined to be a victim
By the Almighty.

Jesus too bears willingly this sore burden,
Which, through sacrifice of the Sacred Body,
Soon shall be a tree of life for the nations,
Richest in blessing.

For as, once of old in the desert planted,
Moses' brazen serpent brought healing to those who
Looked on it,—salvation, blessing and comfort
This Tree has brought us.

---

of death must be written out and will be read publicly before all the people."

The scribe began to write, and as he wrote, from down the street were heard the voices of the soldiers who were bringing the thieves, driving them forward. "Will you not move on, you wretches? Have you not long ago deserved your fate! Thrust them on, those outcasts of mankind." When the thieves, driven by the soldiers, came to the foot of the balcony they were halted on the other side of the steps to that where Jesus stood. Then said the Rabbi, pointing to the thieves: "That is worthy company for the false Messiah on his last journey." Pilate said to the thieves: "Of you and your misdeeds the earth shall to-day be free. You shall die upon the cross. Let the sentence of death be now read."

Then the scribe stood forward and read thus:—" I, Pontius Pilate, Viceroy in Judæa, of the mighty Cæsar Claudius Tiberius, pronounce, at the ardent desire of the High Priests and the Sanhedrim and the people of the Jews, the sentence of death upon a certain Jesus of Nazareth, who is accused of having stirred up the people to revolt, of having forbidden to pay tribute to Cæsar, and of having proclaimed himself King of the Jews. The same shall be crucified outside the city between two malefactors who have been likewise condemned to death for many robberies and murders, and be brought from life to death. Given at Jerusalem on the eve of the Passover."

When the scribe had read the sentence Pilate broke a staff, flung it among the people, saying, in tones of great bitterness, "Now take him hence and crucify him!" and went rapidly into the house, leaving Jesus in the hands of the Jews.

"Triumph!" cried Caiaphas in wild exultation, "the victory is ours! the enemy of the Synagogue is destroyed." The priests and people shouted, "Away with him to Golgotha! Long live the Synagogue! Long live the nation!" Then said Annas, "Hasten that we may come home in time to eat the Passover." The priests and Pharisees said, "We will keep this Passover with joy, as did our fathers in Egypt." "Now," said Caiaphas, "let our triumphal procession go through the midst of Jerusalem." "Where," asked the Rabbi, "are his disciples? They are invited to cry Hosanna!" Then rushed the multitude away, crying, "Up and away, off to Golgotha! Come and see him perish on the cross! O delightful day, the enemy of Moses is overthrown! So be it done to every one who despises the law. He deserves the death on the cross. O happy Passover! Now joy will return to Israel. There is an end of the Galilean." And so crying with wild and savage clamour, they swept back to the street of the Sanhedrim.

THE WAY TO THE CROSS.—ACT XV. 103

VIA DOLOROSA.

VORBILDER.

Chor.

Betet an und saget Dank!
Der den Kelch der Leiden trank
Geht nun in den Kreuzestod
Und versöhnt die Welt mit Gott.

1. Isaak, zum Opfer bestimmt, besteigt mit dem Holze beladen den Berg.
1 Mos. 2², 1—10.

[Christus steigt den Calvarienberg hinauf, beladen mit der schweren Holzbürde des Kreuzes, um auf solchem Seinem himmlischen Vater geopfert zu werden. Die eherne Schlange ist ein Vorbild des Kreuzestodes Christi. Moses errichtete die eherne Schlange an einem hölzernen Pfahle und Jeder genas bei ihrem Anblicke. Christus wird am Kreuze erhöht, damit der glaubensvolle Hinblick auf ihn die Seelenwunden heile.]

Solo.

Wie das Opferholz getragen
Isaak den Berg hinan,
Wanket mit dem Kreuz beladen
Jesus auch die steile Bahn.

Chor.

Betet an, &c.

2. Moses erhebt eine aus Erz gegossene Schlange auf einem Querholze.
4 Mos. 21, 9.

Choragus.—Recit.

Angenagelt wird erhöhet
An dem Kreuz der Menschensohn.
Hier an Moses Schlange sehet
Ihr des Kreuzes Vorbild schon.

Chor.

Betet an, &c.

HANDLUNG.

CHRISTUS mit dem Kreuze beladen wird nach Golgotha geführt und begegnet seiner betrübtesten Mutter.—SIMON VON CYRENE wird gezwungen, das Kreuz zu übernehmen;—einige Frauen von Jerusalem beweinen JESUM.

ERSTE SZENE.

Die heil. Frauen mit JOHANNES und JOSEPH VON ARIMATHIA, von Bethanien kommend.

Maria. [*Zu JOHANNES.*] O liebster Jünger, wie wird es meinem Jesus ergangen sein?
Johannes. Wenn die Priester könnten, wie sie wollten, so wäre er gewiss schon bei den Todten. Aber sie dürfen das Urtheil ohne Erlaubniss des Statthalters nicht ausführen. Pilatus aber, hoff' ich, wird ihn nicht verurtheilen, da er stets nur Gutes gethan hat.
Magdalena. Allmacht'ger! lenke zur Gerechtigkeit des Richters Herz, dass er die Unschuld schütze!
Maria. Wo geh'n wir hin, o Freunde, ach, wohin, damit ich nochmal den Geliebten sehe? Ich muss ihn sehen! doch wo find' ich ihn? Vielleicht, ach, schmachtet er im tiefsten Kerker.
Magdalena. Der Herr lenke das Herz des Statthalters!
Maria. O Freunde, wo gehen wir hin, dass ich meinen Sohn nochmals sehe?
Joseph. Es lässt sich auch Niemand seh'n, bei dem man sich erkundigen könnte.
Johannes. Das Beste wird sein, wir gehn zu Nicodemus, der weiss sicherlich, wie es um den Meister steht.
Maria. Ja, dahin lasst uns gehn. Jeder Augenblick mehrt meinen Kummer. . . .
Johannes. Sei stark im Glauben, liebe Mutter. [*Man hört Geschrei:* "Weiter, weiter mit ihm!" *Es ist das Volk, das den unter seiner Last erliegenden JESUS antreibt.*]
Joseph. Was ist das für ein furchtbarer Lärm?

[*Sie bleiben lauschend stehn.*]

Worship now, and praise and thank!—
Who the cup of suffering drank
Now the way to death has trod,
Reconciling us to God.

[Two more tableaux bring us to the Crucifixion. The first represents Isaac carrying the wood with which he was to be burnt, up the slope of Mount Moriah; the second, another scene from the wilderness, full of spirit and life, shows Moses raising the brazen serpent on high so that all who look upon it may live, even though they have been bitten by the fiery serpents. The stage is crowded with life.

Isaac thus on Mount Moriah
Bore the sacrificial wood,
As, beneath the burden fainting,
Christ on Golgotha hath stood.

Worship now, &c.

Pierced by nails, on high is raised,
On the cross the Son of Man,
Here you see, in Moses' serpent,
Shadowed forth the sacred plan.

Worship now, &c.

THE WAY TO THE CROSS.

THEN they took Jesus and led him away, and a great multitude followed him. And when Jesus, bearing the cross, with the thieves also bearing their crosses, was entering the street of Annas, Mary the mother of Jesus, with Mary Magdalene, and John, and Joseph of Arimathea, came down the street by Pilate's house. And Mary said to John, "O beloved disciple, how will it have gone with my Jesus?" Then answered John, "If the priests could do as they will, then sure enough he would be already among the dead. But they could not carry out the sentence without permission of the governor. But Pilate, I hope, will not condemn him, as he has done nothing but what is good." Then prayed Mary Magdalene, "O Almighty God, incline the ruler's heart to justice, that he may protect the innocent." Then said Mary, the mother of Jesus, "Whither shall we go, O friends, oh whither, that I may but once more see my beloved son? I must see him, but where can I find him? Perhaps, oh perhaps, he lies buried in the deepest dungeon." Mary Magdalene said, "May the Lord guide the governor's heart!" Then Mary asked again, "O friends, whither shall we go, that I may see my son once more?" Joseph answered, "There is no one to be seen from whom we can inquire." John said, "The best thing will be to go to Nicodemus, he surely knows what is happening to the Master." "Yes, let us go," said Mary, "every moment increases my grief." "Be strong in faith, dear mother," said John. Suddenly a horrible noise of confused voices and tramping feet was heard in the distance. From the tumult could be heard the words, "On, on, with him!" Mary started, and they all stood listening while the noise came nearer and nearer. "What terrible noise is that?" said Joseph. Then stood they all still, listening to hear what it might signify.

THE WAY TO THE CROSS.—ACT. XV., SC. 1.   105

SIMON OF CYRENE.

THE CENTURION.

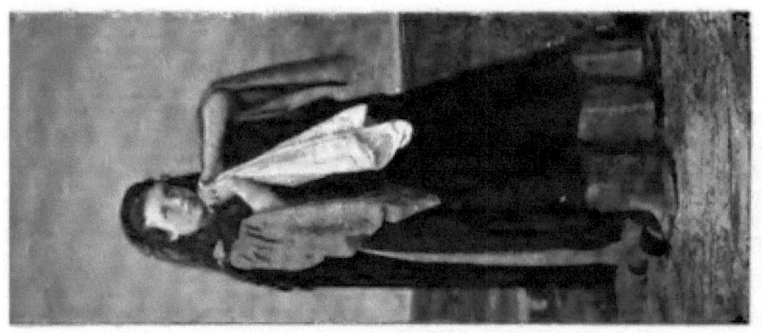

VERONICA.

ZWEITE SZENE.

Der Zug der Kreuztragung, Priester, Pharisäer, Volk, Soldaten, noch innerhalb der "Annasgasse" langsam nach vorne rückend. Voran der Hauptmann mit dem Kommandostab, in der Gruppe ein Reiter mit einer römischen Fahne. Christus mühsam das Kreuz schleppend, ihm zunächst die vier Henker.

Volk. Er sterbe, und Jeder der es mit ihm hält!
1. Henker. Wird dir die Last schon zu schwer?
Volk. Treibt ihn mit Gewalt, dass wir nach Kalvarien kommen!
2. Henker. Haltet an, er will zusammenstürzen. [*Die Gruppe in der Pilatusgasse weiss noch nicht, um was es sich handelt.*]
Joseph. Was thun wir? Bei diesem Gedränge können wir uns nicht in die Stadt wagen.
Maria. Was mag dieser Lärm bedeuten? Er wird doch nicht meinem Sohne gelten?
Joseph. Es scheint eine Empörung ausgebrochen zu sein.
Johannes. Wir wollen uns hier stille halten bis der Sturm vorbrausst. —
Simon von Cyrene. [*Kommt mit einem Korbe eilfertig und ängstlich aus der Mittelbühne nach vorn.*] Ich muss eilen, dass ich in die Stadt komme. Der Abend des Festes rückt heran, ich muss noch einkaufen.
Priester und Volk. [*Von Simon noch ungesehn.*] Lasst ihn nicht ruhen! Treibt ihn mit Schlägen!
Simon. Welches Geschrei! Ich will mich ruhig halten.
3. Henker. Dein Wanken nützt dir nichts, du musst doch auf Golgotha hinaus.
Ahasverus. [*Rasch aus seinem Hause tretend.*] Weg von meinem Hause, hier ist kein Ort zum Ausruhen!
Simon. Der Lärm wird stärker . . . was kommt da? Ich will die Geschichte abwarten.

DRITTE SZENE.

Der Zug mit Christus ist endlich vorne angekommen. Indessen nähern sich vom Grunde der Mittelbühne Veronica und die Frauen Jerusalems.

Johannes. Es scheint, dass Jemand nach Kalvarien zur Hinrichtung ausgeführt wird.
Maria. [*Erblickt Jesum.*] Er ist's, ach Gott, es ist mein Sohn! [*Ihre Umgebung stützt sie.*]
Henker. Er bleibt uns auf den Wege.
Hauptmann. (*Zu dem in äusserster Ermattung herankrankenden Jesum, der wiederholt fällt.*) Hier, stärke dich! [*Reicht ihm eine Flasche,—Jesus nimmt sie, trinkt aber nicht.*]
Maria. Ach, so sehe ich ihn zum Tode geführt, einem Missethäter gleich, zwischen Missethätern!
Johannes. Mutter, es ist die Stunde, die er vorher gesagt hat; so ist des Vaters Wille.
Hauptmann. Willst du nicht trinken? So treibt ihn an!
4. Henker. [*Rüttelt Jesum.*] Rühre dich, trager Judenkönig!
2. Henker. Fort, nimm die Kräfte zusammen.
3. Henker. Thue nicht so zärtlich, es muss gehn!
Maria. O, wo ist ein Schmerz gleich meinem Schmerze!
3. Henker. Er ist zu sehr geschwächt, es muss Jemand helfen, sonst . . . .
Rabbi. [*auf Simon deutend*]. Hier, dieser Fremdling . . . .
Pharisäer. Packt ihn nur!
Hauptmann. Komm' her, du hast breite Schultern.
Simon. Ich muss . . . .
4 Henker. Freilich musst du, oder es giebt Schläge.
Pharisäer. Schlagt drein, wenn er nicht gehen will.
Simon. Ich bin ja unschuldig, ich habe nichts verbrochen!
Hauptmann. Schweige!
Simon. [*Christus betrachtend.*] Was sehe ich, das ist der heilige Mann von Nazareth!

As they listened the procession to Golgotha was already half-way down the street of Annas. In front marched the centurion, holding in one hand the staff of authority, followed by Jesus, staggering painfully under the burden of his cross. Around Jesus stood four executioners who brutally goaded him forward. Behind Jesus came the thieves, each bearing his own cross. Behind them came soldiers carrying spears, in the midst of whom, on a white horse, rode a horseman carrying the Roman banner, on which were the letters S.P.Q.R. By the side of the soldiery walked Annas and Caiaphas followed by all the Council of the Sanhedrim. All around crowded a numerous multitude, whose shouts were heard almost without intermission. "Let him die!" they cried, "and all who hold with him." Jesus who had already fallen under the cross walked slowly and with difficulty. One of the executioners said unto him, "Is the burden already too heavy?" and the people shouted, "Drive him on with violence, that we may get to Golgotha." The second executioner cried, "Take care, or he will be down."

The progress was so slow that not even the head of the procession could be seen from where the two Maries and John were standing, wondering what the noise might mean. Joseph said, "What shall we do? In this commotion we cannot enter into the city." But Mary said, "What may this noise signify? Surely it does not concern my son?" As the noise waxed ever louder, Joseph said, "It seems as if an insurrection had broken out." Then John said, "We had better stop here till the storm passes over."

While they stood waiting and wondering, Simon of Cyrene came hastily into the street that lay between those of Pilate and Annas. He carried a basket, and looking anxiously around him, said, "I must hasten in order to get into the city. The eve of the feast is coming, and I have still some purchases to make." Hardly had he said this than he heard the sound of a great outcry, amid which he could only distinguish the words, "Let him not rest! urge him on with blows!" "What an outcry," said Simon, "I will keep quiet for a time." Jesus had fallen faint and had staggered up against the house of Ahasverus, and was there endeavouring to support himself. The third executioner said to him roughly, "It is no use thy fainting. Thou must keep on to Golgotha." Then Ahasverus came out of his house, and said, "Be off from my house, here is no place for resting." Simon, who was listening, without being able to see the cause of the commotion, said, "The noise waxes louder. What comes there! I will wait and see what happens."

Then, as the procession turned the corner of Annas's street, John, seeing the cross, said, "It appears that someone is being led out to Golgotha for execution." Mary, the mother of Jesus, saw him, and cried out with a piercing wail, "It is he! Oh, God! It is my son!" Jesus meanwhile staggered under the cross, but was forced forward by the executioners, grumbling as they did so; "He will drop on the road." The Centurion, seeing that Jesus from sheer exhaustion had again fallen, reached him a bottle, saying, "Here, strengthen thyself!" Jesus took it, but did not drink of it. Mary cried, weeping, "Ah! there I see him led to death, even as a malefactor, between malefactors." Then said John, as he tenderly supported her, "Mother, it is the hour of which He has told us before. Such is the will of the Father." Then said the Centurion to Jesus, "Wilt thou not drink?" Then drive him on." Then one of the executioners shook him, saying, "Rouse thyself, lazy King of the Jews!" Another of the executioners said, "Forward! pull thyself together!" and the third said, "Do not act thus weakly; we must get on."

Then Mary cried as she looked upon the scene, "Oh, where is any sorrow like unto my sorrow?"

The third executioner, seeing that all the efforts to compel Jesus to move forward had failed, said, "He is too much exhausted; someone must help him, otherwise——." Then the Rabbi, seeing Simon of Cyrene, pointed him out, saying, "Here, this stranger——." The Pharisees said, "Just seize him!" Then said the Centurion, "Come hither, thou hast broad shoulders." Simon, protesting, said, "I must——." "Truly you must," said one of the executioners, "otherwise there will be blows." "Flog him if he refuse to go!" said a Pharisee. Simon struggled, crying, "Indeed I am innocent; I have committed no crime!" "Silence!" said the Centurion. Simon then beholding Christ, said, "What

2. Henker. Deine Schultern her!
Simon. Dir zu liebe will ich es tragen, o könnte ich mich dadurch dir werth machen!
Christus. [*Erschöpft zur Seite stehend.*] Gottes Segen dir und den Deinen!
Hauptmann. Jetzt vorwärts, du folge mit dem Kreuzesbalken nach!
1. Priester. [*Zu Christus.*] Nun kannst du schon geschwinde Füsse machen!
3. Henker. [*Jesum beim Nacken fassend und schüttelnd.*] Sieh' was wir auf dich halten, sogar das Strafwerkzeug wird dir abgenommen.
2. Henker. Bist du noch weiter bedürftig?
Hauptmann. Lasst das gut sein. Wir wollen noch ein wenig Inne halten, dass er sich erhole, ehe es den Hügel hinan geht. [*Veronica und die Frauen Jerusalems nahen sich dem Zuge.*]
Kaiphas. Schon wieder ein Stillstand! Wann werden wir nach Kalvarien kommen?
Veronica. [*Vor Jesus knieend und ihm ihr Schweisstuch bietend.*] O Herr, wie ist dein Angesicht von Blut und Schweiss überronnen! Willst du dich nicht abtrocknen?
Christus. [*Trocknet sein Antlitz und giebt das Tuch zurück.*] Mitleidige Seele! Der Vater wird es dir vergelten.
Frauen Jerusalems. [*Dem Herrn mit ihren Kleinen nahend.*] Du guter Lehrer! — Unvergesslicher Wohlthäter! — Edelster Menschenfreund, so wird dir gelohnt! [*Sie weinen.*]
Christus. Töchter Jerusalems! Weinet nicht über mich, sondern über euch weinet und über eure Kinder! Denn sehet! Es werden Tage kommen, an welchen man sagen wird: Glücklich die Unfruchtbaren und die Leiber, die nicht geboren, und die Brüste, die nicht gesäugt haben. Dann werden sie den Bergen zurufen: Fallet über uns! Und den Hügeln: Bedecket uns. Denn wenn das am grünen Holze geschieht, was wird am dürren geschehen?
Hauptmann. Entfernt nun das Weibervolk!
3. Henker. Was nützen eure Weiberthränen? Zurück!
2. und 4. Henker. Fort mit dir auf den Todeshügel!
Volk. Frisch hinauf nach Kalvarien!
Rabbi. Geht es doch endlich einmal vorwärts?
Nathanael. Der Hauptmann ist allzu milde.
Priester. Schont seiner nicht so sehr! [*Der Zug setzt sich wieder in Bewegung, da erscheint ein Diener des Pilatus.*]

VIERTE SZENE.

Diener des Pilatus. Halt! Auf Befehl des Statthalters soll der Hauptmann alsogleich bei ihm erscheinen und weitere Befehle einholen. [*Der Zug steht stille.*]
Kaiphas. Was soll dies? Wozu neue Befehle? Das Todesurtheil ist gesprochen und muss unverweilt vollzogen werden.
Hauptmann. [*Streng.*] Nein, dies wird nicht geschehn, bis ich die Befehle meines Herrn werde vernommen haben. [*Zu den Soldaten.*] Ihr haltet indessen Wache und richt mit den Verurtheilten nach Golgotha. Dann entlasst ihr [*auf Simon deutend*] diesen Mann und wartet meine Ankunft ab. [*Geht mit dem Diener. Der Zug setzt sich wieder in Bewegung, nach der Tiefe der Mittelbühne zu.*]
Volk. [*Wild durcheinander.*] Hinauf nach Golgotha! An's Kreuz mit ihm! Heil Israel, der Feind ist überwunden! Wir sind befreit, es lebe das Synedrium! —
Johannes. Mutter, wollen wir nicht nach Bethania zurück? Du wirst den Anblick nicht ertragen können!
Maria. Wie könnte eine Mutter ihr Kind verlassen in der bittersten letzten Noth! Ich will mit ihm leiden, Hohn und Schmach mit ihm theilen, mit ihm sterben.
Johannes. Wenn nur die Kräfte des Leibes nicht erliegen!
Maria. Fürchte nichts! Ich habe zu Gott um Kraft gebetet, der Herr hat mich erhört. Lasst uns nachgehn.
Alle. Beste Mutter, wir folgen dir.
[*Gehen langsam dem Zuge nach.*]

is this I see? This is the holy man from Nazareth!" "Place thy shoulders here!" said an executioner. Then said Simon, "For the love of thee will I carry it. Oh, could I thereby make myself useful to thee!" Christ, who stood exhausted on one side, looked upon Simon, and said, "God's blessing be upon thee and thine!"

"Now forward!" said the Centurion; "follow thou with the beam of the cross." The first priest, addressing Jesus, said, "Thou canst come quickly enough now." The third executioner, seeing that Jesus still stood, unable to move, seized him by the neck, and shook him, saying, "See, with what consideration we treat thee! even the cross has been taken from thee." "Dost thou need anything else?" said another of the men. "Let him be," said the Centurion. "We will now halt a little, that he may recover before we ascend the hill."

While the procession halted, Veronica and the women of Jerusalem approached. Caiaphas, meanwhile, chafing with vexation at the delay, exclaimed, "What, still another stoppage!—when shall we come to Calvary?" Veronica, coming up to Christ, kneeled before him, and offering him her handkerchief, said, "O Lord, how is thy face covered with blood and sweat! Wilt thou not wipe it off?" Jesus took the handkerchief and wiped his face and gave it back to her, saying, "Compassionate soul! the Father will reward thee for this!"

Then spoke the women of Jerusalem, who drew near to the Lord with their little ones, "Thou good teacher, never-to-be-forgotten benefactor, noblest friend of men, thus art thou rewarded!" Then they wept. Christ, looking upon them in their tears, said, "Daughters of Jerusalem, weep not for me but for yourselves and your children. For behold the days are coming in the which they shall say, Blessed are the barren and the wombs that never bare, and the paps that never gave suck. Then shall they call to the mountains, Fall on us, and to the hills, Cover us. For if they do these things in the green tree, what will be done in the dry?"

By this time the patience of the Centurion was exhausted, and he cried out, "Clear out now these women-folk!" The third executioner, pushing them roughly away, said, "What use are your women's tears? Back!" While the other executioners cried, as they pushed Jesus forward, "On with thee to the hill of death!" The crowd took up the cry, and said, "Quick, forward to Calvary!" "Are we really going forward again," said the Rabbi, and Nathanael said, shrugging his shoulders, "The Centurion is far too mild." "Do not spare him so much," said a priest.

The long procession was once more in motion when there appeared a servant from Pilate. This man cried "Halt!" and the procession stopped. "By command of the Governor the Centurion must appear before him as quickly as possible and receive further orders." Caiaphas exclaimed, "What does this mean? What new orders are required? The death sentence is pronounced and must be carried out without delay." Then said the Centurion bluntly, "No, this will not happen until I have received the further orders of my lord." Then, turning to the soldiers, he said, "Keep watch meanwhile and go with the condemned to Golgotha. Then dismiss this man (Simon) and await my arrival." The Centurion then went with the warrant to Pilate, and the procession set forth again.

The people cried wildly, "Up to Golgotha, to the cross with him! Hail to Israel! The enemy is vanquished! We are free! Long live the Sanhedrim!"

Jesus looked upon his mother as the procession passed the corner of Annas's street, but spoke not.

Then said John, when the dolorous procession had passed, "Mother, shall we not go back to Bethany? Thou wilt not be able to bear the sight?" But Mary answered, "How can a mother leave her child in the last and bitterest need? I will suffer with him, bear scorn and shame with him; die with him!" "Only," said John, "if the strength of the body does not give way." "Fear not," said Mary, "I have asked strength of God and He has heard me. Let us go after them." And they slowly followed the procession to Calvary.

XVI.—VORSTELLUNG.

Jesus auf Golgotha.

[*Der Chor erscheint in Trauergewändern.*]

PROLOG DES SAENGERCHORES.

Choragus.—*Recit.*

Auf, fromme Seelen, auf und gehet,
    Von Reueschmerz und Dank durchglüht.
Mit mir zum Golgatha und sehet,
    Was hier zu eurem Heil geschieht!
Dort stirbt der Mittler zwischen Gott
Und Sünder den Versöhnungstod.

Ach! nackt, von Wunden nur bekleidet,
    Liegt er hier bald am Kreuz für dich!
Die Rache der Gottlosen weidet
    An seiner Marter frevelnd sich.
Und er, der dich, o Sünder, liebt,
Schweigt, leidet, duldet und vergibt.

Ich hör' schon seine Glieder krachen,
    Die man aus den Gelenken zerrt.
Wem soll's das Herz nicht beben machen,
    Wenn er den Streich des Hammers hört,
Der grausam, ach! durch Hand und Fuss
Die Nagel schmetternd treiben muss!

[*Hört man hinter dem Vorhange dröhnende, markdurchdringende Hammerschläge.*]

Nun, Seelen, kommt, zum Kreuzesstamme,
    Erbarmungsvoll die Blicke lenkt
Hinauf zum mildem Gotteslamme,
    Das euch sein Blut und Leben schenkt.
Seht. zwischen Mördern schwebend hängt
Der Gottessohn, vom Spott umdrängt!

Wollt ihr ihm keine Thräne weihen?
    Nun öffnet er den Mund und fleht
Für seine Mörder um Verzeihen.
    Und spricht zu Gott sein letzt' Gebet.—
Den Speer man in die Seite stösst—
Da liegt das heilige Herz entblösst.

Wer kann die hohe Liebe fassen,
    Die dieses Herz beseelt,
Das Güte gibt für alles Hassen;
    Sein Leben für die Welt.
O, seht durch alle Zeiten
Am Kreuz die Arm' ihn breiten!
    Er zieht auch dich
    Voll Lieb an sich.

HANDLUNG.

Jesus wird, an das Kreuz geheftet, erhoben.— Spott über ihn.— Jesu letzte Worte und Hinscheiden.— Vorkehrung der Juden zur Bewachung des Grabes.— Beerdigung des Leichnams Jesu.

ERSTE SZENE.

Die Szene ist auf der Mittelbühne. Wie der Vorhang sich erhebt, werden eben die beiden Kreuze mit den Schächern aufgerichtet. Christus liegt, an sein Kreuz genagelt, am Boden. Lictoren, Henker, Hohepriester, Pharisäer, Volk; im Hintergrunde die heil. Frauen mit Johannes, Joseph und Nicodemus.

Die Henker. [*Auf die aufgerichteten Schächer deutend.*] Mit diesen sind wir nun fertig. Jetzt muss auch der Judenkönig auf seinem Throne erhöht werden.

Priester. Nicht König! Betrüger! Hochverräther!

Hauptmann. Zuvor muss aber nach dem Befehle des Statt-

CHAPTER XVI.

PROLOGUE.—Act XVI.

Ye pious souls, rise up and go,
    With grateful penitence aglow,
    With me to Golgotha, and see
    What shall be done your souls to free.
See how the Mediator dies
    The atoning death of sacrifice.

Ah! see—with wounds His only covering—
    He hangs for you upon the cross,
And Belial's sons, in godless triumph,
    Drink in the sight of His pain and loss,
While He, whose love for sinners lives,
Is silent, suffers, and forgives.

With horror of dread the sound I hear,
    The rending of joints from sockets torn.
When the strokes of the hammer reach the ear;
    Where is the heart that was ever born
Sickens not at the blows that beat
The cruel nails through the hands and feet?

Come ye, and lift to the Tree of Shame,
    O souls of men, your pitying eyes,
And look on the face of the gentle Lamb
    Who has given His blood for you, and dies.
See, between murderers lifted up,
God's Son has drained the bitter cup.

Oh! grant ye him no pitying tears?
    Now lifts He up His voice, and prays
Forgiveness on his murderers,
    And His last words of prayer He says.
They thrust the spear into His side,
And forth there flows His heart's red tide.

Oh! who can know the love that lives
    In this Heart now laid bare,
That kindness back for hatred gives,
    And saves us from despair?
He through unnumbered years
With outstretched arms appears.
    Thee, too, His pain
    And love constrain.

THE CRUCIFIXION.

And when they came to Golgotha, which is, by interpretation, the Place of the Skull, they crucified him there. But first they hanged the two thieves each on his cross, the one on the left, the other on the right. Their arms were tied over the cross by the hands, and their feet were tied with cord to the beam. But Jesus was nailed to the central cross while it yet lay with the head slightly raised upon the ground. One nail was driven through the palm of each hand, and one through the two feet, which were placed tho one above the other, and the sound of the hammer-strokes was horrible. Jesus lay silent without moving. On his head was the crown of thorns, from which a little blood trickled over his brow. His hands and his feet bled a little, but the rest of his body was pale and colourless; a light cloth only being cast around his loins.

The Centurion, who had returned from Pilate, stood on the right of the cross giving orders. The lictors stood near the soldier on the white horse, who held on high the Roman standard with the letters S.P.Q.R. Caiaphas, Annas, and all the members of the Sanhedrim stood on the left exulting. A great crowd of sight-seers thronged the place. Among them, coming from behind the centurion, were the holy women from Bethany with Mary the mother of Jesus, and John, and Joseph of Arimathea and Nicodemus.

Then said the executioners to the centurion, "We have finished with these," pointing to the thieves. "Now, must the King of the Jews be exalted upon his throne!" Which hearing, the priests cried angrily. "Not king! deceiver, traitor!" The centurion, who held in his hand a scroll or escutcheon, said, "First, by command of the Governor, this writing must be fastened to the cross. Faustus," he added,

THE CRUCIFIXION.—ACT XVI., SC. 1. 109

ON CALVARY.

halters diese Aufschrift an's Kreuz geheftet werden. Fanstus!
Hefte diesen Schild oben an das Kreuz.

Faustus. Ein Aushangeschild! Ha, da geht es schon
königlich her! [*Heftet die Aufschrift an.*

Hauptmann. Greift nun zu und erhebt das Kreuz! Nur
nicht nachgelassen!

3. Henker. Auf, verdoppelt eure Kräfte! [*Sie heben.*
4. Henker. Nun gut, das Kreuz steht fest.

Hauptmann. Der peinliche Akt ist vollzogen.

Kaiphas. Und zwar trefflich vollzogen. Dank und Beifall
von uns Allen!

Pharisäer. Dank und Beifall von uns Allen!

Kaiphas. Dieser Tag soll für ewige Zeiten ein Festtag sein.

Pharisäer. Ja, feierlich werde er für alle Zukunft begangen.

Annas. Und ich will nun gerne zu den Vätern hinabgehen,
weil ich noch die Freude erlebt habe, diesen Bösewicht am
Kreuze zu sehen. Aber die Kreuzesaufschrift scheint mir
ganz kurz verfasst zu sein?

Rabbi. [*Näher tretend.*] Das ist eine Beleidigung für Synedrium und Volk!

Kaiphas. Was steht geschrieben?

Rabbi. Es heisst: Jesus von Nazareth, König der Juden!
[*Die 4 Henker lagern sich unter dem Kreuze.*

Kaiphas. [*Liest.*] Wahrhaftig, da ist die Ehre der Nation
angegriffen.

Priester. Man reisse die Aufschrift herunter!

Kaiphas. Selbst dürfen wir nicht Hand anlegen. [*Zu zwei Priestern.*] Geht zum Statthalter und fordert im Namen des
Hohen Rathes und des gesammten Volkes die Abänderung
dieser Aufschrift. Er soll schreiben, dass er gesagt hat: ich
bin der König der Juden. Dann stellt auch das Ansuchen,
dass den Hingerichteten noch vor dem grossen Abend die
Beine gebrochen und ihre Leiber abgenommen werden dürfen.
[*Die Beiden ab.*

3. Henker. Nun, Kameraden, lasst uns unsere Erbschaft
theilen [*Nimmt Christi Rock und Mantel zur Hand.*] Seht, sein
Mantel giebt oben vier Theile. [*Die vier Henker fassen den
Mantel und reissen ihn mit einem Ruck in 4 Stücke.*] Aber der
Rock ist nicht zusammengenäht, wollen wir ihn doch zerstückeln?

2. Henker. Nein; besser ist es, wir werfen das Loos über
ihn.

1. Henker. Hier sind Würfel. Ich will gleich mein Glück
versuchen! [*Wirft.*] Das ist zu wenig. Ich habe verloren.

3. Henker. [*Zu Christus empor.*] Wie? Wenn du am
Kreuze Wunder wirken kannst, so begünstige meinen Wurf!
[*Wirft.*

Die übrigen Henker. Was weiss er um uns?

4. Henker. Sollte ich nicht glücklicher sein! Fünfzehn!
Bald genug. Nun versuche du es!

2. Henker. Ich muss ihn haben [*Wirft.*

8. Henker. [*Die Würfel betrachtend.*] Achtzehn! Das ist
das Beste.

1. Henker. Dein ist er, nimm ihn hin.

4. Henker. Du bist eben nicht darum zu beneiden.

turning to one of the hangmen named Faustus, "make fast
this title over the cross." Faustus took the scroll from the
centurion, and going to the cross, nailed it with one hammerstroke over the head of Jesus, saying, "Ah, an escutcheon
displayed, this is right royal!" When this was done according to the command of the Governor, the Centurion said to the
executioners, "Now, up with the cross! not carelessly, but
lay hold firmly." Then two hangmen, taking the cross by
the arms, lifted it up so that its foot fell into the hole prepared
for it. But as the cross bearing the body of Jesus was
heavy the third hangman placed his back under it near
to the feet of Jesus, saying, "Come, now, all together,"
and so helping raised it on high. The fourth then filled in
the hole at the foot, saying when he finished, "All right, the
cross stands firm." Then said the Centurion addressing the
chief priests, "The execution is accomplished." "Quite
admirably so," said Caiaphas with radiant face. "Thanks
and applause from us all!" "Yes, thanks and applause from
us all," echoed the Pharisees, looking up at the cross.
Caiaphas then declared, "This shall be a feast day for ever."
And the Pharisees said, "Yes, for all time to come it shall be
kept every year with grateful jubilation." "And now," said
the aged Annas, "now gladly will I go down to my fathers since
I have lived to have the joy of seeing this wretch on the cross."
And as he gazed long, as if exultantly drinking in the pleasure of
satisfied vengeance, he saw, for the first time, the writing on the
title. But his old eyes could not decipher the words. Turning to
Caiaphas he said, "The superscription seems to be very short."
Then the Jews drew nearer to see what was written. The
hangmen seated themselves on the ground at the foot of the
cross and looked up at Jesus. Then the Rabbi reading the
words written by Pilate exclaimed, "That is an insult, an
outrage upon the people and the Sanhedrim!" Caiaphas,
hearing him, asked, "What is written?" Then said the
Rabbi, "It is written, Jesus of Nazareth, King of the Jews."
Caiaphas, as if incredulous, approached the cross, and reading
it himself, started back with indignation. "Verily," he cried,
"that is an affront upon the honour of our nation." "Down
with it at once," cried the priests. But Caiaphas said,
"We dare not touch it ourselves. But do you two," addressing the Rabbi and Saras, "hasten at once to the Governor to
demand from him, in the name of the Sanhedrim and of the
assembled people, that the superscription shall be altered.
Say to him, 'Write not, The King of the Jews, but that he
said, I am King of the Jews.'" "We are off at once," said the
Rabbi and Saras. "Stay," said Caiaphas, "also request
from the Governor that he may order the bones of the crucified to
be broken and their bodies taken down from the cross before the
eve of the Passover." When the Rabbi and Saras departed on
their mission, the hangmen, who had been sitting at the foot
of the cross, bethought themselves, and the first, who was
named Agrippa, standing up said, "Now comrades, let us
divide our share." Taking the mantle of Jesus they seized
each one corner, and then pulling all together rent it into four
parts.

The coat remained. Agrippa held it up; "The mantle has
made just four pieces, shall we rip up the coat also? See, it is
without seam!" "No," said Faustus, who had fastened
the superscription over the head of Jesus; "it would be better
to cast lots for it." "Look," said Agrippa, as he went to the
foot of the cross and took up his basket; "see, here are dice!"
Then the four hangmen standing at the foot of Jesus threw the
dice. Agrippa throw them first, saying, "I will try my luck
first. Alas, that is too little," he added, as he counted up the
result of his throw. "I have lost." Catiline, the third hangman, as he rattled the dice in his hand looked up at Jesus and
said, "Hi! you up there, if you can do anything give me
good luck;" the others shrugged their shoulders and said,
"What does he care about us!" Catiline's throw was not
high. Then Nero said, "I ought to have better luck," and
throwing the dice he counted fifteen. "Nearly enough; now
Faustus, it is your turn." Faustus threw the dice, saying, "I
ought to get it." They all bent over to see the result. "Eighteen," cried Catiline, "that is the best yet." Then said
Agrippa, "Take it," handing him the mantle, "it is thine,
take it away." And Nero consoled himself by saying, "You
are not to be envied!" Faustus gathered up the coat and
folding it up put it away.

THE CRUCIFIXION.—ACT XVI., SC. 1.

MARY, THE MOTHER OF JESUS

Rabbi. [*Von* PILATUS *zurückkehrend.*] Unsere Gesandschaft war vergeblich. Er wollte uns nicht anhören.

Kaiphas. Hat er euch gar keine Antwort ertheilt?

Rabbi. Diese einzige: Was ich geschrieben habe, bleibt geschrieben.

Annas. [*Für sich.*] Unerträglich!

Kaiphas. Welchen Bescheid gab er euch wegen des Beinbrechens?

Rabbi. Hierüber, sagte er, wolle er dem Hauptmann seine Befehle geben.

Priester. [*Zu* CHRISTUS.] So bleibt es also geschrieben: König der Juden. Ei, wenn du König in Israel bist, so steige jetzt, vom Kreuze herab, dass wir es sehen und an dich glauben.

2. Priester. Du, der du den Tempel Gottes niederreissest und in drei Tagen wieder aufbauest, hilf dir nun selbst!

Kaiphas. Ha, Andern hat er geholfen, sich selbst kann er nicht helfen.

Falsche Zeuge. Komm herab, du bist ja der Sohn Gottes!

Annas. Er hat auf Gott vertraut. Der rette ihn jetzt, wenn er Wohlgefallen an ihm hat.

4. Henker. Wie, hörst du nicht?

1. und 3. Henker. Zeige deine Macht, erhabener Judenkönig!

Christus. [*Dessen Haupt die ganze Zeit über still gesenkt gewesen, wendet es jetzt schmerzlich.*] Vater, verzeihe ihnen, denn sie wissen nicht, was sie thun!

Der Linke Schächer. [*Zu* CHRISTUS.] Hörst du? Bist du der Gesalbte, so rette dich jetzt und uns mit dir!

Der Rechte Schächer. [*Zum linken.*] Auch du fürchtest Gott nicht, da du doch zu derselben Strafe verurtheilt bist? Uns geschieht Recht, denn wir empfangen den Lohn, den wir durch unsere Missethaten verdient haben — er aber hat nichts Böses gethan. [*Zu* CHRISTUS.] Herr, gedenke meiner, wenn du in dein Reich kommst.

Christus. Wahrlich, ich sage dir, heute noch wirst du mit mir im Paradiese sein. [MARIA *und* JOHANNES *nähern sich dem Kreuze.*]

Kaiphas. Hört, er thut noch dergleichen, als ob er über die Pforten des Paradieses zu gebieten hätte!

Rabbi. Ist ihm sein Hochmuth noch nicht vergangen, da er hilflos am Kreuze hängt?

Christus. Frau, sieh deinen Sohn. Sohn, sieh deine Mutter.

Maria. So sorgst du sterbend noch für deine Mutter!

Johannes. Heilig sei mir dein letzter Wille! Du meine Mutter! und ich dein Sohn!

Christus. [*Mit Zeichen des herannahenden Endes.*] Mich dürstet.

Hauptmann. Er leidet Durst und ruft um einen Trunk.

2. Henker. Geschwind will ich ihn reichen. [*Nimmt die Stange mit dem Schwamm, auf der Hauptmann aus seiner Flasche giesst.* CHRISTUS *nippt an dem Schwamme.*] Hier, trinke!

Christus. [*Mit dem Ausdrucke des höchsten Leidens.*] Eloi, Eloi, lama sabachtani!

Pharisäer und Volk. Seht, er ruft dem Elias.

Kaiphas. Nun, wir wollen sehen, ob Elias komme, ihn herabzunehmen.

Christus. [*Wiederholt tief aufathmend.*] Es ist vollbracht! Vater, in deine Hände empfehle ich meinen Geist [*Neigt langsam das Haupt und stirbt. Man hört Getöse, es wird finster.*]

By this time the Rabbi and Saras returned from Pilate, and coming back to Caiaphas they said, "Our mission was in vain. The governor would not listen to us." Caiaphas indignantly asked, while the priests and Pharisees crowded around, "Did he give you no answer at all?" "This only," said the Rabbi. "What I have written I have written." "Intolerable!" said Annas. Caiaphas also was much perturbed. But collecting himself he asked, "What did he order about the breaking of the bones?" "About this matter, he said, he would give his orders to the Centurion," answered the Rabbi.

Then seeing that no more could be done, the Jews began to revile Jesus, going up to the cross and wagging their heads and scoffing at him. Jesus, the priest, went up first and said, "So then it remains written, King of the Jews. Behold, if thou art King of Israel, come down now from the cross, that we may see and believe." And all the Jews laughed together.

Then said Eliezer, "Thou that destroyest the Temple and buildest it again in three days, save thyself!" And Caiaphas said, "Ha! thou that savedst others, thyself thou canst not save." "Come down," cried one of the witnesses. "Art thou not the Son of God?" And Annas said, "He trusted in God; let Him deliver Him now if He will have Him." Then cried the hangmen, "What! don't you hear? Show Thy power, mighty King of the Jews!" And so the sport went on.

Then Jesus, who all this time had hung motionless and silent, raised slowly and with pain his head, which had been bowed down, and said, "Father, forgive them; they know not what they do!"

Hearing Jesus speak, the Thief who was crucified on his left said unto him, "Hearest thou? If thou be Christ, save thyself and us." But the other Thief, who was crucified on the right, answered and said, "Dost thou not fear God, seeing that thou art in the same condemnation? And we, indeed, justly; for we receive the due reward of our deeds; but this man hath done nothing amiss." Then, turning to Jesus, he said. "Lord, remember me when thou comest into thy kingdom!" Then Jesus looked upon him and said. "Verily, I say unto thee, to-day shalt thou be with me in Paradise."

"Listen to that," cried Caiaphas, scornfully, "He speaks as if he had power over the gates of Paradise." "What," said the Rabbi, "Have not his pride and presumption deserted him even as he hangs helpless on the cross?" And they were wroth with Jesus.

During all this time Mary, the mother of Jesus, and John had been slowly approaching the cross, and now they stood immediately below Jesus, Mary on the right, John on the left. Then Jesus, beholding them, said to Mary, "Mother, behold thy son!" And slowly and with difficulty turning his head to see John, Jesus added. "Son, behold thy Mother!"

Then Mary cried in ecstacy of love and adoration. "Even in dying Thou carest still for Thy Mother!" And John, tenderly supporting Mary, but looking above to Jesus, exclaimed. "Thy last request is sacred to me!" And then to Mary he said. "Thou my mother, I thy son!"

Then Jesus, in a hollow voice, cried hoarsely, "I thirst."

The Centurion hearing him, said, "He thirsts and calls for drink." Then said Faustus, "I will reach him some at once." Then, taking the reed with the sponge, he filled it with vinegar and passed it to the Centurion, who, taking a small phial from his dress, poured hyssop on the sponge. Faustus then reached the sponge up to the lips of Jesus. But Jesus turned away his head and would not drink. "Here, drink!" said Faustus. "What, wilt thou not?" and seeing that Jesus would not touch the sponge, he took it away.

Then Jesus cried in agony, "Eli, Eli, lama sabachthani!"

But those bearing him did not understand, but imagined he cried for Elias.

"Hark!" said they; "he crieth for Elias."

Then Caiaphas laughed and said, "Let be, let us see whether Elias will come to save him."

Then Jesus, raising his head with a great effort to heaven, and breathing heavily, cried with a loud voice and said, "It is finished. Father, into thy hands I commend my spirit!"

And as Jesus spoke these words his head fell forward on his breast and he gave up the ghost. Then was there a great earthquake and thunder and lightning, and a great darkness, at which all were astonished.

THE CRUCIFIXION.—ACT XVI., SC. 1.

CHRIST IN THE BOSOM OF MARY.

THE DESCENT FROM THE CROSS.

Priester und Volk. Welch' fürchterliche Erschütterung! Hört ihr das Gekrache der einstürzenden Felsen? Wehe uns!
Hauptmann. Wahrlich, dieser Mann war ein Gerechter!
Soldaten. Die Gottheit selbst giebt ihm Zeugniss durch diese Schrecken der Natur.
Hauptmann. Diese Geduld in den heftigsten Leiden, diese edle Ruhe, dieser laute, fromme Ruf zum Himmel im Augenblicke vor seinem Hinscheiden—das lasst etwas Höheres ahnen. Wahrlich, er ist ein Gottessohn!
Volk. Kommt, Nachbarn, ich bleibe nicht mehr an diesem Orte des Schreckens. Lasst uns noch Hause gehen. Gott sei uns gnädig!
Andere. [An die Brust schlagend.] Allmächtiger! Wir haben gesündigt! [Das Volk zerstreut sich mit Zeichen von Angst und Reue.]
Tempeldiener. [Kommt eilends.] Hohepriester und gesammter Rath! Im Heiligthume hat sich ein schrecklicher Auftritt ereignet. Ich zittere an allen Gliedern.
Kaiphas. Was ist es, doch nicht der Tempel....
Annas. Eingestürzt?
Diener. Das nicht, aber die Scheidewand des Tempels ist mitten entzwei geborsten. Es schien, als spalte sich die ganze Erde.
Priester und Pharisäer. Schrecklich!
Kaiphas. [Auf den todten Jesus deutend.] Das hat uns dieser Bösewicht durch seine Zauberkünste angethan! Gut, dass er aus der Welt ist, sonst brachte er noch alle Elemente in Unordnung.
Priester und Pharisäer. Fluch dem Verbundeten des Belzebub!
Kaiphas. Lasst uns eilends heimgehn und sehen, was sich ereignet hat, dann wollen wir sofort hieher zurückkehren. Denn ich habe keine Ruhe, bis ich gesehen habe, dass diesem Menschen die Gebeine zerschlagen sind und sein Leichnam in die Grube der Missethäter hinabgeworfen ist.

[Die Priesterschaft ab.

ZWEITE SZENE.

Nicodemus. [Zu Joseph von Arimathia.] So soll denn der heilige Leichnam des Gottgesandten so schrecklich verunehrt, in die Grube der Missethäter geworfen werden?
Joseph. Freund, höre meinen Entschluss. Ich gehe geraden Weges zu Pilatus und will ihn herzlich bitten, dass er mir die Leiche Jesu schenke. Diese Gnade wird er mir nicht versagen.
Nicodemus. Thue das, Freund! Ich will Gewürze bringen, ihn einzubalsamiren. [Gehen ab.
Hauptmann. [Zu den heiligen Frauen.] Fürchtet euch nicht, gute Frauen. Es darf euch kein Leid geschehen.
Magdalena. [Das Kreuz umfassend.] O, liebster Lehrer, mein Herz hangt mit dir am Kreuze!
Diener der Pilatus. [Eintretend zum Hauptmann.] Auf Befehl meines Herrn sollen den Gekreuzigten die Beine gebrochen und dann ihre Leichname abgenommen werden. Vor Anbruch des grossen Abends muss alles vorüber sein.
Hauptmann. Sogleich wird es geschehen. Leute, brechet zuerst diesen Zweien die Gebeine!
3. Henker. Lasst uns dieses herzbrechende Geschäft schnell vollbringen!
2. Henker. Schlag zu, dass er sterbe!
3. Henker. [Der auf einer Leiter zum rechten Schächer emporgestiegen und mit vier Keulenschlägen ihm die Beine gebrochen.] Dieser erwacht nicht mehr!
4. Henker. [Steigt zum linken Schächer empor.] Den andern will ich aus der Welt hinausbefördern.
Maria. [Schaudernd.] Ach Jesus, man wird doch mit deinem heiligen Leibe nicht so grausam verfahren?
4. Henker. [Zum linken Schächer.] Rührst du dich nicht mehr? Nein, er hat seinen Lohn.

The priests and the people cried out saying, "What a dreadful earthquake. Do ye hear the crash of falling rocks? Woe, woe be to us!" But the centurion said, "Certainly this was a righteous man." Another soldier replied, "God himself bears him witness by these convulsions of nature." The centurion said, "Oh, his patience in his agony, his noble calm, this last loud cry to heaven at the moment before death, all betoken his divine origin. Verily he is a son of God!"

The people in alarm departed. "Come, neighbours," said Osiel; "I will remain no longer in this terrible place." "Yes," cried Halon, "let us go home, and may God have mercy on us." And others, smiting their breasts, cried, "Almighty God, we have sinned. Forgive us!"

And so it came to pass that no one remained round the cross but the holy women and John, and the friends of Jesus, with the hangmen.

The chief priests and the rulers still stood together marvelling, near the cross of the repentant thief, when suddenly a temple servant came rushing into their midst, breathless with haste.

"High priests and assembled council!" he exclaimed, "a fearful thing has occurred in the Holy Place! I tremble in every limb!" "What is it?" cried Caiaphas in alarm. "Not the Temple?" "Has it fallen?" said Annas. "No," said the Servant, "Not that, but the veil of the Temple has been rent in twain from the top to the bottom. It seemed as if the whole world was bursting asunder." "Dreadful!" exclaimed the priests and Pharisees, throwing up their hands. But Caiaphas said, "It is that wretch who has done this by his magic arts. What a blessing it is that he is out of the world! otherwise he would bring all the elements into disorder."

Then all the priests and Pharisees raised up their voices and cried, shaking their fists against Jesus, "Cursed be the ally of Beelzebub!"

"Now," said Caiaphas, "let us hurry home and see what has happened; then we will come back at once. For I cannot rest until I have seen this fellow's bones broken and his corpse flung into the grave of the transgressors."

When Caiaphas and Annas and all the rulers of the Jews had departed, then said Nicodemus to Joseph of Arimathea, having overheard the parting words of Caiaphas, "Shall the holy body of the Son of God be delivered over to such dishonour as to be flung into the grave of the 'Evil-doers'?" "Listen, friend," said Joseph, "what I have decided to do. I will go straightway to Pilate, and will implore him to give me the body of Jesus. He can hardly refuse me this favour." "Do so, by all means," said Nicodemus. "Hasten thither and I will bring the spices to embalm him." They having departed, the holy women, trembling, drew round the cross. "Fear not, good women," said the Centurion, "no harm shall happen to you."

Then Mary Magdalene clasped the cross with both her arms, pressed it to her breast, and cried through her tears as she looked up at the silent and lifeless form above, "Oh, dearest Master, my heart hangs with thee on the cross!"

Then entered a servant of Pilate, and, addressing the Centurion, said unto him, "This is the command of my lord: Break the legs of the crucified, and take down their bodies. Everything must be over before the eve of the Passover begin."

The Centurion said, "It shall be done at once. Men, first break the legs of these two." Catiline said, "Come, let us put this business through without more delay." Then the hangmen took ladders and placed them against the crosses of the thieves. Catiline, seizing a strong club, then mounted the ladder against the cross on the right hand. "Strike," said Faustus, "so as to kill him." Then Catiline smote the penitent thief heavily over each of the thighs and then across the shoulder bone. As the blow fell the man's head fell forward, and he gave up the ghost. "There," said Catiline, "he wakes no more." In like manner did Nero to the thief on the left hand, saying, "I will hasten the other out of the world." When the blows were falling upon the body of the thief, Mary, the mother of Jesus, who had watched with terror the blows of the hangman, cried out, shuddering, "O my Son, they will surely not deal so cruelly with thy holy body!" Nero called out to the thief, "Movest thou no more? No, thou hast had enough. I have given thee thy wages." Then,

THE CRUCIFIXION.—ACT XVI., SC. 2.

Magdalena. [*Da der Henker mit der Keule auf* CHRISTUS *loseilt.*] Ach, schonet doch, schonet doch!

3. Henker. [*Zu* CHRISTUS *aufblickend.*] Er ist schon verschieden, das Brechen der Gebeine ist nicht mehr nothwendig.

2. Henker. Damit wir seines Todes ganz sicher sind, will ich ihm mit der Lanze das Herz öffnen. [*Sticht* JESUM *in die Seite, das Blut quillt hervor.*]

Die heil. Frauen. Ach!

Magdalena. O Mutter! Dieser Stich ist auch durch dein Herz gedrungen!

Hauptmann. Nun nehmt die Leichname von den Kreuzen!

1. Henker. Wohin denn mit ihnen?

Hauptmann. Wie es Vorschrift ist, in die Grube der Verbrecher.

Maria. Welch schreckliches Wort!

4. Henker. Leitern her! Die werden bald abgenommen sein.

Magdalena. [*Zum Hauptmann.*] So dürfen wir unserm Freunde nicht einmal die letzte Ehre erweisen?

Hauptmann. Es steht leider nicht in meiner Macht, euren Wunsch zu erfüllen.

2. Henker. [*Zum ersten, der auf der Leiter steht.*] Steige nur zu, ich will halten.

3. Henker. Und jenen will ich besorgen. [*Steigt hinauf.*]

DRITTE SZENE.

Die Priesterschaft kehrt auf Golgotha zurück.

Kaiphas. [*An der Spitze der Priester herankommend.*] Desto angenehmer wird es uns sein, den Leichnam des Bösewichtes in die Schandgrube werfen zu sehen, nachdem wir die Verwüstung geschaut haben, die er im Tempel angerichtet hat.

Annas. Es würde mir Augenweide sein, seine Glieder von wilden Thieren zerrissen zu sehen.

Kaiphas. Seht, sie werden schon herabgenommen. Da werden wir unser Verlangen sobert erfüllt sehen.

Diener des Pilatus. [*Mit* JOSEPH *von Arimathia eintretend, zum Hauptmann.*] Der Statthalter hat mich gesendet, dich zu fragen, ob Jesus von Nazareth wirklich schon verschieden sei, wie ihm dieser Mann hier berichtet hat.

Hauptmann. Es ist so, sieh selbst.

Diener. So habe ich den Auftrag, dir zu melden, dass dessen Leichnam diesem Manne vom Statthalter als Geschenk überlassen sei. [*Ab.*

Die heil. Frauen. O tröstliche Nachricht!

Rabbi. [*Gegen* JOSEPH *von Arimathia.*] Der Verrather des Synagoge? Da hat er wieder Schleichwege gemacht!

Annas. Und unsere Freude verdorben!

Kaiphas. [*Zum Hauptmann.*] Jedoch gestatten wir nicht, dass er anderswo beigelegt werde, als bei den Missethätern.

Hauptmann. Da der Leichnam diesem Manne geschenkt ist, so versteht es sich von selbst, dass er ihn bestatten kann, wie und wo er will. Das bildet keine Einrede. [*Zu den Soldaten und Henkern.*] Leute! unser Geschäft ist beendet, wir wollen zurückkehren. [*Ab.*

Annas. [*Zu* JOSEPH *von Arimathia.*] Du beharrst also auf deinem Starrsinn! Schämst du dich nicht, einen hingerichteten Verbrecher noch in seinem Leichnam zu ehren!

Joseph. Den Tugendhaftesten der Menschen, den gottgesandten Lehrer, den unschuldig Gemordeten ehre ich.

Nicodemus. Neid und Stolz waren die Triebfedern seiner Verurtheilung. Der Richter selbst musste seine Unschuld Zeugniss geben, er schwor es, dass er kein Theil haben wolle an seinem Blute.

Kaiphas. Der Fluch des Gerechten wird euch, ihr Feinde unserer Väter, zu Grunde richten!

Rabbi. Ereifere dich nicht, Hoherpriester, sie sind mit Blindheit geschlagen.

coming down from the ladder, they made ready to break the legs of Jesus.

But as the hangman approached the foot of the cross with the ladder and the club, Mary Magdalene sprang before him, and, thrusting him back with her slender arm, cried piteously. "Oh! spare him! spare him!" Then Catiline, looking up at Jesus, said: "Behold! he is already dead. There is no need, therefore, to break his legs." "But," said Faustus, "in order to make sure, I will pierce his heart with a spear." Then, grasping a lance, he thrust it into the right side of Jesus, and forthwith there spurted out blood and water. John, who was looking up with the holy women, shuddered as the spear entered the side of Jesus. Mary Magdalene, turning to Mary, said: "Oh, mother, that spear has pierced my own heart also." Then said the Centurion: "Now take down the bodies from the Cross!" "Where," said one of the hangmen, "shall we put them?" The Centurion replied: "As ordered, into the grave of the malefactors." Then said Mary, with a terrible sob: "What a terrible word!" "Ladders here," said the hangmen, "we shall soon have them down." Then the hangmen unfastened the cords which bound the thieves to their crosses, and, mounting the ladder, received their bodies in their arms and bore them away.

While they were busy Mary Magdalene went to the Centurion, and said unto him, "May we not even pay the last honours to our friend?" "Alas," said the Conturion, "it is not within my power to permit this."

Then came back Caiaphas and Annas and all the rulers of the Sanhedrim from the Temple to Golgotha. Caiaphas, speaking as they approached, said, "It will be all the more delightful to see the body of this evildoer cast into a shameful grave, because we have witnessed the destruction he has brought to pass within the Temple." Annas answered, "What joy it would be if my eyes could see him torn limb from limb by wild beasts." "Ha," said Caiaphas, as they saw the hangmen bearing off the bodies of the thieves, "they are already being taken down. Now we shall soon see our ardent desires fulfilled."

Hardly had Caiaphas and the priests approached the cross, when from the other side there came Joseph of Arimathea and with him a servant of Pilate's. The servant said to the Centurion, "The governor has sent me to inquire of thee whether it can really be true that Jesus of Nazareth is already dead, as this man has informed him?" "It is so, indeed," replied the Centurion, pointing to the cross, "look for yourself." Then said the servant, "Then I have orders to inform you that the body is to be delivered over to this man, as a gift from Pilate," and having said this he departed.

"Oh, blessed messenger!" cried the holy women still gathered together around the foot of the cross. But the Jews, hearing the message, waxed furious, and the Rabbi, speaking of Joseph, said to the chief priests and rulers, "The traitor of the Synagogue, he has foiled us again." "And spoiled our triumph," said Annas. But Caiaphas would not submit, and said, haughtily, "We shall not tolerate it that his body shall be laid anywhere else than in the grave of the transgressors."

The Centurion replied, "As the body is given to this man, it is obvious that he can bury it where and how he will. There is no disputing that."

Then said he to the soldiers and executioners, "Men, our work is done. We must go."

Then the hangmen gathered up their basket and their cord, their dice, and the fragments of Christ's mantle, and departed. With them went the Centurion and his band, leaving Caiaphas and the Jews face to face with the holy women and their friends at the foot of the cross. The Jews were exceeding wroth, and raged among themselves against the Centurion. Annas cried out to Joseph of Arimathea, "Dost thou still persist in thy headstrong obstinacy? Art thou not ashamed to do honour to the very corpse of an executed malefactor?" Joseph replied, "I, indeed, honour this noblest of men, the teacher sent from God, whom, being innocent, you have murdered." And Nicodemus added, "Envy and pride slew him. The judge himself was forced to bear witness to his innocence, and swore he would have no part in his death."

Then said Caiaphas, furiously, "The curse of our law will overwhelm you, ye enemies of our Fathers!" The Rabbi said, "Do not excite thyself about them, O High Priest; they are

Kaiphas. Verflucht seid ihr vom ganzen Rathe. Eurer Würde beraubt, sollt ihr's nicht mehr wagen, in unserm Kreise zu erscheinen!

Nicodemus. Das wollen wir auch nicht mehr.

Annas. [Mit den Priestern nach vorne tretend.] Da der Leichnam in den Handen seiner Freunde ist, so müssen wir auf unserer Hut sein, denn dieser Verführer hat bei seinen Lebzeiten gesagt, er werde nach drei Tagen wieder erstehn.

Rabbi. Wie leicht könnte da dem Volke ein neuer Betrug gespielt, uns aber neue Verlegenheit bereitet werden! Seine Jünger konnten ihn heimlich entwenden und dann die Sage verbreiten, er sei erstanden.

Kaiphas. Dann wäre der letzte Irrthum ärger als der erste. Lasst uns daher sogleich zu Pilatus gehen und bei ihm um Mannschaft nachsuchen, damit das Grab bis zum dritten Tage bewacht werde.

Annas. Ein kluger Gedanke!

Rabbi. So werden ihre Pläne vereitelt werden.

[Die Priesterschaft ab.

VIERTE SZENE.
Kreuzabnahme und Begräbniss.

Magdalena. Sind sie endlich fort, die Wüthenden! Tröste dich, geliebte Mutter! Das Gespötte und die Lästerungen sind verstummt und heilige Abendstille umfängt uns.

Maria. Er hat es vollbracht, er ist eingegangen in die Ruhe des Vaters. Ruhe ist in meinem Herzen.

Magdalena. Er ist uns nicht für immer entrissen, er hat es uns versprochen. . . .

Maria. [Zu den mit der Kreuzesabnahme beschäftigten Männern.] Edle Männer! Bringt mir bald den Leichnam meines lieben Kindes!

Salome. Gefährtinnen, kommt, bereitet diese Leinwand zu seinem Empfang. [Sie setzen MARIA auf einen Stein und breiten Leinwand zu ihren Füssen.

Joseph. [Den Leichnam Jesu auf seine Schulter nehmend.] O süsse, heilige Bürde, komm' auf meine Schultern! [Trägt den Leichnam herab.]

Nicodemus. [Die Arme zum Empfang des Todten ausbreitend.] Komm', heiliger Leichnam meines einzigen Freundes! Lass' dich umarmen! Wie hat die Wuth deiner Feinde dich zerfleischt! [Der Leichnam wird zu Mariens Schoss gelehnt].

Johannes. Hier soll der beste Sohn nochmals im Schoose der besten Mutter ruhen.

Maria. O mein Sohn, wie ist dein Leib mit Wunden bedeckt!

Johannes. Mutter, aus diesen Wunden floss Heil und Segen für die Menschheit.

Magdalena. Sieh', Mutter, Himmelsfriede ruht auf dem erblassten Angesichte.

Nicodemus. Lasst uns ihn salben und in diese neue Leinwand einwickeln.

Joseph. In mein neues Grab soll er gelegt werde, das ich mir in der Felsengrotte meines Gartens habe zubereiten lassen.

Salome. Bester Meister! Noch eine Thräne der Liebe auf deinen entseelten Leib!

Magdalena. O lasst mich nochmals die Hand küssen, die mich so oft gesegnet!

Johannes. Wir werden ihn wiedersehn!

smitten with blindness." But Caiaphas, refusing to be silenced, cried, "Cursed are ye by the whole Council. Deprived of all your honours, never more shall you take your seats in our midst." "Neither do we desire to do so," said Nicodemus. Then said Annas, "As the body is now in the hands of his friends, we must be on our guard, for this deceiver, while he was yet alive, said that in three days he would arise again."

The Rabbi said. "They could easily practise a new deception on the people and make fresh trouble for us. His disciples might take his body away secretly and then give out that he had risen from the dead." "In that case," said Caiaphas, "the last error would be worse than the first. Let us go at once to Pilate and ask him for a guard of soldiers to keep watch over the grave till the third day." "A prudent thought!" cried Annas, and the Rabbi added, "Thus their schemes will be foiled." Then they departed to go to Pilate.

His enemies, having left his friends alone round the cross, Nicodemus and Joseph of Arimathea set about taking down the body of Jesus. Bringing the ladders, Joseph mounted on the shorter one that was placed in front, while Nicodemus ascended the longer one behind. Nicodemus had with him a roll of linen so long, that after putting it round the body of Jesus, the ends, hanging over the cross, reached to the ground, where they were held by Simon of Bethany and Lazarus. Then after taking off the crown of thorns, Nicodemus took the pincers and began to pull out the nails from the hands of Jesus and bent the stiffening arms lovingly away from the Cross. While they were thus engaged the Magdalen and Mary talked together. "At last," said Mary Magdalene, "the madmen have departed! Be comforted, beloved mother, the mockery and the blasphemy is past, and a holy evening stillness surrounds us." Mary said, "Now he has finished his work and entered into the rest of his Father. Peace also and trust from heaven fills my soul." Magdalene comforted her, saying, "He is not taken from us for ever; that he promised." "Oh, noble men!" said Mary to Joseph and Nicodemus, "make haste and bring me the body of my beloved son." Then seating herself on a stone a little to the right of the cross, Mary waited while her friends made ready to receive the body of Jesus. "Come, my companions," said Salome, "and help me to prepare the winding sheet to receive the body." They spread the linen on the ground at Mary's feet, placing one end upon her lap.

By this time Nicodemus had extracted the second nail which was in the left hand, and Joseph had taken the nail from the feet of Jesus. Then Simon and Lazarus, holding the ends of the linen roll, slowly lowered the body into the arms of Joseph of Arimathea. "Oh, come!" said Joseph, "thou sweet and holy burden; let me take thee upon my shoulders." Then with the body of Jesus resting upon his shoulders Joseph began to descend the ladder. Nicodemus had already come down and awaited him at the foot of the cross. Spreading out his arms to receive the body of Jesus, he said, "Come, thou holy body of my only friend, let me embrace thee. How the rage of thy enemies hath torn thy flesh." Then they carried the body of Jesus and placed it on the linen winding sheet that was prepared for it on his mother's lap.

"Now," said John, "the best of sons rests once more on the bosom of the best of mothers." Mary looked down upon the pale, blood-spotted face of Jesus, and then, sighing heavily, she said, "Oh, my son, how is thy body covered with wounds." "Mother," said John, "from these wounds flowed salvation and blessing for mankind." "See, mother," said the Magdalen, who stood on her right hand, "how the peace of heaven rests in death upon his face." Then said Nicodemus, who had brought some ointment, "let us anoint him, and then wrap him in this new linen." He then poured the ointment into all the wounds on the body of Jesus. "He shall be laid," said Joseph of Arimathea, "in my new grave which I have prepared in the rock in my garden." But before they could fold him in the winding sheets, Salome came near, and, kneeling, raised to her lips the pierced left hand of Jesus, saying, "Oh, best of Masters! One more loving tear upon thy lifeless body." Then came the Magdalen on the right hand, and kneeling down, stooped low and kissed the right hand, saying, "Oh, let me once more kiss the hand which has so often blessed me." Then said John, "We shall see him again!"

Joseph. [Zu Nicodemus.] Du hilf mir, ihn in den Garten hintragen.
Nicodemus. Ich Glücklicher, der ich die Hülle des Gottgesandten zur Ruhe senken darf. [Sie tragen den Leichnam zum Grabe.]
Johannes. Lasst uns folgen.
Maria. Es ist der letzte Dienst, den ich meinem Jesu erweisen kann. [Alle folgen. Man sieht nun im Hintergrunde das Grab.]
Alle. Freund, ruhe sanft im stillen Felsengrabe!
Johannes. Jetzt wollen wir uns zurückziehn. Komm', beste Mutter! [Ab mit den Frauen.
Joseph. Mit diesem Steine hier lasst uns das Grab verschliessen, hilf mir.
Nicodemus. Nach dem Festtage wollen wir das Liebeswerk vollenden.
Joseph. Nun komm, Freund, seinen Tod zu beweinen.
Nicodemus. O dieser Mann voll Geist und Wahrheit, wie hat er solch' ein Schicksal verdient! [Ab.

XVII.—VORSTELLUNG.
Die Auferstehung.

Tenor.
Ruhe sanft aus, heil'ge Hülle
Solo.
Ruhe in des Grabes Stille
Von den Leidensmühen aus
Chor.
Ruhe sanft in Schoos der Erde
Bis du wirst verkläret sein
Der Verwesung Opfer werde
Nie dein heiliges Gebein.—
Christen, senkt am Pilgerstabe
Hin das Haupt in Ehrfurcht still;
Denn ihr steht am heil'gen Grabe
Dessen, der statt gold'ner Gabe
Nur ein Herz voll Einfalt will.

ERSTE SZENE.
Garten mit der Felsengrotte. Titus, Pedius, Rufus, Kajus.
[Am Felsenhügel um das Grab her sitzend oder liegend.]

Titus. Wie ist euch, Bruder? Mir wird's bald zu lange, so hierzusitzen als Todtenwächter.
Rufus. Habt nur Geduld! Es ist die letzte Nacht. Bis an den dritten Tag, so hiess es ja, soll die Bewachung dauern.
Pedius. Nun, so wird uns bald Erlösung werden.
Titus. Wahrlich ist's doch lacherlich, wie diese Leute noch den Todten fürchten.
Rufus. Der Mann von Nazareth, so wird erzählt, hat ausgesagt, er werde wiederkehren am dritten Tage aus der Unterwelt. Daher die Furcht.
Kajus. [Der bisher im Schlafe gelegen, erwachend.] Brüder! ist die Nacht nicht bald vorüber?
Titus. Bald! Schon fangt der Himmel an, im Osten sich zu röthen. Ein schöner Frühlingstag lacht uns entgegen. [Erdbeben.
Pedius. [Aufspringend.] Unsterbliche! welch furchterlicher Eridstoss!
Rufus. Die Erde spaltet sich! [Blitz und Donner.
Titus. Hinweg vom Felsen! Hinweg! er wankt! er stürzet ein! [Ein Engel stösst den Stein weg; Christus erscheint.
Pedius. Ihr Götter! Was seh' ich.
Titus. Ich erblinde! Ach! ein Feuer hat mich ergriffen!
[Sie stürzen nieder, die einen auf die Knie, sich das Angesicht verhüllend; die andern neigen das Haupt bis zur Erde.]
Kajus. [Ueber eine Weile—noch auf den Knieen.] Brüder! was ist uns begegnet!
Rufus. Keinen Augenblick will ich hier langer bleiben.
Titus. [Aufsehend.] Die Erscheinung ist verschwunden. [Nimmt seine Waffe und steht auf.] Brüder! fasset Muth! [Alle erheben sich.
Titus. [Der sich dem Grabe genähert hat.] Seht her! der Stein ist abgewalzt vom Grabe. Das Grab ist offen.

"Help me," said Joseph to Nicodemus, "to bear him into the garden." "Blessed am I." said Nicodemus, "that I may lay to rest the remains of him who was sent from God." Then, taking up the body, they bore it away. Then said John to Mary and the other women, "Let us follow." "It is the last honour," said Mary, "that I can do my Jesus." Then they bore the body to the grave. All then said, "Friend, rest sweetly in the quiet rock-tomb." John said to Mary, "Now let us depart. Come, dear mother," and led her away, the women following. Joseph then said to Nicodemus, "Help me to close the grave with this stone." Nicodemus, having done so, replied, "After the feast-day we will finish the work of love." Joseph said, "Now come, friend, and weep for his death," and Nicodemus, as they departed, said, "Oh! this man full of wisdom and truth!—how has he deserved such a fate?"

CHAPTER XVII.
Act XVII.

Tenor.
Softly rest now, sacred body.
Solo.
Rest in peace from pain and labour
In the stillness of the grave.
Chorus.
Softly rest within Earth's bosom
Till that Thou art glorified.
Never shall Thy flesh corruption
See, though Thou like us hast died.
Christians, low in adoration
Bow your heads as here ye stand:
By His grave ye have your station,
Who, for gifts of consecration
Doth a simple heart demand.

THE RESURRECTION.

On the morning of the third day since Jesus had been crucified, before the sun had arisen, the four soldiers who were appointed to watch the grave sat outside the tomb where the body of Jesus had been laid. One watched, the others were asleep. Then said one of the watch, who was named Titus, to his neighbours, as they stretched themselves, "How goes it, brothers? As for me I am getting very weary of sitting here to watch the dead." Then said Rufus unto him, "Have a little more patience. It is the last night, for it is only until the third day that the watch had to continue." Then said another soldier, "We shall be soon released now!" "Truly it is laughable," said the first who had spoken, "how these people fear the dead body." "Oh," said Rufus, "the Man of Nazareth has predicted, so they say, that he would return from the under-world on the third day." The fourth soldier, awaking, cried, "Brothers, is not the night nearly over?" Then said Titus, "The sky is already reddening in the east; a beautiful spring day is beginning to dawn."

Hardly had he said these words when there was a great earthquake. Pedius, springing up, exclaimed, "Immortal gods! what a fearful shock." "The earth is splitting!" cried Rufus. Then there was a peal of thunder. Titus called out, "Away from the rock!—it is tottering—it is falling!" and the stone which had been rolled up into the mouth of the sepulchre fell down with a crash.

Jesus arose. For a moment he appeared at the mouth of the sepulchre, radiant in white apparel, while the Watch fell on their faces to the ground, crying out, "Ye gods, what do we see? The fire is blinding my eyes!" Jesus then passed out through the door of the sepulchre, and went down the garden out of sight.

After a while the soldiers, who were lying prostrate on the ground, said to each other, "Brother, what has happened to us!" Then said one of the soldiers, "I will not stop here another moment." But Titus, looking up, said, "The apparition has vanished;" and grasping his spear, he rose to his feet, saying, "Brothers, take heart!" They then stood up and saw the open door of the sepulchre, from which the stone had fallen. Then said Titus, "The stone is rolled away from

THE ASCENSION.

Kajus. [*Am Eingange des Gartens.*] Und die Gartenthür verseperrt. [*Alle gehen zum Grabe.*
Rufus. [*In die Höhle hineinsehend.*] Ich sehe keine Leiche mehr.
Pedius. [*Geht weiter hinein.*] Hier liegt noch die Leinwand, die der Leiche zur Hülle diente. Er ist aus dem Grabe.
Titus. Er muss erstanden sein. Es kann kein Mensch herein.
Rufus. So ist geschehen, was die Priester befürchteten.
Titus. Er hat sein Wort erfüllt.
Rufus. Und wir?—was bleibt uns nun zu thun?
Pedius. Nichts And'res, als hinzueilen und den Pharisäern zu melden, was geschah.
Alle. Das wollen wir. [*Sie gehen zu* ANNAS, *Seite ab.*

the grave. The grave is open." "Yes," said another, "and the garden door is bolted." Then they went with fear and trembling to the door of the sepulchre, and one, looking in, said, "I do not see the corpse." Then another, going farther inside, said, "Here is the linen cloth lying, in which the body was wrapped. He has gone out of the grave." Titus said, "He must have risen again, as no one came into the garden." Then said the third soldier, "It has happened thus, as the priests feared." And Titus answered, "He has fulfilled his word!" "Now what shall we do?" said the soldiers. "There is nothing else to be done," said one, "excepting to hasten to the Pharisees, and tell them what has happened." All replied at once, "That we will," and they hastened away.

SCHLUSS-VORSTELLUNG.

HALLELUJA.

Ueberwunden—überwunden
Hat der Held der Feinde Macht.
Todt—hat Leben er gefunden
In der düstern Grabesnacht.
Singet ihm in Jubelpsalmen!
Streuet ihm des Sieges Palmen!
Auferstanden ist der Herr!
Jauchzet ihm, ihr Himmel an!
Preis, den Sieger, Erde du!
Halleluja Dir, Erlöser!
Anbetung bringet dem Heiland dar,
Dem Lamme, das getödtet war!
Halleluja!
Das, schreitend aus dem Grab hervor,
Zum Leben siegreich steigt empor.
Halleluja! Halleluja!
Ueberwunden—überwunden (wie oben).

Preis Ihm, dem Todesüberwinder,
Der durchgeführt, wozu Er kam,
Vom Tod erlöst die Gotteskinder,
Und ihm der Sünde Stachel nahm.
Lasst uns dem Kranz dem Sieger bringen,
Der auferstand und ewig lebt!
Lasst hell das neue Lied erklingen,
Dass Freude durch die Welten bebt.
"Lös' die Siegel, Herr! vom Buch,
Oeffne es—das ist Dein Recht!"
Frei sind wir vom alten Fluch
Und ein priesterlich Geschlecht.
Lobsinget, alle Himmelsheere!
Dem Herren sei Ruhm und Herrlichkeit!
Anbetung, Macht und Kraft und Ehre
Von Ewigkeit zu Ewigkeit!

Das Schlussbild stellt Christi Himmelfahrt dar, wie er von den Jüngern und den heil. Frauen umgeben, auf dem Oelberg steht.

CONCLUDING ACT.

HALLELUJAH CHORUS.

Overcome, yea, overcome
Has our Hero-Lord the might
Of his foes, and from the gloom
Of the grave brought life and light.
Sing to Him in joyous psalms,—
Strew before Him victory-palms!
Risen, risen is the Lord!
Cry, ye Heavens, to Him in praise,
Earth! the victor-anthem raise,
Hallelujah! Thou Adored!
Oh! worship Him! we cry again.
Worthy the Lamb that once was slain!
Hallelujah!
Who, rising from the darksome earth,
Ascends unto His place of birth,
Hallelujah! Hallelujah!

Oh! praise the Victor over death,
Who finished the work for which He came,
And all God's children ransometh,
Taking away all sin and shame.
Let us, the crown of victory bringing
To Him who rose and lives for aye,
The new, glad song of triumph singing,
Spread joy throughout the world to-day.
Open, Lord, the sealed scroll,
Loose the seals—it is Thy right!
Now away the curse doth roll,—
We are priests and kings in might.
Oh! join Him! all ye hosts of heaven,
Sing praise and glory to the Lord;
All honour, might and power be given
To Him eternally adored!

THE ASCENSION.

THE closing tableau represents the Ascension. It is as if Raffaelle's famous picture in the Vatican had suddenly become instinct with life. Christ robed in white, holding a palm-branch in his hand, stands in the midst of his disciples. Close to him are his Mother and Mary Magdalene, and John and Peter. As he blesses them, he slowly and almost imperceptibly begins to ascend into the air, the Apostles and the Holy Women following him with looks of intense adoration. When he reaches the centre of a great company of angels the curtain falls, and the "Passion Play" is over, except for the last jubilant song of the Schutzgeister, who resume their semicircle on the stage and sing the last line with as much vigour as if they had not been off and on the stage some twenty times.

THE END.

V.—THE GOSPEL ACCORDING TO ST. DAISENBERGER.

THE gospel according to St. Daisenberger as unfolded on the stage at Ober Ammergau is his version of the story that transformed the world, and that will yet transform it again. It is the old, old story in a new and, to Protestants, somewhat unfamiliar dress. It is as if the Gospel from the stained windows of our cathedrals had suddenly taken living bodily shape and transacted itself once more before our astonished eyes.

Wherein does it modify orthodox opinions? Chiefly in humanising them, in making the Gospel story once "palpitate with actuality," to quote the French phrase which Matthew Arnold loved to use. These people on the stage at Ober Ammergau are not lay figures, mere abstract representations of the virtues or the opposite. They live, breathe, and act just as if they were actors in a French or Russian novel. That is the great difference. These poor players have brought our Lord to life again. In their hands He is no mere influence or abstraction, no infinite and Almighty ruler of the universe. He may be, and no doubt every one of the Ober-Ammergauers would shrink with horror from the suggestion that he was any other than the second person of the Trinity. But they have done more than repeat the Athanasian Creed. They have shown how it came to be believable. If that poor carpenter's son, by getting himself crucified as one part fool and three parts seditious adventurer, could revolutionise the world, then the inference seemed irresistible that He must have been Divine. If the illegitimate son of a Bengalee peasant, hanged by order of our Lieutenant-Governor in the North-West provinces because of the mischief he was making among the Moslems of Lahore, were to establish his faith on the ruins of Westminster Abbey, and instal the successor of his leading disciple on the throne of the British Empire, we should not wonder at his Apotheosis. To do so much, with so little material, compels the inference that there is the Infinite behind. Nothing but a God could control such a machine. It needed a fulcrum in Eternity to make such a change in the things of time with so weak a lever as the life of this Galilean.

But it is not only Christ himself who becomes real to us, but, what is almost as important, we see his contemporaries as they saw themselves, or as he saw them. Caiaphas—who that has seen Burgomaster Lang in that leading rôle can feel anything but admiration and sympathy for the worthy Chief of the Sanhedrim? He had everything on his side to justify him. Law, respectability, patriotism, religious expediency, common sense. Against him there was only this poor vagabond from Nazareth—and the Invisible! But Caiaphas, like other men, does not see the Invisible, and he acts as, according to his lights, he was bound to act. He is the great prototype of the domineering and intolerant ecclesiastic all the world over. Since the Crucifixion he has often changed his clothes, but at heart he is the same. He has worn the three-crowned hat of the successor of Peter; he has paraded in a bishop's mitre; he has often worn the gown and bands of Presbyterian Geneva. Caiaphas is eternal. He produces himself in every church, and in every village, because there is a latent Caiaphas in every heart.

Perhaps the character who comes out best is Pilate. He is a noble Roman, whose impartiality and rectitude, coupled with an anxious desire to take the line of least resistance, and find out some practical middle course, is worthy of that imperial race, to whose vices, as well as to many of their virtues, we English have succeeded. Pilate did his best to save Jesus—up to a point. Beyond that point he did not go, and, according to the accepted ethics of men in his position, it would have been madness to have gone. Why should he, Pontius Pilate, Procurator of Judæa, risk his career and endanger the tranquillity of Jerusalem merely to save a poor wretch like that Galilean? What Englishman who has ever ruled a province in India, where religious ferment was rife, who would not have felt tempted to act as Pilate acted—nay, would not have acted as he acted without even the hesitation he showed, if the life of some poor devil of a wandering fakir stood between him and the peace of the Empire? Would to God that British magistrates, even at home in our own land, would give the despised and unpopular poor man the same number of chances Herod gave to Jesus! With Downing Street eager for the conviction of a Socialist agitator, and the whole of Society and the mob savage against him, a man would be a fool who would not appeal from Bow Street or Old Bailey to so just a judge as Pilate. To the last Pilate never made himself the willing instrument of popular frenzy. He argued against it, he denounced it, he resorted to every subterfuge by which he could save the prisoner's life, and it was only when the Sanhedrim threatened to denounce him to Cæsar as an enemy of the Emperor, that he unwillingly gave way. Here and there, no doubt, there are among our English magistrates and judges fanatical believers in abstract right, who would have risked the Empire rather than let a hair of Christ's head be touched ; but the average English magistrate—especially if the accused was " only a nigger "—would shrug his shoulders at such Quixotism as folly and worse. It is better, they would say, that one man should die even unjustly than that everything should be upset.

And that brings us to another point. Nothing stands out more clearly than the fact that on the technical point of law, it is, to say the least, doubtful whether Jesus was not rightly condemned. The great trial scene, where one scribe after another read out the text of the law governing the case, brought home very forcibly to the mind that the Sanhedrim was, after all, not going very far out of its way in order to condemn Jesus. He had, from a worldly point of view, been recklessly imprudent. He had played into the hands of his enemies as if he had actually been working for a conviction. His contumacious silence at the trial, broken only by a declaration that must have honestly appeared the most outrageous blasphemy to his judges, would have produced the very worst possible effect on the minds of an English judge and jury. The law takes no account of motives. The law lays down a set of maxims which must be applied without respect of persons. There is not a single one of the wise saws, such as the British press delight to quote when some particularly abominable piece of iniquity is about to be enacted in Ireland or in London, that would not have fitted admirably the mouth of Caiaphas or of Annas.

Then, if this be so ; if Jesus were legally condemned by the Sanhedrim for offences against the Jewish law, it becomes a grave question whether, on the accepted principles of imperial policy, it was really Pilate's duty to do more than he actually did. The Romans allowed the Jewish nation a considerable measure of home rule. To have absolutely refused to execute a prisoner whom they had tried by their own tribunals, and declared to be guilty, not only of offences which by their law merited death, but of entertaining designs against the imperial supremacy which they felt it incumbent upon themselves to denounce, would have been a very serious step to take. So serious that, having regard to the larger questions of the preservation of the liberties of the subjugated provinces, and the maintenance of the responsibility of the local authorities, it is easy to see that Pilate would have exposed himself to very grave censure had he gone further than he did in the attempt to save the life of one whom he could not have regarded as other than an amiable but slightly cracked enthusiast. Life was cheap in those days, and a Roman governor, as Caiaphas sarcastically reminded Pilate, thought little of the slaughter of the hecatomb of Jews. At any rate, before condemning Pilate I should like to see how the British viceroy will act when he is asked to interfere with the first act of flagrant injustice insisted on by an Irish Home Rule administration, when Downing Street is occupied by a Ministry that will give anything for an easy life, and when there is no outside public opinion to invoke in favour of the innocent oppressed.

Another person who comes out better than might be expected is Judas. The conception of his character is very fine and very human. Judas, as the treasurer of the little band, naturally felt indignant at the apparent wanton extravagance which led Mary Magdalene to pour ointment worth 300 pence upon the head of her Master. There is real human nature and sound practical common-sense in his reply to those who told him not to worry about the money, when he retorted, Who is there to take care about it if I don't ? Judas never from first to last really meditates betraying his Master to death. The salves which he lays to his conscience when consenting to identify Jesus at night are very ingenious. Judas was a smart man who calculated he stood to win in any event. He got the indispensable cash ; all that he did was to indicate what could perfectly well have been discovered without his aid : if Jesus were what he believed him to be, he could easily have baffled his enemies ; if he were not, well then he had deceived them. But the moment Judas learns that he has really endangered his Master's life, his whole demeanour changes. He flings back the blood-money at the feet of those who had given it him, and in the madness of despair he hangs himself. So far from Judas being callous to Christ's fate, his suicide was a proof that his penitence was far more agonising than that of Peter. To hang yourself is one of the severest proofs of the sincerity of your sorrow. One who had no conscience, or one incapable of intense feeling, would not have acted as did Judas.

Simon Peter also comes in for a share in the general rehabilitation. It was impossible not to feel sympathy for the hasty old man, hustled from side to side by a pack of violent soldiery. Knowing, moreover, that he had cut off one of their ears but a few hours before, and that if they recognised him, his own ears would be cropped, even if he didn't share the fate of the Crucified, his denial is so natural under the circumstances, that you cease to marvel that even the cock crow on the roof failed to remind him of his Master's warning.

The Passion Play has at least done this—it sets us discussing the conduct of Caiaphas and Pilate and Judas, as if they were our contemporaries, as if they were statesmen at Westminster, judges at the Old Bailey, or administrators in India. And this, no doubt, is no small service, for these men are types of human character, who are eternally re-embodied amongst us.

VI.—SOME GENERAL REFLECTIONS.

I shrink from setting down exactly what I thought during the Passion Play and what I have thought of it since. But if I may be pardoned for describing an experience that although personal is at least genuine, I may as well set down what it suggested to me. The story of the Passion has ever been real to me in another than a Catholic sense. It has been the perpetual re-incarnation of the Divine story in the history of our own times that has absorbed my attention. These ancient figures on the stage of New Testament history were but of importance in so far as they lived again in our own life. Of their mystical theological significance I am, of course, not speaking. That is a thing apart. But the perpetual re-incarnation of God's Messiah in the great causes of Justice, Freedom, and Humanity, it is that which has made the Gospel story ever new to me. Hence when I saw the old personages walk on the stage in their ancient conventional garb, I was for a time almost puzzled by the confusing multitude of associations which they awoke.

One of my earliest recollections, born as I was in the house of a Nonconformist minister, was of the struggle of the Nonconformists against all manner of religious disabilities inflicted and enforced by the State at the behest of the Established Church. The first Annas and Caiaphas whom I remember meeting in daily life were Anglican Churchmen who thrust Quakers into jail to extort payment of Church-rates, who barred the doors of the Universities against Nonconformists and then taunted us for our ignorance, and who even at the graveside insisted upon depriving us of the last poor consolation of a parting word of prayer by the grave of our dead. The Sanhedrim was Convocation, and the priests and Pharisees were the Established clergy.

When a mere schoolboy, Annas and Caiaphas passed into the secular sphere. The American war was raging, the end of which was to be the extirpation of American slavery. The war for the Union became, in Lowell's phrase, "God's new Messiah," and all those who aided and abetted the South and helped it, as did Mr. Roebuck by his speeches, Mr. Laird with his *Alabama*, or the *Times* by its constant taunts levelled against the North, seemed to be only too faithful followers of those who, nineteen hundred years ago, had betrayed Jesus of Nazareth.

When I entered journalism, the supreme crime which tempted the English to ruin was war with Russia. When the Russo-Turkish war was over, and the Jingo fever was at its height, I remember writing a leading article entitled "Reflections on Good Friday," in which I set out, in plain outspoken Saxon, my reasons for believing that if Lord Beaconsfield were permitted to plunge us into war in order to prevent the liberation of Bulgaria, we should, as a nation, be more guilty, because sinning against greater light, than were the Jews who crucified Jesus, or the Romans who allowed him to be put to death. So strongly was this impression upon me that, when Nicodemus and Joseph of Arimathea got up and left the Sanhedrim rather than share in the blood-guiltiness of those who pressed for the crucifixion of Christ, I was reminded irresistibly of the great struggle of 1878, in which Lord Carnarvon and Lord Derby played the rôle of Nicodemus and Joseph of Arimathea, leaving the Cabinet which Lord Beaconsfield then seemed to be hurrying into war as resolutely as Caiaphas pressed forward the Crucifixion.

After I left Darlington and came to London, the causes which have seemed to me to have most of Christ in them have been the cause of Woman and the cause of the Poor. The struggle against injustice the most foul, and of hardships compared with which those of men seem trivial, has had many vicissitudes, and is still far from being fought out. But I felt somewhat as if an injustice had been done when the same crowd that acclaimed Christ's entry in Jerusalem was brought on to the stage—even the children—to demand His crucifixion. Jerusalem was big enough to afford two crowds. I remember not so many years ago a cause which was cheered from Hyde Park to Charing Cross, shortly afterwards being hooted from Bow Street to Clerkenwell gaol. But it was not the same people who cheered in the one case and hooted in the other. Incidents in the struggle for the cause of woman would form as effective illustrated tableaux leading up to the incidents in the Passion as any of those which Herr Daisenberger selected from the Old Testament.

There was one scene in the Passion Play that reminded me irresistibly of Trafalgar Square. When the money-changers were cleared out of the Temple, they rushed indignantly to make complaint to the Sanhedrim, where they poured their sorrows into the sympathetic ear of Nathanael. It was just like the deputation of Charing Cross shopkeepers to the Home Secretary, which led to the filching of the Square from the people. And when watching the development of the drama, how often it reminded me of what passed three years ago at our very doors. Balbus and Malchus hustle Christ roughly along to the guardroom, pretty much as Sir Charles Warren's Endicotts marched off the victims of Bloody Sunday to the nearest police-station. But our police were more brutal than the soldiers of Ober Ammergau. And even the scourging seemed to recall memories of the Black-hole in Scotland Yard when on the night of Bloody Sunday the police entered the cells where the prisoners lay helpless and batoned them until they were black and blue and bloody, without any redress ever having been afforded them from that day to this. Our Pilates and Herods and money-changers were well content that such things should be. It was well that the mob should be taught a lesson. As it was in Palestine, so it is in London, and so it ever will be where helpless justice pleads in vain before the insolent tribunal of wealth and power.

The cause of Ireland is another of those Christs of to-day which were brought vividly before me at Ober Ammergau. Nathanael, the fierce, bitter, unscrupulous foe of the Nazarene, who went out and suborned false witnesses to come and testify against the accused, was he not the very image of the *Times* newspaper in a horned hat? It was the Parnell Commission all over again, with half-a-dozen Pigotts all in a row.

When the rulers met and conspired together as to how they could destroy Jesus the tableau that illustrated it to me was not the old-world story of Joseph and his brethren, but a scene which I witnessed not many years ago in Basingstoke. The success of the Salvation Army in reclaiming drunkards had so seriously jeopardised the trade of the publicans that they determined to crush the obnoxious evangelists by foul means. In this they found active sympathisers in high places. A brewer was Mayor at the time, and when I arrived in the town I came by the merest chance upon a clump of his friends who were eagerly discussing how to make a put-up job of a riot so as to justify his worship in reading the Riot Act in order to call out the soldiery and disperse the Salvationists. The plan was ingenious and simple, and I afterwards saw it carried out in the full light of day. "You push me," said one worthy, "when the Army comes along. I will push back. You cry 'Violence, violence!' The Mayor will read the Riot Act, and then out come the soldiers, and we shall crush the Salvation Army!" As it was said, so it was done. The publican's Skeleton procession, with tin kettles and banners of rags and newspapers, marched backwards and forwards in front of the Salvationists' barracks. The moment the procession of the Salvationists came out the prearranged comedy was gone through; the Mayor read the Riot Act, and in a few minutes a troop of artillerymen, mounted and armed, were trampling their way through the crowd, which fled in all directions. But there is no end to the tableaux that might be prepared from the record of the struggle of the Salvation Army against the publicans and their backers on the Bench. Christ before Herod received quite as kindly a treatment as that which many a Salvationist captain has received from the hands of an English magistrate.

Then the scene changed, and I was in Russia. Whose features were those that I saw under the gorgeous head-dress of the President of the Sanhedrim? Surely, none other than those of the Pobedenostaeff, the Procurator of the Holy Synod, raging in his orthodox zeal against the sectaries who dared to obey Christ in their own fashion. Exile, imprisonment, punishment are meted out by him as by a second Caiaphas to all who oppose the most holy law and the orthodoxy which is the pillar and mainstay of the Russian State. The ridicule and scorn with which Herod greeted "the King of the Fools," whom he dismissed with jeers from his judgment-seat, were faint echoes of the derision with which cultivated St. Petersburg hailed the propaganda of the Paschkoff-ski. It is ever so. In England, in Russia, as in Palestine—

> By the light of burning heretics Christ's bleeding feet I track,
> Toiling up new Calvaries ever with the cross that turns not back.

It is easy to recognise the traditional and conventional Christ who lived and was crucified in the centuries long since departed. It is another thing to identify Him to-day in the causes which He inspires, and in the great movements which are the Gesta Christi of our time. Most of us who worship Him to-day would make short work of Him if He came to earth once more as He came in Palestine. As an Englishman said to the Tzarewitch, "If Jesus Christ came to the world again, and attempted to deliver the Sermon on the Mount in the streets of St. Petersburg, General Gresser would clap Him in prison in no time." The Christ is ever in the front. It is as easy to be Christian when Christianity is triumphant as it is to be wise after the event.

> For Humanity sweeps onward! Where to-day the martyr stands,
> On the morrow crouches Judas with the gold within his hands;
> Far in front the cross stands ready, and the crackling faggots burn,
> While the hooting mob of yesterday in silent awe return,
> To glean up the scattered ashes into History's golden urn.

Thus the whole drama of contemporary history lives once again in these old-world figures. The faces under the head-dresses are continually changing, but the spirit is the same. And only in proportion as I identify these types with the men and causes in the midst of which we live and struggle from day to day does the battle of life have much zest or meaning for me.

Leaving Ober Ammergau, I returned by Switzerland to London. At Lucerne, while waiting for the train, I turned over the book in the waiting-room that describes the construction of the Gotthard Railway. About one thousand tons of dynamite, it is said, had sufficed to pierce the tunnels through the mountain barrier that separated Italy from Switzerland. Blasting powder could never have done the work. That helped to level the military roads for the legions of Suwarrow. It needed dynamite to tunnel the St. Gotthard—dynamite directed by Science—and, as I read this, I fell a-thinking. The old story, that mediæval Christ in magenta and pearl grey, with his disciples in artistic symphonies of harmonious and contrasted colour, no doubt, transformed the world. But a new world has arisen which sorely needs transforming again, and is it not possible that the conventional Christ, who, no doubt, did mighty things in the past, may have become as obsolete as blasting powder? May we not hope that if the conventional Christ did so much, the real Christ may do much more; that the realisation of the Christ as he actually lived and died amongst us may be as much superior in its transforming efficacy as the dynamite of the modern engineer is to the powder sack of the soldiers who marched under old Suwarrow? Of one thing we may at least be certain, and that is, if every one of those who call themselves by the Christian name could but say one Christ-like word, and do one Christ-like deed between every sunrise and sunset, it would lift a very Alpine mass of sorrow and anxiety from the weary heart of the world. What then might not be done if in very truth, and with all sincerity, we, each of us, tried to be a real Christ in his or her sphere, the sent of God in the midst of those with whom we pass our lives?

One word more and I have done. I have spoken of the endless shifting of features under the same turban. In this also Ober Ammergau supplies a timely lesson. The actors play different parts as they grow old. They begin with being children in the tableaux, and they pass in turn from one rôle to another. The Judas of this year was the Apostle John of 1880. The Apostle John of to-day will probably be the Christ of 1900. When the Christ was selected in 1870, he was chosen out of four competitors. One of the unsuccessful to-day plays King Herod, the other Pontius Pilate. So is it ever in real life. Few indeed are those who are always Christs. When Christians ceased to be martyrs they martyred their enemies. The Church came from the catacombs to establish the Inquisition. In our own lives we may be Christs to-day and atheists to-morrow. Power and opportunity destroy more Christs than the dungeon and the stake. And perhaps one reason why the Ober-Ammergauers have been able to give us the Christ we see this year is because in their secluded valley they have remained poor and humble in spirit, and have never ceased to remember the story that transformed the world.

APPENDIX.

HOW TO GET TO OBER AMMERGAU.

If you are in a hurry you can leave London by the eight-o'clock train from Charing Cross or Victoria on Thursday night, and get to Ober Ammergau by six o'clock on Saturday night. If you have time to spare you will not rush through in any such fashion, but do as I did, that is to say, you will take four days over the journey and arrive at the village of the Passion Play in a condition that renders it possible for you to appreciate the scene which you have travelled across Europe to see.

This is the way in which my son and I went to Ober Ammergau, and if we were to go again we should take the same route. I cannot do better than briefly indicate the line of route for the information of subsequent travellers.

First and foremost, before you start, book your places in advance. The throng is immense, the number of beds very limited. You can write to the Burgomaster or to the committee, or to any of the householders; but if you are wise you will do nothing of the kind. You will go to Gaze's office in the Strand, say what seats you want and what day you expect to be at Ober Ammergau, and ascertain from the office exactly whether or not the seats can be obtained. I say Gaze's, rather than Cook's, because, having inquired at both offices, I found that Gaze's could speak with greater certainty and were able to secure me seats within seven days of the performance. I travelled, therefore, with Gaze's coupons, stayed at Gaze's hotel, and was provided for at Ober Ammergau by Gaze's agents. It would be invidious to enter into comparisons, but my experience certainly did not lead me to regret that I took this course. If for nothing else, it is worth while making arrangements in this way, because you thereby become the guests of King Herod, and are waited upon at table by the Apostle John and King Herod's pleasant and obliging niece, St. Theresa. Herr Diemer, as King Herod is called in private life, and his indefatigable and obliging wife are admirable hosts; and as Mr. Schembri, the resident agent of the great tourist agency, is his right-hand man, the visitor has only himself to blame if he leaves Ober Ammergau with anything but the most pleasant and grateful recollections of the Hotel Osterbichl. Not that you are certain to sleep in the hotel—the chances are much greater that you will be put out to board at one or other of the dependences—but you breakfast, lunch, and dine at the hotel. Considering the enormous pressure of visitors, it is quite surprising that so little occasion is given for dissatisfaction. Visitors have themselves largely to blame for such small disappointments as they experience. Ober Ammergau is six miles from the nearest railway station. Conveyances have to be sent down the pass to Oberau to meet the trains, by which visitors state they will arrive; but as often as not visitors do not turn up as promised. They prefer another hour at lunch or another hour at the museum, or there is another picture gallery to be seen, so they will not leave Munich till a later train. The result is the carriages ordered to meet them according to appointment have been driven empty away, and when the late train comes in there are no carriages to be had. Hence fierce wrath, objurgations loud and deep, special conveyances hired at heavy expense, and a most unprofitable wrangle on the eve of the Passion Play. You never quite appreciate how inconsiderate the travelling Briton can be until you witness the scenes that take place at Oberau railway station. If you send notice in time and stick to your appointments you will be put through all right. If you do not, you must take the consequences, of which a six-mile tramp through rain and mud, with the chance of finding no bed at the end of it, is one of the least agreeable.

When you go to Gaze's office you must take places at the Hotel Osterbichl for Saturday and Sunday night; the cost is 30s., providing a bed for two nights, supper on Saturday night, breakfast on Monday, and breakfast, lunch, and dinner on Sunday, exclusive, of course, of wine or beer. The railway return fare within eight days between Munich and Oberau, is :—1st Class, 13s. 2d.; 2nd Class, 8s. 4d. The omnibus fare from Oberau to Ammergau is 2 marks 40 pfenigs. If you bespeak tickets—for which you pay on arrival, as they are not allotted until Saturday evening—you can order what places you like and take your chance of getting them. As there has never yet been found a foreman printer capable of placing everyone's advertisement at the head of the first column in the papers, so no agency in the world can secure first seats for each of five hundred applicants. The seats are thus distributed :—

1st place, right, at 10s.	1st place, left, at 10s.
2nd „ „ „ 8s.	2nd „ „ „ 8s.
3rd „ „ „ 6s.	3rd „ „ „ 6s.
4th „ „ „ 5s.	4th „ „ „ 5s.
5th „ „ „ 3s.	5th „ „ „ 3s.
6th „ „ „ 1s.	6th „ „ „ 1s.

The front seats of No. 2 are better than back seats of No. 1, although the latter cost 2s. more. Most English people order 10s. seats, and if their numbers are bad, try to exchange them for 8s. seats nearer the stage.

After having got your hotel coupon for the Saturday and Sunday night, there is the question of route. There are, broadly speaking, several routes. You can go to Munich, viâ Harwich, Queenborough, or Dover. Here are the fares and times by the different routes:—

Viâ Harwich, Rotterdam, Cologne, Mayence, Munich: leave Liverpool Street at 8 o'clock Tuesday evening; sleep at Cologne and Mayence; arrive Munich at 8.25 p.m. on Friday evening. Fare—Single, 1st, £5 3s. 7d.; 2nd, £3 13s. 6d. Hotel bills, 10s. per day. Return tickets by same route—1st Class, £7 16s. 6d.; 2nd, £5 10s. 9d.

Viâ Harwich, the same route, but without stopping at Cologne and Mayence and omitting the sail up the Rhine; leave Liverpool Street Thursday night, arrive Munich Saturday morning, 8.30. Fares—Same as above.

Viâ Queenborough, Flushing, Cologne, Mayence, Munich.

Viâ Dover, Calais, Laon, Bale, Lucerne, Zurich, Romanshorn, Lindau, Munich; leave Victoria or Charing Cross at 11 a.m. on Thursday morning, arrive Munich at 7.45 p.m. on Friday evening. Fare—1st, £7 8s. 5d.; 2nd, £5 8s. 8d.

The Special Cheap Return Ticket between Munich and Oberau, available for eight days, is—1st Class, 13s. 2d.; 2nd, 8s. 4d.

Viâ Dover, Calais, Paris, Bale, Lucerne, Romanshorn, Lindau, Munich; leave Victoria or Charing Cross at 8.40 a.m. on Wednesday morning; sleep at Paris and Lucerne, leave 7.20 a.m., arrive Munich, Friday night, 7.45 p.m. Fare—Single, 1st, £7 18s. 2d.; 2nd, £5 18s. 8d.

When I went to Ober Ammergau I travelled by the Rhine and came back by Lucerne. I would strongly advise all who can afford the time to do the same. In any case do not go by Lucerne and come back by the Rhine. To go up the Rhine after leaving England and journeying across Holland is to take the great German river in the best way. To take it after Switzerland is to take it in the worst possible mood. Going, the Rhine is a romantic and noble stream winding round the base of precipitous and vine-clad cliffs; returning, after the eye has been accustomed to Alpine heights and Swiss loveliness, the Rhine is but a great arterial drain passing through a plain studded here and there with dwarfish hills.

If you leave London on Tuesday night, Gaze's courier meets you as you get out from the steamer at Rotterdam into the tender that conveys you to the railway station. For the untravelled and also for the travelled Englishman a courier is exceedingly handy. M. Delacour is an unobtrusive Frenchman, familiar with German, who spends this summer oscillating between Munich and Rotterdam. Like a ghost he only speaks when spoken to, but if you want to know anything or have to find out anything or have any difficulty about your luggage, he is your man. The railway and steamboat people all know him. The whole route is as familiar to him as an old glove. If you don't want him, you need not notice his existence. If you get into any trouble he is invaluable. He is a kind of peripatetic encyclopædia limited, a Bradshaw in official uniform, a universal referee as to table d'hôtes, times of departures, posts, &c.

If the weather is as fine as it was when we crossed, Rotterdam is reached at nearly two hours before the train leaves for Cologne. Go down by the tender to the station, leave your bag with the portmanteau, and then take either a drive in an open cab or landau (cost 2s., and 6d. tip) through the city, or if it is not too hot, prowl round the old city and the canals until it is time for the train to start. The train leaves at 10.20 a.m. You cross the Rhine by a floating bridge, an incident which agreeably diversifies a ride that is not particularly interesting. You pass Cleves, with its reminiscences of Anne of Cleves who married Henry VIII. and onwards, traverse the flat but prosperous manufacturing district of Elberfeld, and reach Cologne at 4.40 p.m. We stayed at the Victoria Hotel, and after table d'hôte, served within half an hour of our arrival, went to the Cathedral. The great Dom, the more romantic St. Peter's of northern Europe, is open till eight. But although the setting sun irradiates the western windows with the glories of a celestial vision, you have not time to visit the Cathedral at night. You had better go and see the western windows and the sunset, and then revisit the Dom early next morning before breakfast.

We arrived on the eve of Corpus Christi Day. Everything was beflagged as if for a great festival. Next morning crowds filled the Cathedral, and an immense procession after Mass obstructed traffic in a way that would have made Mr. Monro wild. The Cathedral is open in the morning at seven, so that there is time to visit it before the Rhine boat leaves at nine. On Corpus Christi Day, however, solemn service was going on, and the Dom, closed to sightseers, was only accessible to worshippers. There was thus a curious and not unwelcome association that linked together the celebration of Corpus Christi in the Cathedral and the Passion Play at Ober Ammergau. In my native district, nearly every guild in Newcastle-on-Tyne used to perform a mystery or miracle play at Corpus Christi. Now the very festival has so utterly disappeared from our midst, that probably not nine Englishmen in ten know when Corpus Christi Day is, or why it is celebrated? It has gone under like the miracle plays. But now we were in a land where strange survivals lingered, and it seemed not inappropriate that on the threshold of Catholic Germany, whither we were hastening to witness the Passion Play, we should have been reminded of the ancient splendour of Corpus Christi.

The bells in the Cathedral spire were ringing merrily out over the festive town when we steamed off up the Rhine. The bells that gave forth such sweet music roused strange echoes. For, according to Baedeker, they were cast from the cannon captured from the French in the last war. Even in the melody that peals from heaven-piercing belfry there seems to linger some reminiscence of the cannon thunder. Yet as we steamed slowly up the wide and winding Rhine and noted castle after castle

APPENDIX.

crumbling into ruin, whose destruction dated with almost wearisome monotony to the devastating presence of the French invaders, it seemed very natural that the Germans should sling up the French cannon in their church towers. If French cannon never found themselves in worse places it would be well for the world. Nor could we wish them better employment than in summoning the Germans to praise and prayer.

At Mayence, where we arrived in the midst of a magnificent thunderstorm after sunset, we found good quarters at the Englischer Hof. Here also the festival had been well observed. How many hundreds of years have passed since our good St. Boniface converted the heathen Teuton to the Christian faith, and in the flags overhead and the crowded streets we have living contemporary evidence of the deepness of the dint which that propagandist Englishman made on the character of Europe.

As you arrive in Mainz at about nine o'clock there is not much opportunity of seeing the town till next morning. If you can get a back room in the hotel, for the streets are very noisy, you had better go to bed, and be up betimes next day. Mainz is one of the most ancient and famous towns in the Fatherland, and celebrated, moreover, as having been the birth-place of the invention of printing. The Cathedral, which is now being repaired and re-beautified internally, although not for a moment to be compared to the Dom of Cologne, has a great deal of interest of its own. The frescoes on the wall and the monumental tombs are well worth closer examination than you will be able to spare, seeing that your train starts for Munich at 10.27. From Mainz to Munich is a run of about ten hours, and as the German arrangements for feeding the travellers en route are most barbarous, you had better provide yourself with a lunch basket before leaving Mainz. There is not a stoppage anywhere of more than ten minutes, and the food is not good. Sour cabbage with German sausage is a very poor substitute for a mid-day meal. We stopped at Darmstadt, Aschaffenburg, Wurtzburg, and then the line runs right across Western Bavaria, crossing the Danube at Ingolstadt, and reaching Munich at about half-past eight, after a run of 280 miles. The only place between Darmstadt and Munich at which anything can be got to eat is Anspach. The scenery is varied, and you pass many small fortified towns surrounded by crumbling towers and ancient walls, bearing mute witness to the wars which, only two hundred years ago, were the normal condition of German life.

On arriving at Munich you go straight to the Hôtel de Bavière and remain there, for by the time you have washed and got something to eat you are about ready to go to bed. You will have a good long morning next day, during which you can see the Museum, which is the glory of Southern Germany, the old and new art galleries, returning in time to have an early lunch—not at the table d'hôte, for that is too late for the train—and then start from Munich Station by the special train to Oberau, leaving at 2 o'clock.

It is usually a very long train, and it is just as well to be there in good time if you want to get a seat by the window. It is worth while doing this, as the country through which the line passes is very pretty. The journey takes three hours and a half, and the line rises upwards into the mountains, passing on the way two beautiful lakes, the Wurm See, usually known as the Starnberger See, and the Staffel See. As the train approaches Oberau you reach the higher mountain scenery of the Bavarian Highlands.

As soon as the train stops you have no time to think about scenery, as there is a general rush for vehicles. If you have done as you instructed to do when you took your ticket and advised Messrs. Gaze's agent, you will find him and an omnibus waiting. But if you have lost your train, and arrive at an hour at which no one expects you, you will have to take a carriage to Ober Ammergau or walk ten miles. The seat in the 'bus only costs 2 marks 40, but a one-horse carriage costs 10 marks, and a two-horse 16 marks, a shilling or one-and-six extra for the driver. The road from Oberau to Ober Ammergau is one long ascent, until you come close to Ettal. The road winds up the side of the hill, and enables you to have a beautiful view of the valley below. Ettal is the first place of interest. It contains a wonder-working image and a large monastery, now turned into a brewery. But you press on to the village, and learn where you will be billeted for the night. You will sup at the Hotel Osterbichl. There is no bell when supper is served, but you can sit down as soon as you arrive, and can go to bed as soon as you have supped.

On "Passion Play" Day you have to rise early. Ober Ammergau gets up at five o'clock in the morning on Sunday, and crowds the parish church till half-past seven. The bands parade the village at six o'clock, and at seven the theatre already begins to fill. You do not, however, need to go until half-past seven, and when it is wet an omnibus will take you from the hotel to the theatre for one shilling. You can walk comfortably in ten minutes if it is dry. You get your tickets the previous night, paying sixpence extra above the published price of the tickets for the cost of booking. You will have no difficulty in finding your way to the numbered seat allotted to you. If it is at all cold, take a rug, put on a couple of pairs of trousers, or an extra petticoat, for nothing is more calculated to spoil your enjoyment of the spectacle than insufficient clothing. I took a very warm possum skin rug, and found it none too warm. There are no footstools, so that if you can carry anything to put your feet on, so much the better for you. If the sun is high, you can dispense with wrappings. The play commences punctually at eight o'clock, and goes on till about a quarter to twelve. Then there is a break of an hour and a half for luncheon, and the play begins again at ten or quarter past one, and goes on till half-past five. No one, except a few very ill-bred people here and there, indulge in applause as if they were witnessing an ordinary melodrama. But there are many who do not recognise the duty of coming in time, especially if they have tickets which necessitate passing the whole row of seats in order to gain those at the end. Every one is bound to be in time, if he does not wish to disturb the performance and all those who are witnesses of it. He is specially bound to be in time if his seat is in the centre, a fact which he can discover by looking at the plan on another page. The late comer who holds an end ticket compels every one to rise, and is an unmitigated nuisance.

After the performance of the play you can go back to Munich by the night train, arriving there about midnight. It is very uncomfortable. Or you may stay quietly over the night at Ober Ammergau, and return by the early morning train. The bulk of the visitors leave about eight o'clock in order to catch the 10.29 train to Munich. If you wish to go back by Switzerland— and it is one of the pleasantest railway journeys that are possible—you will have to leave Ober Ammergau at half-past two in

DATES OF PERFORMANCE
OF THE PASSION PLAY.

JULY.
Sunday 13
" 20
Wednesday 23
Sunday 27

AUGUST.
Sunday 3
Wednesday 6
Sunday 10
" 17
Wednesday 20
Sunday 24
" 31

SEPTEMBER.
Wednesday 3
Sunday 7
" 14
" 21
" 28

Second Performances take place on Mondays when the numbers are excessive.

FROM MUNICH TO OBER AMMERGAU.

Excursions.

Among the usual excursions made from Ober Ammergau are:— The pleasant valley of Graswang, the sumptuously appointed chateau of Linderhof, the Ammerwaldalpe, the Plansee, and the Royal Castle of Hohenschwangau. Carriages may be also taken for the journey from Ober Ammergau to Innsbruck, via Partenkirchen, Mittenwald, and Zirl (or *vice versâ*), for the convenience of tourists going to, or coming from, the districts of the Austrian Tyrol.

Admission Tickets are issued as follows:—

Linderhof (the Grotto & Kiosque)	Mk 3.50.
Hundingshütte	" 0.50.
Neuschwanstein	" 3.00.
Hohenschwangau	Gratis.

order to catch the 4.23 train at Oberau. This lands you in Munich about a quarter-past eight. You have then till 11.35 in Munich, when the train leaves for Lindau, reaching it at 4.49. From there you take the boat to Romanshorn, and there take the train to Lucerne, *vid* Zurich, which you reach at 11.15. It is a long journey, but it is agreeably diversified. After staying a day at Lucerne you can come home by Basle and the direct route to Calais. You leave Lucerne at half-past six o'clock, and arrive in London about six o'clock the next evening, taking about twenty-four hours.

For those desiring to remain in Ober Ammergau the following official list of fares will be useful:—

APPENDIX.

Fare (without Return Journey).	Distance	Einspänner		Zweispänner		Mehrwerts á Person		Fare (without Return Journey).	Distance	Einspänner		Zweispänner		Mehrwerts á Person	
	km	M	Pf	M	Pf	M	Pf		km	M	Pf	M	Pf	M	Pf
Oberau—Ettal	6	6	—	10	—	1	50	Oberammergau—Mittenwald	39	24	—	36	—	—	—
,, —Oberammergau	11	10	—	16	—	2	40	,, —Zirl	68	54	—	75	—	—	—
Oberammergau—Linderhof	11	10	—	16	—	2	—	,, —Garmisch— Lermos	50	32	—	48	—	—	—
,, —Plansee	24	16	—	24	—	4	—	,, —Garmisch— Lermos—Imst	84	60	—	96	—	—	—
,, —Reutte	50	32	—	48	—	8	—	,, —S. Jongau	35	20	—	30	—	—	—
,, —Füssen	60	34	—	51	—	—	—	,, —Peissenberg	35	20	—	30	—	—	—
,, —Hohenschwangau	65	36	—	54	—	—	—	A Day's Drive	—	16	—	24	—	—	—
,, —Kohlgrub— Murnau	26	16	—	24	—	—	—	Trinkgeld 10 %.							
,, —Garmisch— Partenkirchen	22	14	—	20	—	—	—								

Three Persons are allowed to a One-Horse, Fifteen to a Two-Horse Carriage.

MUNICH, STARNBERG, AND OBERAU RAILWAY.

							†			‡				
Munich	dep.	3 10 5	29 6	35 10	0 10 3	2 0 2	15 7 0	Oberau	dep.	4 23	10 5 10 29 2	27 5 21 7 25	7 55 8 7
Starnberg	arr.	3 50 6	16 7	19 10 44 11 3	2 52 3 14 8 0			Tutzing	arr.	6 38	11 39 12 39 4 52 8 45 9 19	9 46 10 5	
,,	dep.	3 51 6	19 7	21 10 46 11 33	2 58 3 23 8 10			,,	dep.	6 45	12 1 12 41 4 59 8 50 9 2	9 48 10 7	
Tutzing	arr.	4 8 6	45 7	41 11 6 noon	3 20 3 50 8 36			Starnberg	arr.	7 11	12 21 1 10 5 25 9 16 9 43	10 8 10 27	
,,	dep.	4 9 6	56 7	43 11 7 12	6 3 27 3 58 8 45			,,	dep.	7 16	12 23 1 15 5 35 9 25 9 45	10 13 10 32	
Oberau	arr.	6 19	3 9	35 1 0 2	0 5 2 3 12 11 2			Munich	arr.	8 12	1 10 2 15 6 10 10 25 10 10	11 0 11 20	

* Only runs when supplemental performance is required, on day following ordinary representation.
† Runs on day previous to every representation; also on every Sunday and Saint's Day.
‡ Runs on day previous to, and day of, representation.

• Every day following representation.
† Every day when principal representation is given.
‡ After every ordinary or principal representation.

NOTICE.

The Concessionaires, Messrs. Faller, Buchmüller, and Stockmann, have requested me to act as their representative in this country for the reproduction of their photographs. Anyone, therefore, who wishes to reproduce woodcuts or electros of these Passion Play pictures must communicate with me. I am informed that the Concessionaires contemplate publishing a reproduction of the whole series of quarto pictures in an album, which will form a valuable memorial of the Passion Play as it was played in 1890.

The illustrations in this book are reproduced by special authorisation from the photographs taken by Mr. Carl Stockmann, Court Photographer of Vienna, and published by the Kunst und Verlags Anstalt, of Ober Ammergau.

The official photographs are all stamped in the corner. The unstamped photographs are worthless reproductions of those taken in 1870 and 1880. There are some eighty and more photographs published by the Kunst und Verlags Anstalt. The cabinet sizes mounted or unmounted are sold at a shilling. The quarto size at half-a-crown.